PENGUIN SHAKESPEARE

Founding Editor: T. J. B. Spencer
General Editor: Stanley Wells
Supervisory Editors: Paul Edmondson, Stanley Wells

T. J. B. SPENCER, sometime Director of the Shakespeare Institute of the University of Birmingham, was the founding editor of the New Penguin Shakespeare, for which he edited both *Romeo and Juliet* and *Hamlet*.

STANLEY WELLS is Emeritus Professor of the University of Birmingham and Chairman of the Shakespeare Birthplace Trust. He is general editor of the Oxford Shakespeare and his books include *Shakespeare: The Poet and His Plays*, *Shakespeare: For All Time*, *Looking for Sex in Shakespeare* and (with Paul Edmondson) *Shakespeare's Sonnets*.

PETER DAVISON has written or edited forty books on Orwell, Shakespeare and drama; he was appointed an OBE in 1999 for services to English Literature, and was awarded the Gold Medal of the Bibliographical Society in 2003.

ADRIAN POOLE is Professor of English Literature and a Fellow of Trinity College, Cambridge. His publications include *Shakespeare and the Victorians* and *Tragedy: Shakespeare and the Greek Example*.

William Shakespeare

HENRY IV, PART II

Edited with a Commentary by Peter Davison
Introduced by Adrian Poole

PENGUIN BOOKS

PENGUIN BOOKS

Published by the Penguin Group
Penguin Books Ltd, 80 Strand, London WC2R ORL, England
Penguin Group (USA) Inc., 375 Hudson Street, New York, New York 10014, USA
Penguin Group (Canada), 10 Alcorn Avenue, Toronto, Ontario, Canada M4V 3B2
(a division of Pearson Penguin Canada Inc.)
Penguin Ireland, 25 St Stephen's Green, Dublin 2, Ireland (a division of Penguin Books Ltd)
Penguin Group (Australia), 250 Camberwell Road, Camberwell, Victoria 3124, Australia
(a division of Pearson Australia Group Pty Ltd)
Penguin Books India Pvt Ltd, 11 Community Centre, Panchsheel Park, New Delhi – 110 017, India
Penguin Group (NZ), cnr Airborne and Rosedale Roads, Albany, Auckland 1310, New Zealand
(a division of Pearson New Zealand Ltd)
Penguin Books (South Africa) (Pty) Ltd, 24 Sturdee Avenue, Rosebank 2196, South Africa

Penguin Books Ltd, Registered Offices: 80 Strand, London WC2R ORL, England

www.penguin.com

This edition first published in Penguin Books 1977
Reprinted with a revised Further Reading and Account of the Text 1996
Reissued in the Penguin Shakespeare series 2005

This edition copyright © Penguin Books, 1977, 1996
Commentary copyright © Peter Davison, 1977
Further Reading and Account of the Text copyright © Peter Davison, 1996
General Introduction and Chronology copyright © Stanley Wells, 2005
Introduction, The Play in Performance and revised Further Reading copyright © Adrian Poole, 2005

All rights reserved

The moral right of the editors has been asserted

Set in 11.5/12.5 PostScript Monotype Fournier
Typeset by Palimpsest Book Production Limited, Polmont, Stirlingshire
Printed in England by Clays Ltd, St Ives plc

Contents

General Introduction vii
*The Chronology of
    Shakespeare's Works* xvii
Introduction xxi
The Play in Performance lxi
Further Reading lxxi

HENRY IV, PART II 1

An Account of the Text 119
The Songs 145
Commentary 147

General Introduction

Every play by Shakespeare is unique. This is part of his greatness. A restless and indefatigable experimenter, he moved with a rare amalgamation of artistic integrity and dedicated professionalism from one kind of drama to another. Never shackled by convention, he offered his actors the alternation between serious and comic modes from play to play, and often also within the plays themselves, that the repertory system within which he worked demanded, and which provided an invaluable stimulus to his imagination. Introductions to individual works in this series attempt to define their individuality. But there are common factors that underpin Shakespeare's career.

Nothing in his heredity offers clues to the origins of his genius. His upbringing in Stratford-upon-Avon, where he was born in 1564, was unexceptional. His mother, born Mary Arden, came from a prosperous farming family. Her father chose her as his executor over her eight sisters and his four stepchildren when she was only in her late teens, which suggests that she was of more than average practical ability. Her husband John, a glover, apparently unable to write, was nevertheless a capable businessman and loyal townsfellow, who seems to have fallen on relatively hard times in later life. He would have been brought up as a Catholic, and may have retained

Catholic sympathies, but his son subscribed publicly to Anglicanism throughout his life.

The most important formative influence on Shakespeare was his school. As the son of an alderman who became bailiff (or mayor) in 1568, he had the right to attend the town's grammar school. Here he would have received an education grounded in classical rhetoric and oratory, studying authors such as Ovid, Cicero and Quintilian, and would have been required to read, speak, write and even think in Latin from his early years. This classical education permeates Shakespeare's work from the beginning to the end of his career. It is apparent in the self-conscious classicism of plays of the early 1590s such as the tragedy of *Titus Andronicus*, *The Comedy of Errors*, and the narrative poems *Venus and Adonis* (1592–3) and *The Rape of Lucrece* (1593–4), and is still evident in his latest plays, informing the dream visions of *Pericles* and *Cymbeline* and the masque in *The Tempest*, written between 1607 and 1611. It inflects his literary style throughout his career. In his earliest writings the verse, based on the ten-syllabled, five-beat iambic pentameter, is highly patterned. Rhetorical devices deriving from classical literature, such as alliteration and antithesis, extended similes and elaborate wordplay, abound. Often, as in *Love's Labour's Lost* and *A Midsummer Night's Dream*, he uses rhyming patterns associated with lyric poetry, each line self-contained in sense, the prose as well as the verse employing elaborate figures of speech. Writing at a time of linguistic ferment, Shakespeare frequently imports Latinisms into English, coining words such as abstemious, addiction, incarnadine and adjunct. He was also heavily influenced by the eloquent translations of the Bible in both the Bishops' and the Geneva versions. As his experience grows, his verse and prose become more supple, the patterning less apparent, more ready to accommodate the rhythms of ordinary speech, more colloquial in diction, as in the speeches of the Nurse in *Romeo and Juliet*, the characterful prose of Falstaff and Hamlet's soliloquies. The effect is of increasing psychological realism, reaching its greatest heights in *Hamlet*, *Othello*, *King Lear*, *Macbeth* and *Antony and Cleopatra*. Gradually he discovered ways of adapting the regular beat of the pentameter to make it an infinitely flexible instrument for matching thought with feeling. Towards the end of his career, in plays such as *The Winter's Tale*, *Cymbeline* and *The Tempest*, he adopts a more highly mannered style, in keeping with the more overtly symbolical and emblematical mode in which he is writing.

So far as we know, Shakespeare lived in Stratford till after his marriage to Anne Hathaway, eight years his senior, in 1582. They had three children: a daughter, Susanna, born in 1583 within six months of their marriage, and twins, Hamnet and Judith, born in 1585. The next seven years of Shakespeare's life are virtually a blank. Theories that he may have been, for instance, a schoolmaster, or a lawyer, or a soldier, or a sailor, lack evidence to support them. The first reference to him in print, in Robert Greene's pamphlet *Greene's Groatsworth of Wit* of 1592, parodies a line from *Henry VI, Part III*, implying that Shakespeare was already an established playwright. It seems likely that at some unknown point after the birth of his twins he joined a theatre company and gained experience as both actor and writer in the provinces and London. The London theatres closed because of plague in 1593 and 1594; and during these years, perhaps recognizing the need for an alternative career, he wrote and published the narrative poems *Venus and Adonis* and *The Rape of Lucrece*. These are the only works we can be certain that Shakespeare himself was responsible for putting into print. Each bears the author's dedication to Henry Wriothesley, Earl of Southampton (1573–1624), the second in warmer terms than the first. Southampton, younger than Shakespeare by ten years, is the only person to whom he personally dedicated works. The Earl may have been a close friend, perhaps even the beautiful and adored young man whom Shakespeare celebrates in his *Sonnets*.

The resumption of playing after the plague years saw the founding of the Lord Chamberlain's Men, a company to which Shakespeare was to belong for the rest of his career, as actor, shareholder and playwright. No other dramatist of the period had so stable a relationship with a single company. Shakespeare knew the actors for whom he was writing and the conditions in which they performed. The permanent company was made up of around twelve to fourteen players, but one actor often played more than one role in a play and additional actors were hired as needed. Led by the tragedian Richard Burbage (1568–1619) and, initially, the comic actor Will Kemp (d. 1603), they rapidly achieved a high reputation, and when King James I succeeded Queen Elizabeth I in 1603 they were renamed as the King's Men. All the women's parts were played by boys; there is no evidence that any female role was ever played by a male actor over the age of about eighteen. Shakespeare had enough confidence in his boys to write for them long and demanding roles such as Rosalind (who, like other heroines of the romantic comedies, is disguised as a boy for much of the action) in *As You Like It*, Lady Macbeth and Cleopatra. But there are far more fathers than mothers, sons than daughters, in his plays, few if any of which require more than the company's normal complement of three or four boys.

The company played primarily in London's public playhouses – there were almost none that we know of in the rest of the country – initially in the Theatre, built in Shoreditch in 1576, and from 1599 in the Globe, on Bankside. These were wooden, more or less circular structures, open to the air, with a thrust stage surmounted by a canopy and jutting into the area where spectators who paid one penny stood, and surrounded by galleries where it was possible to be seated on payment of an additional penny. Though properties such as cauldrons, stocks, artificial trees or beds could indicate locality, there was no representational scenery. Sound effects such as flourishes of trumpets, music both martial and amorous, and accompaniments to songs were provided by the company's musicians. Actors entered through doors in the back wall of the stage. Above it was a balconied area that could represent the walls of a town (as in *King John*), or a castle (as in *Richard II*), and indeed a balcony (as in *Romeo and Juliet*). In 1609 the company also acquired the use of the Blackfriars, a smaller, indoor theatre to which admission was more expensive, and which permitted the use of more spectacular stage effects such as the descent of Jupiter on an eagle in *Cymbeline* and of goddesses in *The Tempest*. And they would frequently perform before the court in royal residences and, on their regular tours into the provinces, in non-theatrical spaces such as inns, guildhalls and the great halls of country houses.

Early in his career Shakespeare may have worked in collaboration, perhaps with Thomas Nashe (1567–*c.* 1601) in *Henry VI, Part I* and with George Peele (1556–96) in *Titus Andronicus*. And towards the end he collaborated with George Wilkins (*fl.* 1604–8) in *Pericles*, and with his younger colleagues Thomas Middleton (1580–1627), in *Timon of Athens*, and John Fletcher (1579–1625), in *Henry*

VIII, *The Two Noble Kinsmen* and the lost play *Cardenio*. Shakespeare's output dwindled in his last years, and he died in 1616 in Stratford, where he owned a fine house, New Place, and much land. His only son had died at the age of eleven, in 1596, and his last descendant died in 1670. New Place was destroyed in the eighteenth century but the other Stratford houses associated with his life are maintained and displayed to the public by the Shakespeare Birthplace Trust.

One of the most remarkable features of Shakespeare's plays is their intellectual and emotional scope. They span a great range from the lightest of comedies, such as *The Two Gentlemen of Verona* and *The Comedy of Errors*, to the profoundest of tragedies, such as *King Lear* and *Macbeth*. He maintained an output of around two plays a year, ringing the changes between comic and serious. All his comedies have serious elements: Shylock, in *The Merchant of Venice*, almost reaches tragic dimensions, and *Measure for Measure* is profoundly serious in its examination of moral problems. Equally, none of his tragedies is without humour: Hamlet is as witty as any of his comic heroes, *Macbeth* has its Porter, and *King Lear* its Fool. His greatest comic character, Falstaff, inhabits the history plays and *Henry V* ends with a marriage, while *Henry VI, Part III*, *Richard II* and *Richard III* culminate in the tragic deaths of their protagonists.

Although in performance Shakespeare's characters can give the impression of a superabundant reality, he is not a naturalistic dramatist. None of his plays is explicitly set in his own time. The action of few of them (except for the English histories) is set even partly in England (exceptions are *The Merry Wives of Windsor* and the Induction to *The Taming of the Shrew*). Italy is his favoured location. Most of his principal story-lines derive from printed writings; but the structuring and translation of these narratives into dramatic terms is Shakespeare's own, and he invents much additional material. Most of the plays contain elements of myth and legend, and many derive from ancient or more recent history or from romantic tales of ancient times and faraway places. All reflect his reading, often in close detail. Holinshed's *Chronicles* (1577, revised 1587), a great compendium of English, Scottish and Irish history, provided material for his English history plays. The *Lives of the Noble Grecians and Romans* by the Greek writer Plutarch, finely translated into English from the French by Sir Thomas North in 1579, provided much of the narrative material, and also a mass of verbal detail, for his plays about Roman history. Some plays are closely based on shorter individual works: *As You Like It*, for instance, on the novel *Rosalynde* (1590) by his near-contemporary Thomas Lodge (1558–1625), *The Winter's Tale* on *Pandosto* (1588) by his old rival Robert Greene (1558–92) and *Othello* on a story by the Italian Giraldi Cinthio (1504–73). And the language of his plays is permeated by the Bible, the Book of Common Prayer and the proverbial sayings of his day.

Shakespeare was popular with his contemporaries, but his commitment to the theatre and to the plays in performance is demonstrated by the fact that only about half of his plays appeared in print in his lifetime, in slim paperback volumes known as quartos, so called because they were made from printers' sheets folded twice to form four leaves (eight pages). None of them shows any sign that he was involved in their publication. For him, performance was the primary means of publication. The most frequently reprinted of his works were the non-dramatic poems – the erotic *Venus and Adonis* and the more moralistic *The Rape of Lucrece*. The *Sonnets*, which appeared in 1609, under his name but possibly without his consent, were less successful, perhaps because the vogue for sonnet sequences, which peaked in the 1590s, had passed by then. They were not reprinted until 1640, and then only in garbled form along with poems by other writers. Happily, in 1623, seven years after he died, his colleagues John Heminges (1556–1630) and Henry Condell (d. 1627) published his collected plays, including eighteen that had not previously appeared in print, in the first Folio, whose name derives from the fact that the printers' sheets were folded only once to produce two leaves (four pages). Some of the quarto editions are badly printed, and the fact that some plays exist in two, or even three, early versions creates problems for editors. These are discussed in the Account of the Text in each volume of this series.

Shakespeare's plays continued in the repertoire until the Puritans closed the theatres in 1642. When performances resumed after the Restoration of the monarchy in 1660 many of the plays were not to the taste of the times, especially because their mingling of genres and failure to meet the requirements of poetic justice offended against the dictates of neoclassicism. Some, such as *The Tempest* (changed by John Dryden and William Davenant in 1667 to suit contemporary taste), *King Lear* (to which Nahum Tate gave a happy ending in 1681) and *Richard III* (heavily adapted by Colley Cibber in 1700 as a vehicle for his own talents), were extensively rewritten; others fell into neglect. Slowly they regained their place in the repertoire, and they continued to be reprinted, but it was not until the great actor David Garrick (1717–79) organized a spectacular jubilee in Stratford in 1769 that Shakespeare began to be regarded as a transcendental genius. Garrick's idolatry prefigured the enthusiasm of critics such as Samuel Taylor Coleridge (1772–1834) and William Hazlitt (1778–1830). Gradually Shakespeare's reputation spread abroad, to Germany, America, France and to other European countries.

During the nineteenth century, though the plays were generally still performed in heavily adapted or abbreviated versions, a large body of scholarship and criticism began to amass. Partly as a result of a general swing in education away from the teaching of Greek and Roman texts and towards literature written in English, Shakespeare became the object of intensive study in schools and universities. In the theatre, important turning points were the work in England of two theatre directors, William Poel (1852–1934) and his disciple Harley Granville-Barker (1877–1946), who showed that the application of knowledge, some of it newly acquired, of early staging conditions to performance of the plays could render the original texts viable in terms of the modern theatre. During the twentieth century appreciation of Shakespeare's work, encouraged by the availability of audio, film and video versions of the plays, spread around the world to such an extent that he can now be claimed as a global author.

The influence of Shakespeare's works permeates the English language. Phrases from his plays and poems – 'a tower of strength', 'green-eyed jealousy', 'a foregone conclusion' – are on the lips of people who may never have read him. They have inspired composers of songs, orchestral music and operas; painters and sculptors; poets, novelists and film-makers. Allusions to him appear in pop songs, in advertisements and in television shows. Some of his characters – Romeo and Juliet, Falstaff, Shylock and Hamlet – have acquired mythic status. He is valued for his humanity, his psychological insight, his wit and humour, his lyricism, his mastery of language, his ability to excite, surprise, move and, in the widest sense of the word, entertain audiences. He is the greatest of poets, but he is essentially a dramatic poet. Though his plays have much to offer to readers, they exist fully only in performance. In these volumes we offer individual introductions, notes on language and on specific points of the text, suggestions for further reading and information about how each work has been edited. In addition we include accounts of the ways in which successive generations of interpreters and audiences have responded to challenges and rewards offered by the plays. The Penguin Shakespeare series aspires to remove obstacles to understanding and to make pleasurable the reading of the work of the man who has done more than most to make us understand what it is to be human.

Stanley Wells

The Chronology of
Shakespeare's Works

A few of Shakespeare's writings can be fairly precisely
dated. An allusion to the Earl of Essex in the chorus to
Act V of *Henry V*, for instance, could only have been
written in 1599. But for many of the plays we have only
vague information, such as the date of publication, which
may have occurred long after composition, the date of a
performance, which may not have been the first, or a list
in Francis Meres's book *Palladis Tamia*, published in 1598,
which tells us only that the plays listed there must have
been written by that year. The chronology of the early
plays is particularly difficult to establish. Not everyone
would agree that the first part of *Henry VI* was written
after the third, for instance, or *Romeo and Juliet* before
A Midsummer Night's Dream. The following table is based
on the 'Canon and Chronology' section in *William
Shakespeare: A Textual Companion*, by Stanley Wells and
Gary Taylor, with John Jowett and William Montgomery
(1987), where more detailed information and discussion
may be found.

The Two Gentlemen of Verona	1590–91
The Taming of the Shrew	1590–91
Henry VI, Part II	1591
Henry VI, Part III	1591

Henry VI, Part I (perhaps with Thomas Nashe)   1592
Titus Andronicus (perhaps with George Peele)   1592
Richard III   1592–3
Venus and Adonis (poem)   1592–3
The Rape of Lucrece (poem)   1593–4
The Comedy of Errors   1594
Love's Labour's Lost   1594–5
Edward III (authorship uncertain,   not later than 1595
    not included in this series)   (printed in 1596)
Richard II   1595
Romeo and Juliet   1595
A Midsummer Night's Dream   1595
King John   1596
The Merchant of Venice   1596–7
Henry IV, Part I   1596–7
The Merry Wives of Windsor   1597–8
Henry IV, Part II   1597–8
Much Ado About Nothing   1598
Henry V   1598–9
Julius Caesar   1599
As You Like It   1599–1600
Hamlet   1600–1601
Twelfth Night   1600–1601
'The Phoenix and the Turtle' (poem)   by 1601
Troilus and Cressida   1602
The Sonnets (poems)   1593–1603 and later
Measure for Measure   1603
A Lover's Complaint (poem)   1603–4
Sir Thomas More (in part,
    not included in this series)   1603–4
Othello   1603–4
All's Well That Ends Well   1604–5
Timon of Athens (with Thomas Middleton)   1605
King Lear   1605–6

Macbeth (revised by Middleton)   1606
Antony and Cleopatra   1606
Pericles (with George Wilkins)   1607
Coriolanus   1608
The Winter's Tale   1609
Cymbeline   1610
The Tempest   1611
Henry VIII (by Shakespeare and John Fletcher;
    known in its own time as *All is True*) 1613
Cardenio (by Shakespeare and Fletcher; lost)   1613
The Two Noble Kinsmen (by Shakespeare
    and Fletcher)   1613–14

Introduction

DOUBLE DOUBLE

What does it mean to 'succeed'? This is a great play about what gets into history and what gets left out, and how. It is also about the difference between winners and losers, about the relations between predators and prey, about the passage of time, about growing up and growing old, about memory and forgetting, about expectation and disappointment, about deception, self-deception and the possibilities of enlightenment.

The play we now know as *Henry IV, Part I* was an instant hit with audiences when it was first performed, probably in 1597. We do not know for certain whether Shakespeare originally planned to make two plays out of the material he got from the historians, especially Raphael Holinshed, and from a popular anonymous play from the 1580s, *The Famous Victories of Henry V*. But we do know that the character the world knows as Falstaff was first called Sir John Oldcastle, and that his descendants objected to Shakespeare's comic treatment of their revered ancestor, a Lollard or proto-Protestant martyr (1378–1417) (see Introduction to *Part I*, pp. xxxv–xxxvi: this helps to explain the curious disclaimer in the Epilogue to *Part II* (30–31). It seems likely that at some point in the process of composing and performing what was at first a single play called *The History of Henry the Fourth* the playwright realized that he was on to a good thing, perhaps the best thing he had ever done – so far. There was at least one good reason for making two plays rather than one: Falstaff. In fact such a good reason that Shakespeare would go on and make yet a third play featuring the character, a comedy unleashed from the restraints of 'history', *The Merry Wives of Windsor* (of uncertain date, between 1597 and 1598).

Taken together as a single unit, the two *Henry IV* plays tell a story about the transformation of Prince Henry from reprobate youth to responsible ruler, and the success with which he succeeds his father and assumes the throne as King Henry V. They tell other stories about the threats to the realm the two Henrys must govern, the overt political and military challenge headed by the Percys in the North and Owen Glendower in the West, and the menace of lawless disorder represented by Falstaff and his low-life cronies. The two King Henrys succeed in overcoming these threats, and this victory is staged for us at the climax of each play when the son slays his prime antagonists, Hotspur at the end of *Part I* and Falstaff at the end of *Part II*. If only it were as simple as this.

'Comparisons are odorous', as Dogberry reminds us in *Much Ado About Nothing* (III.5.15), but they are essential to the very form and matter of *Henry IV, Part II*. The first part of *Henry IV* gets an essential element of its structure from the invidious comparison the King makes between his own son, the Prince of Wales, and the son of his rival, the Earl of Northumberland, also named Henry or Harry but best known as Hotspur. Shakespeare aids and abets the King by reducing the real Hotspur's age to make it the same as the Prince's and pitting them against each other in single combat during the final battle at Shrewsbury. In killing Hotspur the Prince seems to free himself from the 'double' to whom his father has bound him. But Shakespeare has provided other doubles outside his father's control, including a double of the Prince's father himself. It is not only Hotspur's corpse that the Prince contemplates on the ground at Shrewsbury but also that of his false father: Falstaff. And it is a false corpse. The Prince is not yet rid of him, nor is the King, nor is anyone. This is one good reason for needing another play, a double of *Henry IV*. 'I am not a double-man', Falstaff claims (*Part I*, V.4.136). But he is, he is.

There are other doubles in the first part of *Henry IV*, including all the 'shadow' kings at Shrewsbury tricked out to look like the real one, who meet their end at the hands of the rebel Douglas. 'Another king!' he exclaims in dismay. 'They grow like Hydra's heads' (V.4.24). By giving this play a sequel Shakespeare raised the whole principle of doubling and comparison to a new level. In one sense there are two Falstaffs, two Kings and two Princes. Readers and audiences are bound to compare the rebel leaders in *Part I* with those in *Part II*. They will compare the battle scenes, or rather the climactic battle of Shrewsbury in *Part I* with the anti-climactic non-battle at Gaultree in *Part II*. They will compare the tavern scenes in both plays and the scenes of confrontation between father and son, between King and Prince. They will see the false death of Falstaff at Shrewsbury mirrored in *Part II* by the seeming death of the King – by both of which the Prince is deceived.

Part II takes the greatest interest of all in the likeness and difference between fathers and sons and brothers. The Prince spends a large part of these plays trying to establish that he is *not* like his father, the guiltily usurping King. This is why he chooses a paternal surrogate, from whom in turn on assuming the throne he will mark his absolute difference by adopting yet another – the Lord Chief Justice. Yet we can understand the fears of his brothers and chief advisers, when he emerges for the first time in the 'new and gorgeous garment, majesty' (V.2.44), that he will prove to be a tyrant. He seeks to reassure them: 'This is the English, not the Turkish court; | Not Amurath an Amurath succeeds, | But Harry Harry' (47–9). For a moment we could be forgiven for thinking the new King was oddly called 'Harry Harry' – especially modern readers and audiences who require an editor's help with the topical reference to the successive Sultans who disposed of potentially rivalrous brothers by having them murdered (see note to V.2.48). Then we realize that there are of course two different Harrys, father and son. Yet this Harry is saying something quite complicated: that the two Harrys are like the Amuraths in being like each other, and at the same time quite different from them because they do not kill their rivals (well, not their brothers at least). It is a brave assertion, but is English history really so different from Turkish? Anyone who knows Shakespeare's other English history plays – *Richard III* for example – might reasonably doubt it. The trouble with likenesses is that once the connection has been made you can never be sure you have erased it for good and left it behind. One minute the new King is saying he is his father's true son, Harry Harry; the next he is disowning him by announcing that 'My father is gone wild into his grave' (V.2.123).

'And is old Double dead?' asks Shallow of his fellow Justice Silence (III.2.51). Old Double 'drew a good bow' and 'shot a fine shoot' (42–3), and was well loved by

John of Gaunt, as Shallow likes to think he was himself. 'Dead, sir', comes the answer (41). But in *Part II* new doubles live on.

GREAT EXPECTATIONS

Henry IV, Part II is more certainly Falstaff's play than *Part I*. But if the old rogue was bound to pull the crowds in again his author had also set himself some tricky challenges. More mirth was all very well, but what about the serious history? And what, in particular, about the story of the young Prince, and his vexed relations with his father, the King? *Part I* had reached a tremendous climax with the battle of Shrewsbury and the duel between Harry and Harry, Hotspur and Monmouth. In saving the King from the Earl of Douglas, the Prince seems to win the vindication for which he has been planning: 'Thou hast redeemed thy lost opinion,' his father assures him (V.4.47). The Prince had confided in us near the start of the play that he was planning to throw off his 'loose behaviour' and 'falsify men's hopes . . . Redeeming time when men think least I will' (I.2.193–215). Is not this what he has done at Shrewsbury? If so, then where does this story go from here?

One answer would be that it does not move on, that it simply stalls, at least for a time. One of the many oddities or inconsistencies about *Part II* is that neither the Prince nor his father seems to remember Shrewsbury at all (see The Play in Performance). There is something nightmarish about the relations between the Prince and his father, and something dreamlike about the whole play as a reprise of *Part I*. At the end of *Part II* the new King Henry V will say he has awoken from his dream

(V.5.52–4), but he can only do so when his fathers have been sent 'wild' to the grave. This is a play that does not follow its predecessor with perfect continuity; it doubles back, repeating itself with a difference. In this respect it repeats at a formal level one of the key themes of its own action: the question of 'succession', of how one king follows on from another, or one son from a father. There is a mystery at the heart of historical process and change, a mystery that braces itself against the possibility that things might never really change at all or move on. As one of the rebels puts it:

> And so success of mischief shall be born,
> And heir from heir shall hold this quarrel up
> Whiles England shall have generation. (IV.2.47–9)

'Success of mischief' to the end of time: that is the nightmare prospect.

There is more than one kind of story being told in *Henry IV, Part II*. There is the story of the great expectations invested in the Prince – the hopes both for good and for ill that come to a climax in the big scene with the King (IV.5), and then resolve themselves in Act V when he succeeds his father, vindicates the Lord Chief Justice, announces his reformation and throws off his old loose companions, above all the 'tutor and the feeder of my riots' (V.5.65). This is the story of the Prodigal Son, the official, upbeat, morally approved story of the reform of the heir apparent and his transformation into the mirror of all Christian kings. The difficulty – and the interest – is that this story is simply put on hold for the first two-thirds of the play, until Act IV, scenes 4 and 5. In fact it can seem more ominous than this: because the play seems to have forgotten the 'success' that this story made in its predecessor, the effect is of stealthy regression. This feeds the nightmare alternative possibility that the Prince will *not* after all be able to redeem the time or his promise, and that under Harry Harry, England will get stuck in a murderous and licentious chaos from which there is no escape.

This is the extreme, even lurid vision the play entertains. Or to be exact, it is the vision to which, as we shall see, the two most prominent and literal fathers – the King and Northumberland – give expression. But there is a third, less spectacular kind of story no less important to the play's whole temper. This too is set against the optimistic story of the Prince's graduation to manhood, uprightness and kingship, but instead of a descent into chaos, it is a more temperate story of disappointment, of things not coming to fruition, of expectations that are thwarted, aborted or just peter out. The play is riddled with anticlimax, as when the festivities at the Boar's Head are cut short before they ever get going, and Falstaff laments: 'Now comes in the sweetest morsel of the night, and we must hence and leave it unpicked' (II.4.362–3). This is echoed in Justice Shallow's 'now comes in the sweet o'th'night' (V.3.49–50), where again the party is interrupted by news from the court. On a larger scale the audience is likely to feel a terrible anticlimax at Gaultree Forest. This should be the equivalent of the battle of Shrewsbury, save that the rebels have no Hotspur and the loyalists have no Prince. Where *is* the Prince? At Windsor, hunting, as his brother Humphrey vaguely suggests (IV.4.14)? Hanging out with his low cronies? Waiting for his father to die? The insurrection does get crushed by a prince, not by Henry, but by his double, young brother John, the cool, ruthless strategist who defeats the rebels not with swords but with words.

'THE ENDING FATHER'

Someone else is absent from the battle at Gaultree, but in this case it is his second failure, for he was missing from Shrewsbury as well. Hotspur's father, the Earl of Northumberland, ought to be leading the rebels. After listening to his two womenfolk he confesses that he cannot bring himself to action: ''Tis with my mind | As with the tide swelled up unto his height, | That makes a still-stand, running neither way' (II.3.62–4). This swollen but undischarged energy characterizes much of the play. Characters seem uncertain of their own direction, design or plot, as for example the rebels who fear that their hopes will be 'still-born' (I.3.64). In this same scene Lord Bardolph has a long-winded speech that is almost bound to be abbreviated when the play is performed. Ironically so, given that its very subject is the anxiety of being cut short, like 'th'appearing buds' (39) more likely to be destroyed by frost than to reach fruition, so he gloomily imagines. He finishes with the thought of a building that has to be abandoned halfway through by a man who 'leaves his part-created cost | A naked subject to the weeping clouds, | And waste for churlish winter's tyranny' (60–62). These poetic lines are gratuitous, but this is true of so many lines, passages and scenes that do not move the plot forward. They are all the more expressive of the passions, desires and fears that resist the inevitability of plot, and of history as it is officially told: the voice of 'naked subjects', bereft of their purpose and place in the story.

How the rebels miss Hotspur. Now they are led by the well-meaning but bloodless Archbishop of York, who reveals the diffidence at the heart of their enterprise when he describes any plan based on popular approval as 'An habitation giddy and unsure' (I.3.89). This could be the King deploring the way the people have turned against the man they once hailed, for he and the Archbishop sing the same tune about the 'cup of alteration' (III.1.52). The Archbishop is no less unsure about the outcome of the rebellion than about its foundations. He and Hastings are trying to persuade the rightly sceptical but insufficiently forceful Mowbray that the King will not perpetuate civil strife by punishing them. The King will see the advantages of an amnesty,

> So that this land, like an offensive wife
> That hath enraged him on to offer strokes,
> As he is striking, holds his infant up,
> And hangs resolved correction in the arm
> That was upreared to execution. (IV.1.208–12)

The infant is being used by the wife and mother as a hostage to 'hang' – that is, suspend or arrest – the punitive blow of the husband and father: another image of thwarted energy. It is a clever move by the offensive wife to avoid being punished. This does not exactly denote confidence in the justice of the rebels' cause and it also misrepresents the realities of the political situation. The rebels do not have a vulnerable infant to hand. Indeed the historical reality of the confrontation at Shipton Moor on 29 May 1405 seems to have been that the rebels enjoyed a numerical advantage. This is what prompted the Earl of Westmorland's recourse to 'policy', as Holinshed puts it (Shakespeare transfers the responsibility to Prince John). The Archbishop is almost laughably innocent, a pallid, sinewless double of Hotspur, the political innocent who dominated *Part I*.

All the authorities and father figures in this play are profoundly anxious about the origins of their power (except for the nameless Lord Chief Justice). King Henry echoes the Archbishop's giddiness when he thinks envyingly of the ship's boy who sleeps soundly 'upon the high and giddy mast' (III.1.18). Later still, as he nears death, he confesses that his 'brain is giddy' (IV.4.110), and urges his son 'to busy giddy minds | With foreign quarrels' (IV.5.213–14). (In *Henry V* the French Prince who thinks England is governed by a 'giddy' youth (II.4.28) will get his comeuppance.) For King Henry IV, as for Northumberland, the sea represents the wild, untameable element they can never hope to control. It seems cruel to the King that the sea should conspire with the god of sleep to behave so maternally towards the favoured ship's boy. Why should sleep 'rock his brains | In cradle of the rude imperious surge' (III.1.19–20)? The King yearns self-pityingly for the state of mindless innocence from which the fathers have been for ever exiled. It is an illusion, of course, or fantasy projection, just as Gloucestershire only seems like an Edenic idyll (especially under the influence of a few drinks).

Northumberland and the King are on the brink of despair for the loss of their sons – literal in one case and virtual in the other. In the play's opening scene Northumberland greets the messenger – the third and true one – who brings certain news of Hotspur's death. He speaks first of reading the man's brow as if it were the title page of a tragic volume, perhaps a play like this one. Yet what the reader sees in the man's face is the trace of the past: 'So looks the strand whereon the imperious flood | Hath left a witnessed usurpation' (I.1.62–3). 'Usurpation' is scarcely an innocent term when the King has seized power by force. But for both Northumberland

and the King it is the flood or sea that is itself 'imperious', a force in the teeth of which mere human 'empire'
is a fragile and probably vain illusion, 'an habitation giddy
and unsure'. Northumberland stares into the abyss, and
summons the forces of rack and ruin. 'Let heaven kiss
earth! Now let not Nature's hand | Keep the wild flood
confined! Let order die!' (153–4). This terrible speech is
a kind of curse, willing the world to destruction, like
Antony's speech at the centre of *Julius Caesar* or Lear's
on the heath.

The King will 'double' this vision in each of his two
big scenes. First when he longs to read the book of fate,

And see the revolution of the times
Make mountains level, and the continent,
Weary of solid firmness, melt itself
Into the sea ... (III.1.46–9)

Then again, though now the imagery shifts to dry land,
in the climactic scene of confrontation with his son. This
is the moment when he contemplates the state of wild
nature to which his son and heir's depravity will reduce,
he believes, the garden of England:

O my poor kingdom, sick with civil blows! ...
O, thou wilt be a wilderness again,
Peopled with wolves, thy old inhabitants! (IV.5.134–8)

We may seem a long way from John of Gaunt's idealized
vision of the garden of England in *Richard II* (II.1.31–68)
– until we remember that that speech too was a nightmare of the realm gone to ruin. This is what King Henry
fears, that his son will be another Richard, a feckless,
insouciant playboy. Yet there is indeed a difference

between King Henry's lament and John of Gaunt's. The latter portrayed England as a sacred realm that has been desecrated, a paradise lost. For King Henry IV the Holy Land is not here but elsewhere, in 'Jerusalem' (IV.5.234–7).

The King is consumed with care about everything over which he is supposed to rule – his realm, his son, himself. When he deputes young Clarence to be the future king's minder he paints a portrait that reveals as much of himself as it does of his heir. He harps on the Prince's temper and lack of self-control. The best way to deal with him when he's moody is to give him time and space, he counsels: 'Till that his passions, like a whale on ground, | Confound themselves with working' (IV.4.40–41). This is another grotesque image of failing passion. But then the King's mind shifts to the contrary – or complementary – thought of forceful containment. He hopes that brother Clarence will prove to be

> A hoop of gold to bind thy brothers in,
> That the united vessel of their blood,
> Mingled with venom of suggestion,
> As force perforce the age will pour it in,
> Shall never leak, though it do work as strong
> As aconitum or rash gunpowder. (43–8)

Again he thinks of energy 'working', in this case chemical energies, but not working to an *end*. On the contrary, he imagines a barrel so firmly hooped that no matter what violent compounds it holds in it will never explode. The King's 'hoop of gold' is – like the Archbishop's infant – a pathetic fantasy. He imagines a magical container that will let 'the venom of suggestion' in but will never let anything out. A perfect machine for the disposal of toxic waste. Poor Clarence.

Fitting then that it should be Clarence who announces their father's imminent death with the image of a fortress that can barely hold life in:

> Th'incessant care and labour of his mind
> Hath wrought the mure that should confine it in
> So thin that life looks through and will break out.
>   (IV.4.118–20)

This recalls Richard II's memorable speech about antic death boring through the castle wall with a little pin – 'and farewell, king!' (III.2.169–70). It also harks back to the 'worm-eaten hold of raggèd stone', as Rumour calls it (Induction, 35), where we first met the 'crafty-sick' Northumberland (37). Modern editions, including this one, call it a 'hold', yet both early texts print 'hole' (see note to Induction, 35). The uncertainty nicely relates to one of the play's own themes, about the holes within holds.

The Prince shares his father's worries about containment. He thinks of the 'majesty' that a king wears as being like a rich suit of armour on a hot day 'That scaldest with safety' (IV.5.32). It keeps you safe but it hurts and may even burn you up. These double-edged images suggest an authority so nervous about its own vulnerability that it fortifies its natural body to excess. The very thing you were supposed to be protecting gets squeezed and pinched and scalded even to death by the security – the 'safety' – required to defend it.

Who would be a father? As the King's death becomes imminent, old superstitions break out amongst the people. Rumour is hard at work. The two sons, Gloucester and Clarence, swop dire omens about 'Unfathered heirs', about the seasons changing their nature and the river flowing three times without ebbing (IV.4.121–8). The last time this happened was several generations back, round the death of their great-grandfather, Edward III. He is indeed a significant figure. If ever these history plays or their anxious rulers could look back to a point of stable origin, a beginning father, the root of them all, it is Edward III, the last strong king before it all went wrong – the death of his heroic son and heir, the Black Prince, and the calamitous succession to the crown of the whimsical, feckless Richard II. *This* is the father, great and grand, to whom the new King Henry V must look back, from whom he should trace his true descent, of whom he should make himself the new double. This is the king who gives his name to *Edward III*, a play popular in the 1590s, in which Shakespeare is likely to have had a hand of some sort, and a play to which *Henry V* explicitly looks back.

What a multitudinous world these fathers and kings and leaders must try to govern. No wonder it extorts so many expressions of helplessness, so many passive grammatical constructions in which we search in vain for a sense of purposive agency. 'We are time's subjects,' says one of the rebel leaders (Hastings, I.3.110). The King too evades responsibility, even when he's confessing, 'God knows, my son, | By what by-paths and indirect crooked ways | I met this crown' (IV.5.183–5). Not 'seized this crown' or 'took it' or even 'found it', but '*met* it', as if for all the world it were a stranger travelling in the opposite direction.

THE THRONG OF
WORDS AND BODIES

The Lord Chief Justice reproves Falstaff for 'wrenching the true course the false way. It is not a confident brow,

nor the throng of words that come with such more than
impudent sauciness from you, can thrust me from a level
consideration' (II.1.108–12). But it is not just the throng
of words that the authorities are up against. It is also the
throng of bodies that will not stay still – or apart from
each other.

There are two kinds of women in the play, one on the
margins of official history and the other well beyond
them. There are the Northumberland ladies, wife and
mother, daughter-in-law and widow. They are defined
entirely by relation to their men, the dead Hotspur and
the shifty, ailing Northumberland. Hotspur's widow, Lady
Percy, carries more force with her single but powerful
elegy for a lost heroic icon, a monument (II.3.18–32).
These women are frozen in grief and mourning, and
never to be seen again. There's a perverse, grotesque
image of fertility associated with Lady Percy's grief,
when she thinks of weeping upon 'remembrance' (that
is, rosemary, the herb), 'That it may grow and sprout as
high as heaven | For recordation to my noble husband'
(59–61). The word 'sprout' may not have been quite
as banal in Shakespeare's time as it is now, but he
could easily have made her say 'climb'. The undignified
physicality of 'sprout' belongs with other prosaic nota-
tions of physical effects such as Morton's description of
fair King Richard's blood being *'scraped* from Pomfret
stones' (I.1.205).

At the other end of the social spectrum the Percy
ladies are mirrored by the Hostess and Doll Tearsheet.
(In Shakespeare's time they were probably played by
the same actors.) Fussing over the slightly wounded
Falstaff after his brawl with Pistol, Doll and the Hostess
comically echo the maternal concern of their patrician
counterparts for their vulnerable menfolk. There are few

further such analogies. The Eastcheap women are as ill-regulated as the Percy ladies are contained and sealed up – which is how anxious authority wants things (and people) to be. The play suggests that this is a response to the sense of how open the body is – how vulnerable, penetrable and permeable.

The very first word of the play is 'Open'. There is a radically destabilizing effect to the opening speech by the figure identified as '*Rumour, painted full of tongues*', who spreads fear and war-fever 'Whiles the big year, swollen with some other grief, | Is thought with child by the stern tyrant War, | And no such matter' (Induction, 13–15). This introduces the important idea of giddy and unsure pregnancy. Not simply 'false pregnancy' in the sense of Doll trying to avoid the strong arm of the law by stuffing a cushion up her dress (V.4.14–15). But more ominously, a real pregnancy of which the origins and outcome are both uncertain. In making his laboured jest out of Shadow's name (III.2.128–31) Falstaff is drawing on the hoary old saying that preys so sharply on Leontes in *The Winter's Tale*, '*Pater semper incertus est*' ('the father is always uncertain'). Unlike maternity, paternity is by its very nature uncertain, a matter of 'surmises, jealousies, conjectures' (Induction, 16), or to put it less darkly, a matter of faith, hope and trust. Just as the passage of regal power is a matter of faith, trust and hope if you believe Harry Harry, or a matter of surmises, jealousies, conjectures if you believe everyone else. Where *is* the Prince's mother and Bolingbroke's queen by the way?

The play stages a conflict between authority and appetite that looks ahead to the world of *Measure for Measure* (1603). More like Prince John than Prince Henry, Lord Angelo has never set foot in the street, let alone in the stews. The scenes in Eastcheap of *Part II* repeat the eating and drinking of its predecessor, but they have been reinforced with more sex and violence in the shape of Doll Tearsheet and Ancient Pistol, in the free allusions to diseases and bastards, and in the verbal habitation composed – or rather hurled wildly together – by its occupants. 'Occupy' is itself one of the many words to have suffered degradation (II.4.143–6), though it is delightful that Doll should be the champion of verbal rectitude, lamenting the corruption of language in the nasty modern world when a nobody like Pistol can be called 'captain' (136). But this is the Hostess's doing, and she is given to elevating her addressees: 'Master Fang' is too good for a mere constable (II.1.1), and 'your grace' for the Lord Chief Justice (67–8). Doll and the Hostess and even Bardolph are vividly aware that the world of words is in a state of chassis (to borrow a phrase from Sean O'Casey's 1924 play *Juno and the Paycock*), what with new words like 'swaggerer' and 'accommodate' looming large, and pipsqueaks like the Page ingeniously railing 'Away, you scullion! You rampallian! You fusti-larian! I'll tickle your catastrophe!' (57–8). There is nothing ingenious about Bardolph's imperturbably circular definition of 'accommodate', when he is put on the spot by Justice Shallow (III.2.65–80). But the Hostess has an irresistibly nonchalant way with words that looks ahead to Dickens and Joyce: 'he's an infinitive thing upon my score', 'Ah, thou honeysuckle villain' (II.1.22–3, 48), 'methinks now you are in an excellent good temperality' (II.4.22–3), and so on.

When it comes to language the Hostess is an innocent. She can say the opposite of what she means: 'aggravate your choler' (II.4.157) and 'O God, that right should thus overcome might!' (V.4.24). She can utter an endless stream of double entendres without realizing it, about

Falstaff's 'weapon' being out, her 'exion' being entered
and her 'case so openly known to the world' (II.1.13–15,
28–9). It is a different matter with Falstaff and Pistol
however, who know just what they are up to with their
bawdy talk about discharging 'upon mine hostess' and
'are etceteras nothings?' (II.4. 108–11, 179). Doll too is
in far more control than the Hostess and a fair match for
Pistol when it comes to verbal violence. But Pistol adds
a wonderful new dimension to the play's linguistic chaos.
Charged up with fragments of rampaging rhetoric from
popular plays of the 1590s, Pistol is permanently on the
point of explosion. It would be an understatement to say
that he's looking for a fight. He is like a swollen phallic
tongue always ready to burst and spray words in every
direction. No wonder audiences (and actors) love him –
as the title page of the 1600 Quarto suggests when along
with 'the humours' of Falstaff it gives a mention to
'swaggering Pistol'.

This rampant male energy out of control can be
detected elsewhere in the play, as for instance when
Northumberland says that 'Every minute now | Should
be the father of some stratagem' (I.1.7–8). It is also at
work in one of the oddest corners of the play, when the
weary Prince indulges in some obscure riddling banter
at the expense of Poins's loose sexual morals. Poins is a
useful butt, because otherwise we might have thought
the Prince was talking about his own sexual activities
(and that this was why he was weary). He seems to be
accusing Poins's unregulated behaviour of increasing the
population at random: 'Whereupon the world increases,
and kindreds are mightily strengthened' (II.2.25–6). But
the effect of random sexual intercourse and its consequences is not only to strengthen kindred or kinship. It
is also to weaken it. Once you're related to everyone you

can't tell the difference between 'us' and 'them', friend and foe. In Doll's 'openness' the Prince sees the complement to Poins's alleged promiscuity, she being as much a 'kinswoman' of Falstaff's 'as the parish heifers are to the town bull' (150–51).

The connections between unlicensed language and sex have been set in motion from the very start when Rumour speaks of the multitude playing on its pipe. If the pipe sounds phallic, its open 'vents' and 'stops' confusingly associate it with a body that can be entered and played on and worked at will. Such a body is like the promiscuous body of the play itself, in and out and round the margins of which so many enter and exit and lurk. There are all the dead and gone: Hotspur, Douglas, Glendower, King Richard II, John of Gaunt, the Mowbray against whom the man who is now king once fought an abortive duel at Coventry. When we get to Justice Shallow's estate his shadowy domain is vastly extended by the old man's precarious memories of his wild youth with the Clement's Inn gang, little John Doit of Staffordshire, black George Barnes, Francis Pickbone, Will Squele, with Scoggin and Samson Stockfish and Jane Nightwork, and the 'little quiver fellow' at Mile End Green. No less important for the play's present tense are all the figures with whom its underworld teems. Behind the working men and women we see for ourselves, such as Francis and '*another Drawer*', the constables Fang and Snare, Justice Shallow's man Davy and the three Grooms, there lies a whole world of everyday labour. In Eastcheap we hear of Master Dommelton the tailor, old Mistress Ursula (unless this is really the Hostess, Mistress Quickly herself), Master Smooth the silkman, goodwife Keech the butcher's wife, Sneak and his 'Noise', Master Tisick the deputy, and Master Dumb our minister. Gloucestershire introduces

us to Silence's daughter Ellen and son William, to William
(the) cook, to William Visor of Woncot and Clement
Perkes o'th'Hill, and to Goodman Puff of Barson
whoever he is. And 'old Double' of course. This is
'rumour' reduced to domestic everyday gossip, the funny
little worlds of soap opera.

But there is something both more and less than funny
about the extraordinary scene – hilarious, shocking,
outrageous, pathetic – in which five Gloucestershire locals
face being recruited into Falstaff's corps to meet almost
certain death (III.2).

'LACK NOTHING! BE MERRY!'

The first of the King's two big scenes (III.1) ends with
his longing to set off for 'the Holy Land'. If played
without a break this leads us straight to Justice Shallow's
country seat in Gloucestershire. The King's second and
final appearance – Act IV, scenes 4 and 5 are effectively
a single scene (see headnotes to these scenes) – also
concludes with reference to the 'Jerusalem' for which the
'ending father' (IV.5.80) must settle, rather than the one
he had in mind. Again we promptly find ourselves in
Gloucestershire. It is not quite the Holy Land nor the
New Jerusalem nor paradise on earth, nor is it overflowing
with milk and honey, but it is a land of comparative
plenty where some at least can eat and drink their fill and
make merry. Shallow's estate is an Elizabethan version
of the moderate dreams, attainable and affordable, that
estate agents now market as a 'highly desirable residence
in a much-sought-after area'. It is a comfortable existence, for some, the nearest thing to festivity and good
fellowship the play can provide. Listen to the dinner

they're going to consume offstage during Act V, scene 2 while the new King is being crowned: pigeons, a couple of short-legged hens, a joint of mutton and some pretty little tiny kickshaws (V.1.22–4) – plus all the sack they can drink.

No wonder everyone breathes a sigh of relief when the play first takes us to Gloucestershire. At last we have escaped – from agonized throne-rooms, urban squalor, the stern arm of the law, the calculations of nervous rebels. What an affable small world of cosy cousins it seems, to begin with, Shallow asking Silence for news of his wife and daughter and cousin William at Oxford. It is a tiny glimpse of the 'normal family life' that is not to be found anywhere else in the play, including Shallow's own wifeless and childless existence.

John of Gaunt was a power in the land when Shallow enjoyed his youth – or tried to, and now thinks he did. Falstaff remembers Gaunt beating young Shallow round the head 'for crowding among the marshal's men' (III.2.312). Gaunt's gorgeous lament for the earthly English Paradise has hung over the subsequent plays. He spoke of the royal kings 'Renownèd for their deeds as far from home | For Christian service and true chivalry | As is the sepulchre in stubborn Jewry | Of the world's ransom, blessèd Mary's son' (*Richard II*, II.1.53–6). This has helped to inspire, as it were, the usurping King Henry IV's dream of self-redemption. But when we encounter Justice Shallow and his domain we also recall Gaunt's vision of 'This other Eden – demi-paradise ... This blessed plot, this earth, this realm, this England' (42–50). Here and now in Gloucestershire we see what the demi-paradise has turned into. It is a tiny fraction of that 'demi' – just as Falstaff imagines himself being sawn into quantities to make 'four dozen of such bearded hermits'

staves' as Master Shallow (V.1.56–8). Gaunt saw Richard's
England being leased out 'Like to a tenement or pelting
farm' (*Richard II*, II.1.60). From his lofty perspective
Shallow's farm might seem 'pelting' or 'paltry', but not
to Falstaff. Miniaturized and thoroughly materialized,
Shallow's domain is the version of an English Eden to
which Gaunt's vision has shrunk. The apples are real and
plentiful, pippins and leather-coats – not the withered old
apple-johns to which Falstaff compared himself in *Part
I* (III.3.3–4), and out of which in *Part II* the Prince made
the cruel jest that angered him to the heart, so the name-
less Drawer remembers (II.4.4–9).

Yet Gloucestershire is not as far away from Eastcheap
as it may seem. Trivial phrase as it is, Shallow echoes the
Drawer when he recalls that as a randy young man he
could anger Jane Nightwork 'to th'heart' (III.2.199).
When he boasts that he and the lads had the best
'bona-robas ... all at commandment' (22–3), he anticipates the phrase that Falstaff will use when he says that
the laws of England are at his commandment (V.3.134–5).
More substantial are the connections between Shallow
and the Hostess, Mistress Quickly. For all the differences
of education and status, they are both garrulous gossips.
The Hostess is probably more cogent and indeed reliable
about the circumstances in which Falstaff allegedly
proposed marriage to her than Shallow is about anything
from the past, and his memories don't have the precision
of detail that hers do to carry conviction. Was Samson
Stockfish really a fruiterer? Did the fight take place
behind Gray's Inn? Did the fight really happen at all?
More convincing is his memory of the 'little quiver fellow'
doing his weapons training at Mile End Green, which
Shallow mimics 'thus' (III.2.269–77) – a comic turn that
can scarcely fail onstage.

Both the Hostess and Justice Shallow are 'old friends' of Falstaff's. Which is to say they are liable to the sentiments generated by shared duration in time with no firmer foundation in friendship, let alone love. She says she has known him 'twenty-nine years, come peascod-time' (II.4.378), and Shallow's acquaintance goes further back to his time at Clement's Inn – according to Silence, fifty-five years ago (III.2.205). If the Hostess provides Falstaff with the nearest thing he has to a home in London, then Shallow looks to Falstaff like the Host who will provide him with a better second residence – this other Eden – in the country. Falstaff would be consumed with envy for Shallow if he couldn't hope to fleece him with ease, or as he puts it, make him 'a philosopher's two stones' (318). Given the sexual meaning of 'stones' – testicles – it is not hard to think of modern equivalents: Falstaff is going to screw him. Isn't this, he asks us, and himself, 'the law of nature' (320)? As it is, the relative luxury in which Shallow lives incites Falstaff to express admiration to his face and envy behind his back. It is outrageous. How has Shallow done it? As a young man he was a nonentity with no more manhood or physical presence than – and this is where Falstaff's expertise in verbal abuse is given full rein – a cheese-paring, a mandrake, a radish, and so on (299–304). How has he stayed so thin? Look at him now with all he needs to eat and drink – no sex, it is true, but some fond memories or fantasies, it scarcely matters which.

The good fellowship supported by Shallow's farm is not a total sham, not at least for the two Justices them-selves, who give no indication that it is anything other than real to them. Nor perhaps for Davy, hard as he has to work. In its small way nothing is more typical of Shakespeare's sociable instincts than the little friendship that wells up between Davy and Bardolph, and the way Shallow chimes in to support it. His characters are always warming or cooling towards each other, rarely static and neutral. It is a wonderful little passage that culminates in Shallow's praise of Bardolph for saying 'I'll stick by him, sir.' 'Why, there spoke a king. Lack nothing! Be merry!' (V.3.67–9). This is promptly followed by the knock on the door with the news from the court that the world has changed. This is the end of the idyll, such as it is, and a return to the world where 'friends' do not stick and perhaps cannot stick by each other, as the new King will not stick by Falstaff.

Compared to Falstaff, Shallow is a comparative innocent. He is certainly innocent of the shameless corruption that Falstaff and Bardolph practise in taking bribes from the locals who can afford it. Shallow correctly identifies the four recruits Falstaff *ought* to take. He also knows that William Visor of Woncot is a knave. But this does not stop him feebly conceding to the worldly wisdom of Falstaff and his man Davy. This is the petty routine corruption on which Shallow's shallow world runs. It receives an unforgettable focus in the recruiting scene (III.2), one of the most brilliant passages Shakespeare ever created, for which the normal connotations of the word 'comic' are scarcely adequate. We don't know whether to laugh or cry. Of course the five potential recruits are ludicrous. Falstaff jeers at them, rather leadenly, and Shallow applauds with risible enthusiasm. Yet it is hard for us not to smile too. Does this not make us partly complicit with Falstaff's chicanery? The scene stages questions that lie at the heart of much comedy, about whom and what you find yourself laughing at and with whom. We know from *Part I* that whoever Falstaff chooses is going to almost certain death. Do they know

it? All of them? How wonderfully Shakespeare distin-
guishes between them. Some make more of an effort to
save their skins than others. Mouldy and Bullcalf have
the means to do it, though in Mouldy's case it is not just
his own skin at stake, but his 'old dame's' too (112). This
may make us more sympathetic towards him – if we
believe him – than towards Bullcalf with his ridiculous
excuse of a cold. Shadow and Wart do not protest at all.
Feeble mutters that he wishes Wart could have been
chosen instead, but in the end he behaves very well,
finding something like courage in the sequence of
commonplaces he utters about a man dying but once,
owing God a death, and no man being too good to serve
his prince (228–32).

But we should spare a thought for the fate of the man
whose only spoken words are 'Here, sir' and 'Yea, sir'
(III.2.137, 139). The first time round Thomas Wart is the
only one of the five to be spared. Even Falstaff can't
make use of him, 'for his apparel is built upon his back,
and the whole frame stands upon pins' (142–3). There's
a good deal of attention to 'apparel' in this play, from
the foul linen the Prince taunts Poins with and Davy
complains about in Falstaff's men to the suits of armour
and the majesty with which power invests itself. Along
with the equally silent but even more unobtrusive Shadow,
Wart is at the lowest end of the spectrum, his appearance that of a derelict ruin – a 'habitation giddy and
unsure' – on the verge of collapse. But then Mouldy and
Bullcalf bribe their way out, and Wart, who had seemed
to be saved, is now doomed. It is on this pathetic figure
that Falstaff fixes to rebut Shallow's feeble complaints
that he has not selected the likeliest men. Given a musket
and made to go through his paces, poor Wart elicits a
further protest from Shallow that he is 'not his craft's

master; he doth not do it right' (III.2.69–70). In a fit of unique generosity Falstaff rewards the doomed Wart with a 'tester' (sixpence). Let us hope he had time to spend it before being 'peppered'. We shall not hear anyone exclaim, as Shallow does about old Double: 'And is old Wart no more?'

The question of money is never far from the surface in Shallow's Gloucestershire, any more than it is in Eastcheap. Davy keeps a close eye on the budget, on the smith's bills that need to be paid, and the cook's wages that ought to be docked for the sack he lost at Hinckley Fair. It is a pity he couldn't catch his master's ear to advise him against lending Falstaff the astronomical sum of a thousand pounds. This is exactly the same amount, as it happens, that Falstaff and his mates stole at Gad's Hill in *Part I* – and had to give up.

REMEMBERING AND FORGETTING

In *Part I* Hotspur speaks bitterly about the erstwhile Bolingbroke as 'this forgetful man' (I.3.159). The first time we see this forgetful man in *Part II* he is pleading with sleep to 'steep my senses in forgetfulness' (III.1.8). The later play is even more concerned than its predecessor with memory and forgetting and the unpredictable relations between the two, their ceaseless interplay. Is such a thing as perfect memory or absolute forgetting conceivable? How far can we trust our own memories, let alone other people's? Can we control them? And what of the past we have not experienced for ourselves, of which our only knowledge comes from others, from stories oral and written, passed on as 'history'? Is memory, both personal and collective, no more stable than a habitation giddy and unsure, no more reliable than the Rumour that posts on the winds? Can we choose and actively summon memories, or are we at their mercy?

Both the King and the rebels are obsessed with the recent past, with 'The dangers of the days but newly gone, | Whose memory is written on the earth | With yet-appearing blood' (IV.1.80–82), as the Archbishop puts it. These writings still need to be read and interpreted. When Westmorland asks Mowbray if he hasn't been restored to all the 'signories' of his 'noble and right well-remembered' father, the haunted son seizes his chance to relive his father's calamitous encounter with Bolingbroke (108–27). For a moment we are back in the world of *Richard II*, when Bolingbroke was still the Duke of Hereford and Mowbray's father Duke of Norfolk. The audience too must remember. But how, exactly? Westmorland's version of the past is not Mowbray's.

As for Hereford-Bolingbroke-King Henry IV, ruefully recalling Richard II's prediction about Northumberland, he appeals for confirmation to his right-hand man, cousin Nevil. Was he not a witness

> When Richard, with his eye brimful of tears,
> Then checked and rated by Northumberland,
> Did speak these words, now proved a prophecy?
> 'Northumberland, thou ladder by the which
> My cousin Bolingbroke ascends my throne' – (III.1.63–7)

But this is not exactly what Richard said, at least not in Shakespeare's play. What Richard said was this: 'Northumberland, thou ladder wherewithal | The mounting Bolingbroke ascends my throne' (*Richard II*, V.1.55–6). His successor has made a small emendation. It purges the record of that ominous epithet 'mounting' and replaces it by the familiar 'cousin', suppressing the hint of a rampant sexuality that would seize the throne by force rather than merely 'ascend' it. Is it deliberate or inadvertent? We can't tell which, nor perhaps can the speaker. But it is hard to resist the suspicion that the King wants to rewrite history, or at least tamper with the detail of its record. At the climax of his last long speech to the Prince he urges his son 'to busy giddy minds | With foreign quarrels, that action hence borne out | May waste the memory of the former days' (IV.5.213–15). Playing the King in the Royal Shakespeare Company production of 1991–2, Julian Glover memorably stumbled on the opening 'w' of 'waste', an emphasis that helped recall the great line spoken by the king he supplanted as he neared his own end: 'I wasted time, and now doth time waste me' (*Richard II*, V.5.49). Unlike Richard II, Henry IV has not wasted time, but the memory of the former days has wasted him.

On his accession to the throne his son makes a formal declaration about memory and forgetting in the scene with the Lord Chief Justice (V.2). Everyone expects the new King to take revenge for the incident when he struck the Lord Chief Justice and was sent to prison for it, a scandal well known to Shakespeare's first audiences, from the historians and, more immediately, from *The Famous Victories*. (Shakespeare chooses not to show it – which helps to protect the Prince's dignity.) 'May this be washed in Lethe and forgotten?' the new King asks (V.2.72). It is conceivable that this is a genuine question, and that it is only the force of the Lord Chief Justice's dignified reply that persuades him to renounce revenge and instead hail the man as the embodiment of 'right justice'. It is no less likely to be a calculated piece of political theatre, designed for the good press the new King is determined to ensure now the stage is at his commandment. This is the way to harness Rumour and try to ride it, to control the news and collective memory.

The Archbishop concludes at one point: 'O thoughts of men accursed! | Past and to come seems best; things present, worst' (I.3.107–8). Not in Eastcheap it doesn't, nor yet in Gloucestershire where past may be best but present is still good. Things present don't usually seem worst to Falstaff. He doesn't much care about the past or the future. Unlike Shallow he does not enjoy wallowing in memory, and there may be a certain curtness to his famous line 'We have heard the chimes at midnight, Master Shallow' (III.2.209–10).

Has Falstaff really forgotten as much as he claims or wishes? Francis and his nameless mate recall the nasty jest the Prince played on Falstaff with the old apple-johns. 'It angered him to the heart. But he hath forgot that' (II.4.8–9). This is magnanimous of Falstaff – or foolish. Perhaps he should *not* have forgotten what the Prince is capable of or what he was trying to tell him. Perhaps he chooses not to remember it, as he certainly chooses to forget the future. The tavern scene enjoys a beautiful moment of transition after the violent expulsion of Pistol, when the musicians start to play and Doll sits on Falstaff's knee. She asks him: 'Thou whoreson little tidy Bartholomew boar-pig, when wilt thou leave fighting a-days, and foining a-nights, and begin to patch up thine old body for heaven?' (II.4.226–8). Those who saw Ralph Richardson's famous Falstaff with the Old Vic Company in 1945 describe his response to these lines as that of a man gazing into the abyss: 'Peace, good Doll, do not speak like a death's-head; do not bid me remember mine end' (29–30). But time is ebbing for Falstaff (and Doll), and it is significant that the Prince makes his entrance at exactly this moment between their two speeches. Doll does speak like a death's-head, but more tenderly than the new King Henry V when he announces in public that 'the grave doth gape | For thee thrice wider than for other men' (V.5.56–7). It is another cruel joke.

There is a special sense in which the idea of remembering and forgetting can be applied to the texts of this play. It comes down to us from Shakespeare's time in two main forms, the Quarto of 1600 and the Folio of 1623 (see An Account of the Text). In fact there are two versions of the former, in the first of which the entirety of Act III, scene 1, the King's first big scene, is absent. Did someone forget to include it? Did Shakespeare add it? Was it deliberately omitted, and if so, by whose choice or command? Had censorship intervened, as seems likely with at least some of the eight passages absent from the Quarto but present in the Folio, and as it certainly did with the deposition scene in *Richard II* (IV.1), omitted from all Quarto texts until the fourth of 1608 (and even then mutilated)? These texts are a part of the history composed by human hands, a matter of remembering and forgetting that is more or less purposive and forcible. So too for that matter is performance, which is the (inevitably imperfect) remembering of a written text in which certain words, lines and passages are omitted, forgotten and altered, both deliberately and inadvertently.

The fact that the most significant differences between Quarto and Folio versions concern the rebels suggests an anxiety in the 1600 text(s) about keeping the challenge to authority in check. Here are the lines 'forgotten' by the Quartos and 'remembered' by the Folio: in Act I, scene 1, two passages in Morton's speech, 166–79 and 189–209; in Act I, scene 3, two passages in Lord Bardolph's, 21–4 and 36–55, and the entire speech of the Archbishop's,

85–108 (including the memory of Richard II trailing after
Bolingbroke into London, and the mob that now yearns
for him then throwing dust on 'his goodly head'); in
Act II, scene 3, Lady Percy's elegy on Hotspur, 23–45;
in Act IV, scene 1, the Archbishop's lines 55–79, and
later in that scene the passage between Westmorland and
Mowbray, 101–37. The pattern suggests a distinct effort
in the earlier texts to 'forget' a good deal of the past associated with Richard II and the adherents to his cause.

Audiences and readers bring their own memories to a
play, including the memory of other related plays, most
obviously, of course, in the case of *Henry IV, Part II*, the
other plays in what is sometimes tendentiously called by
modern critics 'the Henriad'. For Shakespeare's first audiences we would need to add other popular plays of the
time, including the anonymous *Famous Victories of Henry
V* and the uncertainly authored *Edward III* (?1590), and
all the blood-and-thunder hits racing around what passes
for Pistol's brain, including Thomas Kyd's *The Spanish
Tragedy* (c. 1587), Christopher Marlowe's *Tamburlaine
the Great* (also c. 1587) and George Peele's *The Battle of
Alcazar* (c. 1589; the dates are those of composition or
first performance). Some of the readers amongst them
would have brought memories of the historians on
whom Shakespeare drew, the third volume of Raphael
Holinshed's *Chronicles* (1587 edition), Samuel Daniel's
*The First Four Books of the Civil Wars between the Two
Houses of Lancaster and York* (1595), Edward Hall's *The
Union of the Two Noble and Illustre Families of Lancaster
and York* (1548) and John Stow's *The Chronicles of England*
(1580). More generally, audiences would have brought to
the *Henry IV* plays the memory of real bloody events in
the recent past, including the series of major rebellions
against the Tudor monarchy and their violent suppression,

sometimes involving acts of treachery and chicanery by royalty and its officials that bear a family resemblance to the one practised by Prince John in this play. Most notable were the 1536 'Pilgrimage of Grace' and the Northern rebellion of 1569, and amongst the rebel leaders 'Northumberlands' were prominent. Critics point out that Shakespeare could easily have chosen to end the political story of Henry IV's reign with the defeat of the rebels at Bramham Moor in 1408, where the Earl of Northumberland was killed after fighting, as Holinshed reports, 'with great manhood'. If Shakespeare's play chooses not quite to forget this, then it certainly mutes its significance (see Harcourt's speech, IV.4.97–101), and highlights instead the shameful, shameless anticlimax at Gaultree, three years earlier in 1405.

'A GREAT FOOL'

It is hard to speak of Falstaff without being either too generous or too censorious. There are various ways of trying to pin him down. You can stress his provenance in the Vice of the morality plays. You can admire him as a type or an archetype, as the Lord of Misrule, the spirit of Carnival, as rogue, trickster and clown, as the embodiment of infantile and regressive appetite. You can annex him to mythic narratives about scapegoats, about sacrifice, death and rebirth. The idea of him as a sacrificial beast is supported by references in this play to the Prince's 'brawn' (I.1.19), to 'the martlemas' (II.2.95–6) and 'the old boar' (139), and Doll's 'little tidy Bartholomew boar-pig'. But although these frames of reference carry at least a smack of plausibility about them, none of them begins to exhaust his complex vital energy.

Like the recalcitrant Barnardine of *Measure for Measure*
who 'will not die today for any man's persuasion'
(IV.3.57–8), Falstaff resists being wholly appropriated
by anyone's plots or interpretations inside the play or
out – until the play's final moments.

The Falstaff of *Part II* is less buoyant than his earlier
double in *Part I*. He is fighting a rearguard action, a
resourceful but doomed battle against the forces of
gravity. One of his feeblest puns in this second play
seeks to resist precisely this word, when he turns the
Lord Chief Justice's 'gravity' to 'gravy, gravy, gravy'
(I.2.163–4) – a pun so poor that it is almost always omitted
in performance. But a lot of his sallies are now mirthless
and zestless and uninventive – in the Gloucestershire
recruiting scene, for example (III.2). It is a mistake to
suppose we should sit back with fixed grins every time
Falstaff cracks a joke. On the contrary, what makes him
so intriguing is the variability in his powers and resource-
fulness. He can still be wonderfully funny, as for instance
in his scandalous appeal to the Lord Chief Justice against
Mistress Quickly: 'My lord, this is a poor mad soul, and
she says up and down the town that her eldest son is like
you' (II.1.102–3). This is a bit hard on the gullible Hostess.
But in its implication that Shallow is not the only future
Justice to have heard the chimes at midnight and visited
the occasional bona-roba, it is delightfully mischievous.

Does he always know how outrageous he is being?
Much later in the bravura monologue in praise of sack
he claims that 'Prince Harry' gets his valour from
drinking (IV.3.114–20). Does he realize what nonsense
he's talking? Then there are moments when his jests just
fall flat, as for example when he attempts to administer
a blatant snub by inviting Gower to dinner and ignoring
the Lord Chief Justice: 'This is the right fencing grace,

my lord: tap for tap, and so part fair' (II.1.191–2). This is not funny, not clever, just feeble and boorish and frankly embarrassing. But Shakespeare likes to reflect on embarrassment – an essential ingredient of comedy both onstage *and* in the audience. We get a further sense of Falstaff's surprising vulnerability in the scene when he is exposed by Poins and the Prince. Just when we are expecting some typically shameless brilliant riposte, he can only keep repeating, 'No abuse, Hal', 'No abuse, Ned', 'no, faith, boys, none' (II.4.308–19).

The Lord Chief Justice dismisses Falstaff as 'a great fool' (II.1.194), but anyone with a higher opinion of folly and foolery will hear the insult as praise – 'a *great* fool'. If *Part II* is the study of Falstaff in decline, his great powers do not ebb consistently or predictably. On the contrary there is a continuing drama in the question of his mastery over them, the spasmodic and irregular movements by which he triumphantly reclaims and relaxes his grip on them. In this respect he echoes the motifs and rhythms discussed above in the play as a whole. He shares in the predicament of all the older authority figures who try to retain power as it is menaced or shaken or melts away. Falstaff is another 'ending father', though the nature and style of his authority is very different from the King's or Northumberland's.

For one thing he is – like Justice Shallow – childless. The tiny page boy that the Prince has given him serves as a pathetic reminder that he will never have a true son and heir of his own. He has nothing to pass on and nobody to pass it on to. On his first entrance with the Page he announces: 'I do here walk before thee like a sow that hath overwhelmed all her litter but one' (I.2.10–12). For all the enormity of his great belly, it will never give birth to new life – and may even crush it to death: 'my womb, my womb, my womb undoes me', he confesses (IV.3.22), as if it has swallowed up his own manhood. It is a curious little speech. He is standing over an opponent, Colevile of the Dale, who has surrendered himself without a fight on the mere strength of the reputation for valour that Falstaff has gained by 'killing' Hotspur. He boasts that his belly holds 'a whole school of tongues' that speak only his name (18–20). But this leaves no more room for true dialogue or the production of shared new truths than the tongues of Rumour. Indeed Falstaff is Rumour incarnate on earth, a source of endless baseless fictions and fantasies, gossip and scandal and lies. 'If I had a thousand sons', he cries with typical hyperbole (120), just after he has been spinning his ludicrous line about the source of Prince Harry's valour in drink. But it is not a thousand sons he needs. One true one would do.

One of the keys to the Falstaff we see in *Part II* is that he has been 'severed' from the Prince (I.2.204–5). We barely see them together. In *Part I* they were almost inseparable, sharing eight scenes and more than nine hundred lines. They were a great double act, not least in the wonderful improvised theatre they made in the tavern scene (II.4). 'O Jesu, this is excellent sport, i'faith', says the Hostess (383), and everyone agrees with her, onstage and off. There is no such excellent sport in *Part II*. Before the final scene, the Prince and Falstaff only meet once, in the tavern scene, for a mere eighty lines. The Prince turns, from prose to verse and exits from comedy into history, never to return (until perhaps the final scene of *Henry V*). Of course Falstaff has other partners to play with, including the serious Justice in London and the foolish ones in Gloucestershire. The other low-life figures around him seize a greater share of the limelight, especially the new figures of Pistol and Doll, though Mistress

Quickly too is more richly characterized than she was in *Part I*. But Falstaff himself is correspondingly diminished, a great fool pining for the promising apprentice he supposed he'd been teamed up for life with.

Some readers and critics try to take a single uniform stance on Falstaff, of rigid disapproval or no less staunch support. This requires a certain resistance to the experience of the play as it unfolds in performance or the act of reading. Those who yield to this process are more likely to feel a continuous ebb and flow in their sympathies for Falstaff. This has much to do with the sense, at any one moment, of whether he is predator or potential prey. He seems most sympathetic when he is on the defensive, the trickster holding his own in the teeth of authority, or railing against the 'costermongers' times' when 'pregnancy is made a tapster' (I.2.171–2), and tailors like Master Dommelton stand upon 'security' (28–47). It is hard not to take his side in a losing battle against the 'whoreson smoothy-pates' (36–7). He has a fine rally with the Lord Chief Justice in Act I, scene 2, and the abuse he directs at Prince John behind his back at the end of Act IV, scene 3 is likely to be welcome. But the Hostess poses no such real threat to him as these powerful men. And in the Gloucestershire recruiting scene it is impossible whole-heartedly to jeer along with him at the more or less innocent victims whom he is exploiting.

In fact there is a carefully calculated structure to Falstaff's role in this play. In the first half, his main adversary-partners are the Lord Chief Justice and the Prince – weighty opponents. But in the second half things get easy for him – too easy. His victims in Gloucestershire and at Gaultree are simply no match for him. Even he seems depressed by the ease with which Colevile of the Dale yields to his mere name. He is lulled into a false sense of security, and so perhaps are we, even though we know that he is bound to get his comeuppance. This is the point of giving Falstaff the powerful stage effect of three soliloquies in succession in the latter part of the play. Three times he is left alone at the end of a scene so he can be ingeniously abusive of some butt – Shallow (III.2), then Prince John, though he takes off into more than that (IV.3), then Shallow again (V.1). He begins to think he is leisured for life, now that he has found an easy rich prey in the shape of Shallow, and then climactically, when his former pupil assumes the throne: 'I know the young King is sick for me' (V.3.133). But we know he is not. This in turn has the effect of making the King's rejection seem also too easy, so that our sympathies swing back to Falstaff, the victim of his own delusions. To say that our sympathies swing back is not to say that they do not keep vibrating, along with our knowledge that an England in which the laws really were at Falstaff's commandment would be no fun at all, for almost everyone. Even perhaps a wilderness of wolves.

'MY KING! MY JOVE!'

It is an embarrassing moment when Falstaff accosts the new King in all his majesty as 'my royal Hal', 'my sweet boy', 'My King! My Jove! . . . my heart' (V.5.41–9). It is embarrassing for the King and his entourage, and also perhaps for us. Doubly so when crazy Pistol seconds him with 'most royal imp of fame' (42–3). But embarrassment deepens swiftly into humiliation, the King's crushing rejection of an old fat man. This is revenge; this is justice.

Above all it is the redemption of a promise made to the audience by the young Prince Hal near the start of

Part I, the controversial soliloquy in which he confides in us his resolution – and hence makes us complicit with it – in due course to throw off his 'loose behaviour', 'falsify men's hopes' and 'redeem the time' when men least think he will. We have at last reached the 'due course', the conclusion of the story the Prince-King has sought to realize, a story which he now characterizes as waking from a dream: 'I have long dreamt of such a kind of man ... | But being awaked I do despise my dream' (V.5.52–4). It is possible to respect the dreams we leave behind, to remember them with honour rather than to forget them with scorn. But not this one, it seems.

The Prince's story is history in the sense that it is what rulers want to believe and, even more importantly, want their subjects to believe. Here it is the story of controlled, purposive accession to the crown by a prince whose 'reformation' has never been in doubt because he has never really committed himself to the life of riot for which he has been infamous. He has allowed rumour and gossip and scandal to circulate, to infect his reputation and stain his honour, because he is confident that when it comes to the crunch he will be able to persuade everyone he is completely reformed. This is an astonishingly risky strategy, and it is surprising how many critics take the Prince at his word by believing in the absolute stability of his self-belief.

This is one way of reading (and playing) him. But it is less interesting than one which sees him as altogether more vulnerable, needy, uncertain of himself, unpredictable. The soliloquy in *Part I* represents how he thinks he would like to think of himself. He is performing for us but also for himself. The Prince will become a 'good king' because he has studied the role so carefully and knows how to perform the illusion of perfect control

– over himself, his future, his story. It is as if this soliloquy were written in retrospect – and perhaps it was, by
a Shakespeare looking back from the vantage point of
the ending he wanted to create. This doesn't mean that
we have to believe it. In fact you could say that for all
its repetitions and echoes, one of the things that *Part II*
signally lacks is any repetition of that soliloquy in *Part
I*. Shakespeare could easily have provided it if he had
wanted to. Instead the Prince ascends and recedes from
both his old cronies and us, the readers and audience,
into the enigma of 'majesty'.

Yet there is one passage in this play when the Prince
is effectively alone onstage, whether we call it a soliloquy or not. It is the moment when he watches over his
unconscious father (IV.5.22–48). He addresses the crown
– 'O polished perturbation! Golden care!' – and more
abstractly, the concept of 'majesty'. Like his father he
thinks yearningly of the sound sleep enjoyed by the
innocent, 'he whose brow with homely biggen bound |
Snores out the watch of night'. Believing the King to be
dead, he addresses him as 'My gracious lord! My father!'
And again, perhaps more tenderly than at any other
moment, 'O dear father'. He puts the crown on his head,
avowing that God will guard it, and that nothing shall
force 'This lineal honour from me. This from thee | Will
I to mine leave, as 'tis left to me.'

Unlike in his soliloquy in *Part I*, the Prince does not
seem to be addressing us. Yet this is still partly if not
wholly a performance – for himself. Rulers need to
convince themselves that they are right about their rights.
They must also perform this conviction for others. The
whole great scene between the Prince and his ending
father rehearses the performance the new King must
present to the world. This he does to magnificent and

crushing effect in the play's final scenes, first when he adopts the Lord Chief Justice – 'You shall be as a father to my youth' (V.2.118) – and then when he repudiates Falstaff (V.5.50). These performances make something happen 'for real' – like real coronations and judicial sentences. In this sense the new King Henry V answers the Rumour that set this play going. Where Rumour fed parasitically off real events and turned them into endless stories, now the King's words make real things happen, once and for all.

Yet the play does not end quite there, as it might, on the King's exit. As soon as he leaves the stage the 'surmises, jealousies, conjectures' of which Rumour spoke start up again. How can anyone know for certain what the future holds, even the King – even the dramatist? Falstaff bravely assures Shallow that the King will send for him in private. Prince John suggests that Falstaff and his mates will be 'very well provided for', and that there will soon be an expedition to France. For Elizabethan audiences, the Epilogue (rarely heard in modern performances) returned them to an atmosphere of uncertain speculation from which the whole play began – with Rumour.

The new English King seems real enough, wide-awake and very keen to make history. But we have seen that history is also made by the endlessly heterogeneous and finally unknowable lives that have passed before us – made out of them and made up by them. In the subsequent play that bears his own name, King Henry V will demonstrate further what it means to try to govern the process of history, to enjoy the rewards and to count the cost of 'success'.

Adrian Poole

The Play in Performance

From the late 1590s onwards *Henry IV, Part I* has always been more popular and enjoyed more independent performances than its darker sequel. In 1894 at Stratford-upon-Avon Frank Benson produced a free-standing *Henry IV, Part II*, but this was unusual. Over the centuries a more familiar tactic for 'liberating' *Part II* has been to turn it into a Falstaff play either by adaptation, as did Thomas Betterton at Drury Lane in 1720, or by conflation with *Part I*, as in Charles Short's *The Life and Humours of Falstaff* of 1829. As early as, in all probability, 1623 Sir Edward Dering prepared a version of the two *Henry IV* plays for private theatricals that jettisoned most of the comic material from *Part II*. The twentieth century saw a more enduring example of what can be done by cannibalizing the plays in the interest of a new artwork. Orson Welles's film *Chimes at Midnight* (1965; retitled *Falstaff* for the USA the following year) is not only a magnificent retelling of Falstaff's story, but, like all the best translations, a fine commentary on the original texts out of which it is made (including *Henry V*, for Falstaff's death).

If you assume the memory of *Part I* in producing *Part II*, you are faced with some difficulties of continuity, especially as regards the apparent relapse of the Prince's confidence in the new public role he seems to have achieved at the end of the previous play. Faced with creating a continuous narrative that bridges the two parts, Welles ingeniously reversed the sequence after the battle at Shrewsbury to make the King believe that Falstaff has indeed killed Hotspur. This robs the Prince of the credit he ought to have won from his father and motivates the estrangement between them that in Shakespeare's *Part II* has been mysteriously renewed. Theatre productions of the two plays in sequence have been known to adopt this ruse, such as Michael Bogdanov's for the English Shakespeare Company (1986; hereafter ESC).

Larger questions are raised by the possibility of producing *Henry IV, Part II* as part of a sequence leading on to *Henry V* and harking back to *Richard II*. Since the production of these four plays as a tetralogy in 1951 at Stratford-upon-Avon, the Royal Shakespeare Company (hereafter RSC) has put the plays on in sequence at decent intervals, even in a full cycle that paradoxically goes on to the 'earlier' (that is, written earlier) tetralogy of the three *Henry VI* plays and *Richard III*, as in the famous condensed seven-play cycle *The Wars of the Roses* for the quatercentenary of Shakespeare's birth in 1964, directed by Peter Hall, John Barton and Clifford Williams. In 1986 the ESC mounted a touring version of the English history plays that sought quite deliberately to challenge the cultural dominance of the RSC. Whether in sequence or not it has also become something of a habit to use the two *Henry IV* plays to mark moments of theatre history, such as the Festival of Britain in 1951 and the RSC's opening season at the Barbican Theatre in 1982. The plays encourage a statement about 'the condition of England', and perhaps 'of the English theatre': hence their performance as part of the 2000 season entitled 'This England' with which the RSC marked the millennium.

The choice of presenting the plays as part of a sequence has consequences for the actors playing the three principal roles in *Part II*, the King, the Prince and Falstaff. Stretching back to its beginning in *Richard II*, the King's story can be played and perceived as personal tragedy. Conversely the Prince's story looks forward to the unfolding and testing of his kingship in *Henry V*. For Falstaff, however, because his role is confined to the two *Henry IV* plays (despite the ambiguous promise contained in the Epilogue to *Part II*), the aggrandizement enjoyed by the King and the Prince is likely to reduce his significance to the sequence as a whole.

Whether presented as a 'diptych' or part of a longer sequence, the *Henry IV* plays present several possibilities for the significant doubling of roles both across plays and within them. What happens to Hotspur in *Part II*? This can also be a question for the actor playing him. In 1945 Laurence Olivier with the Old Vic Company famously followed his Hotspur in *Part I* by playing Shallow in *Part II*, a tour de force which Roy Dotrice sought to repeat with the RSC in 1964. Another way of thinking about what happens to Hotspur's energy is to turn him into Pistol, as John Price did for the ESC. Other possibilities that suggest comparison and contrast across the apparently separate domains of the play include a famous doubling in 1864 by Samuel Phelps of the King with Justice Shallow – following his Falstaff in *Part I*. Given the comparative paucity of roles for women, there is not much temptation now to double the two Percy ladies with the Hostess and Doll Tearsheet, as was probably the case in Shakespeare's time. By contrast there are all sorts of things you can do with Rumour. You could have Rumour's speech delivered by the actor playing Falstaff, Doll Tearsheet, Pistol or Silence, amongst others. Several modern productions have shared the speech amongst the whole or a large part of the cast to good effect. Trevor Nunn's 1982 production sustained the sense of collective enterprise engendered by this opening by the continued presence of anonymous witnesses watching the action onstage.

The sense of the present and past on which the plays drew for their original Elizabethan audiences is naturally very different from ours. They would have enjoyed a sharp contrast between their consciousness of events belonging to a collective past and the experience of elements from the world around them, such as Boar's Head taverns, corrupt recruiting practices, beadles, apple-johns, Bartholomew boar-pigs, Barbary hens, flap-dragons, half-kirtles, signs of the Leg, testers and the 'four Harry ten shillings in French crowns' with which Bullcalf bribes Bardolph (III.2.216–17), let alone the popular plays spinning round Pistol's head or the Amuraths in the news from whom the new King Henry V is careful to distinguish himself. This was history bursting into the present before their very eyes – unless it was the present leaping into the past. But for us now the plays themselves belong to a past we are unlikely to distinguish sharply from the past dramatized *within* them. We are not going to feel at first hand the distance of nearly two hundred years between the events of the early 1400s and their fictional staging in the 1590s. Faced with our distance from the 1590s in which the plays made their debut, modern performance must choose whether to stress or to mask it, or to settle for some combination of the two, as for example by costume and set designs that position the play in a specific historical time, past or present, or some purposively eclectic combination that keeps the question of historical distance open (as the ESC did, to excellent effect, in the 1980s).

Most modern productions choose to suppress the distance by cutting elements of the text we won't understand without help from an editor. Even editors can be stumped by a phrase as obscure as Falstaff's commendation of Wart's martial valour, his capacity to 'come off and on swifter than he that gibbets on the brewer's bucket' (III.2.256–7). Amongst the candidates for omission are some of Falstaff's references in his opening scene to 'a face-royal', a 'whoreson Achitophel' (I.2.24,34), and the proverbial saying about the dangers of ending up with a whore, a knave and a jade if you choose a wife in Westminster, a servant in St Paul's and a horse in Smithfield (48–52). The Page is unlikely to be allowed his jest at Bardolph's expense about 'Althaea's dream' (II.2.82–5) and Doll her animadversions on the fate of the word 'occupy' (II.4.143–6). But it is not always desirable to cut things a modern audience won't fully or immediately understand – Pistol's scraps from popular plays from the 1590s for instance, and his invocations of 'Atropos' (II.4.194) and 'Alecto's snake' (V.5.37), or indeed his great challenge to Shallow: 'Under which king, Besonian? Speak, or die' (V.3.113).

Other considerations govern the editing of the text for performance. From the 1600 Quarto onwards the rebels have invariably received shorter shrift than the Folio allows them (see Introduction, pp. l–li, and An Account of the Text). Shakespeare's audiences and first readers took far more interest in argumentative and persuasive speech than we do now. They also took more interest in what may now seem gratuitously 'poetic' diction, such as Northumberland's lines about the fall of Troy (I.1.70–75), or the Prince's image on being called away from the tavern: 'When tempest of commotion, like the south | Borne with black vapour, doth begin to melt | And drop

upon our bare unarmèd heads' (II.4.358–60), or the King's
about the 'beachy girdle of the ocean' and the 'cup of
alteration' (III.1.50–52). These are all passages cut for
the RSC production of 1964, so the prompt book records.
The trimming of such 'excess' in the interest of narrative
speed and momentum is characteristic of (though not
unique to) the modern theatre (and all the more so
of film).

Much of the challenge of *Part II* concerns the balance
of power: between the world of history, conducted mainly
in verse, and the world of comedy, conducted entirely in
prose; between the actors playing the King, the Prince
and Falstaff, and the impact made on audiences by the
Prince's relationships with these two 'fathers'; and
between these three principal roles and the wealth of
minor parts in which actors can make a strong impression or steal the limelight.

Though these are mainly to be found in the comic
'underworlds', the actor playing Lady Percy has one big
opportunity in Act I, scene 3, and the actors playing
Prince John and the Lord Chief Justice have several. The
comic roles are far easier, and some of them may seem
a gift. This should certainly be true of Pistol and Shallow.
There have been famous Pistols from Theophilus Cibber
in the early eighteenth century to John Price sporting a
leather jacket with 'Hal's Angels' on the back for the ESC
in 1986, and Albie Woodington for the RSC in 1991. As
for Justice Shallow (and to a lesser extent Silence), theatre
critics regularly melt over 'two of the most cryingly
funny and adorable crumblies that you will ever see', to
quote the *Daily Telegraph* on Michael Attenborough's
production (3 July 2000). This suggests the seductive-
ness of the Gloucestershire scenes, and the edge that
productions can *miss*, whether deliberately or not. It is

tempting for actors and audiences alike to take pleasure in the theatrical bravura of character 'types' and the 'turns' they are offered. There is evidence from the Quarto text that Shakespeare had such pleasures in mind when he cast one of the company's minor players, John Sincklo, as the Beadle in Act V, scene 2. This man's skinny physique would have qualified him well for Shadow too, and all five of the would-be recruits in Act III, scene 2 offer more possibilities than the words they get given to speak would suggest. The Hostess and Doll are also fine parts. Released from the censorship under which it languished throughout the nineteenth century, Doll's role offers the opportunity for a combination of sexiness, sleaziness, warm-heartedness and cold neediness that can seem a clue to the play's whole underworld.

As for the rivalry between the three principals, this is exacerbated by the greater distances separating them than was the case in *Part I*. This has the effect of exposing to even more pressure the two great scenes where the Prince *does* make a final reckoning with the King and with Falstaff (IV.5 and V.5). It raises questions about the relative weight of the two relationships, that sometimes tilts towards the one with his father the King and sometimes towards the one with Falstaff. Critical reactions to Terry Hands's 1975 RSC production suggested that the true climax lay in the scene between Alan Howard's Prince and Emrys James's King, whereas Trevor Nunn's in 1982 seemed to locate the play's centre of gravity in the relationship between Joss Ackland's Falstaff and Gerard Murphy's Prince. The histrionic rivalries here mirror the fictional ones they are representing. We might also note the potential in the role of Poins, whose special relationship with the Prince makes him another rival to Falstaff. Welles's film makes a good deal of the brooding, unsettled rapport between the two young men, while at least one production has given Poins a textually unauthorized place in the new King's entourage at the end of the play so he can cock a final snook at the humiliated Falstaff.

A great deal naturally depends on the strength of the actors you cast as the King and Falstaff. In his excellent short book on *Henry IV, Part I* Simon Callow complains at the 'shortage in the Western world of what might be called "king actors", those who by sheer weight of personality – sometimes by sheer physical weight, or height – can embody the notion of kingship so crucial to the impact of the plays'. The Russians can do it more easily, he thinks. But it was a good role for David Garrick from 1758 to 1770, John Gielgud gives an unforgettable performance in Welles's film, and there have been fine later Kings including Julian Glover (1991) and David Troughton (2000).

As with the King's, the role of the Prince gains complexity if it is part of a sequence that culminates with the conquests in France in *Henry V*. Yet even without the subsequent Falstaff-less play, *Henry IV, Part II* provides the new King with a magnificent climax. From 1739 onwards Covent Garden productions made a big scenic display of the coronation, reaching their zenith in the 1821 production by William Macready with elaborate music by Henry ('Home Sweet Home') Bishop, to coincide with the real-life coronation of George IV. Through the nineteenth century and at least up until Michael Redgrave's production for the Festival of Britain in 1951, performance history took a positive view of the Prince's progress to power. It helped if the actor looked 'princely', as the young Richard Burton certainly did in Redgrave's production and Michael Pennington in Michael Bogdanov's for the ESC. If the British theatre and its audience have lost some of their faith in princes and royalty over the last fifty years, there is still a presumption about what princes should look like, such as made the distinctly unpatrician looks of Gerard Murphy a controversial piece of casting in Nunn's 1982 production. His performance was predictably dismissed with contempt by some and welcomed by others.

In the case of the Prince and Falstaff you have to decide how confident to make them about the way the play is going to end. You can stress the Prince's manipulative powers and make him as coldly calculating as his brother John. But John Dougall, who succeeded Pennington in the role of the Prince, writes well that 'in the depths and heights of his behaviour there is a recklessness, a danger, a need to push situations to extremes and test himself and those around him'. Dougall hoped to retain 'a sense of adolescent vulnerability, to show he was not simply a manipulator but is himself manipulated, by Falstaff his surrogate father, and by the ambivalent nature of kingship, which both attracts and repels him' (quoted in Bogdanov and Pennington, *The English Shakespeare Company*). The test of the Prince's temper comes in the sequence of scenes where he settles his score with his three 'fathers'. You have to decide how much depth and sincerity of feeling to give him when he thinks his father is dead – 'My gracious lord! My father!', 'O dear father' (IV.5.35, 41) – and then again when he pleads for forgiveness. Does he plan in advance the scene with the Lord Chief Justice (V.2), or does he wait to see what happens and then make it up on the spot? Does he foresee the scene in public with Falstaff? Has he prepared himself for it perfectly, or is there some doubt, even a flicker, about exactly what he will say and do?

For Falstaff too it is a question of how confident he really is that when his sweet boy is King the laws of England will be at his commandment. Although some actors have retained the buoyancy of *Part I*, it is hard to keep entirely at bay the deepening melancholy that threatens him throughout *Part II*, especially in the almost complete absence of his best sparring partner and pupil, the young Prince himself. Some memorable modern Falstaffs have come close to making him a tragic figure – Ralph Richardson in 1945, for example, and Welles himself. You must choose how much self-pity to allow him, as well as how much geniality and callousness, especially in his dealings with the Hostess, the recruits and Justice Shallow. You must choose how far to play up or play down what has been described as the class anxiety surrounding him – the marks of degraded gentility, education and learning that distinguish him from the authentically plebeian company it suits him to keep. Many of the most successful Falstaffs have been praised for their intelligence, but the question that animates the role throughout *Part II* is the extent to which he foresees the humiliation that awaits him. You can play his reaction to the King's rejection as thunderstruck shock. Or you can play it as no surprise at all but a long-expected confirmation of his deepest fears. This latter was the way Robert Stephens in 1991 and Desmond Barrit in 2000 both played the part for the RSC, as it seemed to many observers. You could even insinuate a small element of relief that at last the waiting is over. Most effective of all perhaps is to keep the audience guessing to the very end about the varying elements of insight, foresight and self-deception that go to make up this enormous and complex creation.

Adrian Poole

Further Reading

TEXTS, EDITORIAL PROBLEMS, AND SOURCES

The copies chiefly used in the preparation of this edition were those in the British Library, which holds copies of both the four-leaf and six-leaf issues of gathering E (see An Account of the Text). The Folio version can most conveniently and reliably be read in *The Norton Facsimile: The First Folio of Shakespeare* (1968), prepared by Charlton Hinman. This is made up from clear and, where possible, final proof-corrected sheets of many copies of the first Folio. It should be consulted in conjunction with Hinman's study, *The Printing and Proofreading of the First Folio of Shakespeare*, 2 vols. (1963). The 1600 Quarto is reproduced in facsimile in the Malone Society's reprint, ed. Thomas L. Berger (1990), and in *Shakespeare's Plays in Quarto*, ed. Michael J. B. Allen and Kenneth Muir (1981). An edition of Charles Kemble's Coronation production of 1821 (see The Play in Performance) with the text and full details of the staging has been published by the Cornmarket Press (1971); the same publisher has issued several other adaptations of *Henry IV, Part II* in the two series, Acting Versions of Shakespeare. Of great interest, but little textual relevance to *Henry IV, Part II*, is a facsimile of *The History of King Henry the Fourth, as revised by Sir Edward Dering, Bart.* (prepared by G. W. Williams and G. B. Evans (1974)). This is the only surviving manuscript of a play (or rather plays) by Shakespeare from the reign of James I; it conflates both parts of *Henry IV* into a single play. It has been confidently dated as having been prepared not later than February 1623 and probably not much earlier than the beginning of the year by Laetitia Yeandle ('The Dating of Sir Edward Dering's Copy of "The History of King Henry the Fourth"', *Shakespeare Quarterly* 37 (1986), pp. 224–6).

The most helpful editions of the play are the New Variorum, ed. Matthias A. Shaaber (1940); and the Arden, 2nd series, ed. A. R. Humphreys (1966). This edition is deeply indebted to them. Recent editions include those edited by Giorgio Melchiori in the New Cambridge series (1989) and René Weis in the Oxford Shakespeare series (1997). Of editions in one-volume collections of Shakespeare's plays, two are particularly recommended: that in *The Riverside Shakespeare*, ed. G. Blakemore Evans, with introduction by Herschel Baker (2nd edn, 1997), and John Jowett's edition in the Oxford *Complete Works*, ed. Stanley Wells and Gary Taylor (1986); see also their *A Textual Companion* (1987). There are many studies of the text and, as the Account of the Text shows, they are far from being in agreement. I suggest for further reading Shaaber's discussion in the New Variorum edition and in *Shakespeare Quarterly* 6 (1955); Alice Walker's counter-arguments in the *Review of English Studies*, new series II (1951), and *The Library*, 5th series VI (1951); J. K. Walton's *The Quarto Copy for the First Folio of Shakespeare* (1971), which contains much that is relevant to the problem (but see the review by Albert Smith, *The Library*,

5th series XXVII (1972)); and Alan E. Craven's study of
the work of Compositor A who set the Quarto of *Henry
IV, Part II, Studies in Bibliography* XXVI (1973). An important study of the Folio text of *Henry IV, Part II*, Eleanor
Prosser's *Shakespeare's Anonymous Editors* (1981) argued
that eighty-six Folio readings regularly accepted by
modern editors must be rejected (and see An Account of
the Text, p. 128).

Useful summaries of the sources are given in the New
Variorum and Arden editions; the fullest collection is in
Geoffrey Bullough's *Narrative and Dramatic Sources of
Shakespeare*, vol. IV (1962), which includes *The Famous
Victories of Henry V*. The second tetralogy is discussed
by Edna Zwick Boris in *Shakespeare's English Kings,
the People, and the Law: A Study of the Relationship
Between the Tudor Constitution and the English History
Plays* (1978). Peter Saccio's *Shakespeare's English Kings:
History, Chronicle, and Drama* (1977) is a handy intro-
duction to historical matters. Shakespeare's rich indebt-
edness to the Bible is fully documented in Naseeb
Shaheen's *Biblical References in Shakespeare's History Plays*
(1989).

BACKGROUND AND CRITICISM

Several books on the background to the history plays or
considering the history plays as a whole are relevant for
Henry IV. These include E. M. W. Tillyard, *Shakespeare's
History Plays* (1944; repr. 1962); Lily B. Campbell,
Shakespeare's 'Histories': Mirrors of Elizabethan Policy
(1947); Paul A. Jorgensen, *Shakespeare's Military World*
(1956); D. A. Traversi, *Shakespeare: from 'Richard II'
to 'Henry V'* (1957); M. M. Reese, *The Cease of Majesty*

(1961); S. C. Sen Gupta, *Shakespeare's Historical Plays* (1964); Gareth Lloyd Evans, *Shakespeare II* (1969) in the series Writers and Critics; and Robert Ornstein, *A Kingdom for a Stage* (1972). *Shakespeare Survey 6* (1953) includes a survey by Harold Jenkins of work on the history plays between 1900 and 1951; and in *Shakespeare: A Bibliographical Guide*, ed. Stanley Wells (1990), Richard Dutton provides a useful bibliographical guide to the histories as a whole, with particular attention to the *Henry IV* plays, in 'The Second Tetralogy' (*Richard II*, the two *Henry IV* plays and *Henry V*).

Many of the critical studies referred to in the list of Further Reading for *Henry IV, Part I* are also relevant to *Henry IV, Part II*, and this applies especially to Falstaff. A particularly useful survey is Arthur C. Sprague's 'Gadshill Revisited', *Shakespeare Quarterly* 4 (1953), which is reprinted in the Norton Critical Edition of *Henry IV, Part I*, ed. James L. Sanderson (1962). Maurice Morgann's study of Falstaff (1777) is published in *Eighteenth Century Essays on Shakespeare*, ed. D. Nichol Smith (1903), and in other collections (see below). Dr Johnson's comments are also frequently reprinted, as are A. C. Bradley, 'The Rejection of Falstaff', in his *Oxford Lectures on Poetry* (1909); E. E. Stoll, from his *Shakespeare Studies* (1927); and J. Dover Wilson, *The Fortunes of Falstaff* (1943). William Empson's essay in defence of Falstaff was posthumously published in his *Essays on Shakespeare*, ed. David B. Pirie (1986); this is a much revised version of his 'Falstaff and Mr Dover Wilson', published in *Kenyon Review* XV (1953). Harold Bloom has edited a volume on Falstaff in the Major Literary Characters series (1991), and there is a study of Falstaff from a very different perspective by Roderick Marshall, *Falstaff: The Archetypal Myth* (1989). He sees the character recurring in many cultures, in histories and in folklore from India, Egypt and Russia, and sets out to throw light on human characteristics as well as on Shakespeare's character. Gender and sexuality are the standpoint for Valerie Traub's essay, 'Prince Hal's Falstaff: Positioning Psychoanalysis and the Female Reproductive Body' (*Shakespeare Quarterly* 40 (1989), pp. 456–74). Other studies of the plays which are relevant are Caroline Spurgeon, *Shakespeare's Imagery and What It Tells Us* (1935); on the relationship of the two parts of the play, M. A. Shaaber, 'The Unity of *Henry IV*', in *Joseph Quincy Adams Memorial Studies*, ed. J. G. McManaway, G. E. Dawson and E. E. Willoughby (1948), and Harold Jenkins, *The Structural Problem in Shakespeare's 'Henry the Fourth'* (1956); A. P. Rossiter's essay, 'Ambivalence: The Dialectic of the Histories', in his *Angel with Horns* (1961); and C. L. Barber, 'The Trial of Carnival in *Part Two*', in his *Shakespeare's Festive Comedy* (1959).

Two useful collections of essays are available. G. K. Hunter has edited *King Henry IV Parts 1 and 2: A Casebook* (1970). Hunter's introduction is particularly valuable, and the volume includes comments by Johnson, some of the essays noted above (Morgann, Bradley, Dover Wilson, Tillyard and Empson) and H. B. Charlton (extracts from his *Shakespeare, Politics and Politicians* (1920)), J. I. M. Stewart, 'The Birth and Death of Falstaff' (from his *Character and Motive in Shakespeare* (1949)), W. H. Auden, 'The Prince's Dog' (first printed in *Encounter* 13 (1959) as 'The Fallen City'; repr. with the new title in his *The Dyer's Hand* (1962)) and Paul A. Jorgensen ('Redeeming Time in Shakespeare's *Henry IV*', *Tennessee Studies in Literature* (1969)).

The second collection is *Twentieth-Century Interpretations of Henry IV, Part Two*, ed. David P. Young (1968), with a useful introduction. Inevitably the two anthologies overlap to some extent. Among the contributions are L. C. Knights, 'Time's Subjects: The Sonnets and *King Henry IV, Part 2*', from his *Some Shakespearean Themes* (1959); Clifford Leech, 'The Unity of *2 Henry IV*' (from *Shakespeare Survey 6* (1953)); Harold E. Toliver, 'Falstaff, the Prince, and the History Play' (from *Shakespeare Quarterly* 16 (1965)); and a previously unpublished essay by Robert B. Pierce, 'The Generations in *2 Henry IV*'. Barber, Traversi, Bradley, Dover Wilson, Tillyard, Jenkins, Rossiter, R. J. Dorius ('A Little More than a Little', *Shakespeare Quarterly* 11 (1969)), and an extract from A. R. Humphreys's introduction to the Arden edition are also included.

There is a very detailed study of Falstaff's language in ch. 4 of Brian Vickers's *The Artistry of Shakespeare's Prose* (1968). Vickers argues that in the prose, and therefore in the comedy, of *Henry IV, Part I*, 'Falstaff is the central figure and Hal is his Good Angel', while the unholy combination of Falstaff's Appetite, Reason and Conscience . . . represents the devil', an arrangement quite different from the usual morality pattern associated with that play. This means, says Vickers, that 'when Hal has left Falstaff alone' (as happens in *Henry IV, Part II*), 'Sir John sells his soul to the devil for a few syllogisms and half-a-dozen puns'.

Several useful series of student guides have been published. These include T. F. Wharton on both parts of *Henry IV* in the Text and Performance series (1983); and *Part II* is discussed by Barbara Hodgdon in the Shakespeare in Performance series (1993). Collections of essays may conveniently be found in *Shakespeare's History Plays: 'Richard II' to 'Henry V'*, ed. Graham Holderness (1992); as well as a volume of essays on *Henry IV, Part I*,

Harold Bloom has edited another on *Henry IV, Part II* in the Modern Critical Interpretations series (1987). John Wilders discusses *Henry IV, Parts I* and *II* in one of his *New Prefaces to Shakespeare* (1988). *Political Shakespeare: Essays in Cultural Materialism*, ed. Jonathan Dollimore and Alan Sinfield (1985), advertises itself as a book that 'some academies tried to prevent being published and which others have been fulminating about ever since'. It is not *quite* so exciting, but Stephen Greenblatt's essay, 'Invisible Bullets: Renaissance Authority and Its Subversion, *Henry IV* and *Henry V*', does offer a different perspective:

The first part of *Henry IV* enables us to feel at moments that we are like [Thomas] Harriot [a mathematician suspected of atheism though professing Christian belief], surveying a complex new world, testing upon it dark thoughts without damaging the order that those thoughts seem to threaten. The second part of *Henry IV* suggests that we are still more like the Indians, compelled to pay homage to a system of beliefs whose fraudulence somehow only confirms their power, authenticity and truth.

Alexander Leggatt devotes a chapter to *Henry IV* in *Shakespeare's Political Drama* (1988). Susan Bassnett has an interesting chapter on *Henry IV, Part II* in *Shakespeare: The Elizabethan Plays* (1993): 'England, the World's Best Garden' (with *Henry V*). J. L. Simmons is stimulating on the engendering of history in 'Masculine Negotiations in Shakespeare's History Plays: Hal, Hotspur, and "the foolish Mortimer"' (*Shakespeare Quarterly* 44 (1993), pp. 440–63); he draws on both parts of *Henry IV* and *Henry V*. Short references in two books are well worth digging out: Germaine Greer on 'The capacity for change in *Henry V*' in her *Shakespeare* (1986, pp. 48–51); and Brian Gibbons in his *Shakespeare and Multiplicity* (1993, pp. 65–8) on 'The situation of the erect figure gazing at the silent, inert body' in three scenes in both parts of the play.

Peter Davison

Useful recent work on the *Henry IV* plays includes a detailed study by Tom McAlindon, *Shakespeare's Tudor History: A Study of 'Henry IV, Parts 1 and 2'* (2001). Also recommended are books by Benjamin Griffin, *Playing the Past: Approaches to English Historical Drama 1385–1600* (2001); Jean E. Howard and Phyllis Rackin, *Engendering a Nation: A Feminist Account of Shakespeare's English Histories* (1997); Paola Pugliatti, *Shakespeare the Historian* (1996); and Phyllis Rackin, *Stages of History: Shakespeare's English Chronicles* (1990). An important article by John Kerrigan first published in 1990, 'Henry IV and the Death of Old Double', has been collected in his volume of essays *On Shakespeare and Early Modern Literature* (2001).

THE PLAY IN PERFORMANCE

For both *Henry IV* plays in performance Michael Bogdanov and Michael Pennington provide many behind-the-scenes insights in *The English Shakespeare Company: The Story of 'The Wars of the Roses', 1986–1989* (1990), and although addressed to *Henry IV, Part I*, Simon Callow sheds intelligent light on both plays in the series 'Actors on Shakespeare' (2002). On Welles's film *Chimes at Midnight* (or *Falstaff*) there are helpful articles by Samuel Crowl, 'The Long Goodbye: Welles and Falstaff', in

Shakespeare Quarterly 31 (1980), and by Robert Hapgood, '*Chimes at Midnight* from Stage to Screen: The Art of Adaptation', *Shakespeare Survey 39* (1987); the script can be studied in the Rutgers Films in Print series, ed. Bridget Gellert Lyons (1988), and in the expanding literature on Shakespeare and film *The Cambridge Companion to Shakespeare on Film*, ed. Russell Jackson (2000), includes a chapter by Pamela Mason on 'Orson Welles and Filmed Shakespeare'. Also recommended is Kenneth S. Rothwell's *A History of Shakespeare on Screen* (2nd edn, 2004).

Adrian Poole

THE SECOND PART OF
HENRY THE FOURTH

The Characters in the Play

RUMOUR, the presenter
KING HENRY IV
PRINCE HENRY, afterwards crowned KING HENRY V
PRINCE JOHN of Lancaster ⎫ sons of Henry IV
Humphrey Duke of GLOUCESTER ⎬ and brothers of
Thomas Duke of CLARENCE ⎭ Henry V

Of the King's Party
Earl of WARWICK
Earl of WESTMORLAND
Earl of Surrey
Sir John Blunt
GOWER
HARCOURT
The LORD CHIEF JUSTICE
A SERVANT of the Lord Chief Justice

Opposed to the King
Earl of NORTHUMBERLAND
The ARCHBISHOP of York
Lord MOWBRAY
Lord HASTINGS
LORD BARDOLPH
TRAVERS
MORTON
Sir John COLEVILE

LADY NORTHUMBERLAND, Northumberland's wife
LADY PERCY, Percy's widow

'Irregular Humorists'
POINS
Sir John FALSTAFF
BARDOLPH
PISTOL
PETO
Falstaff's PAGE

HOSTESS Quickly
DOLL Tearsheet

Robert SHALLOW ⎫
                ⎬ country justices
SILENCE   ⎭
DAVY, Shallow's servant

Ralph MOULDY   ⎫
Simon SHADOW   ⎪
Thomas WART   ⎬ country soldiers
Francis FEEBLE ⎪
Peter BULLCALF ⎭

FANG ⎫ sergeants
SNARE ⎭
FRANCIS, WILL, and another DRAWER
FIRST BEADLE
Three GROOMS

PORTER
MESSENGER

Speaker of the EPILOGUE

Officers, musicians, a page, soldiers, a captain, lords, beadles

Induction

Enter Rumour, painted full of tongues

RUMOUR

Open your ears, for which of you will stop
The vent of hearing when loud Rumour speaks?
I, from the orient to the drooping west,
Making the wind my post-horse, still unfold
The acts commencèd on this ball of earth.
Upon my tongues continual slanders ride,
The which in every language I pronounce,
Stuffing the ears of men with false reports.
I speak of peace while covert enmity,
Under the smile of safety, wounds the world;   10
And who but Rumour, who but only I,
Make fearful musters, and prepared defence,
Whiles the big year, swollen with some other grief,
Is thought with child by the stern tyrant War,
And no such matter? Rumour is a pipe
Blown by surmises, jealousies, conjectures,
And of so easy and so plain a stop
That the blunt monster with uncounted heads,
The still-discordant wavering multitude,
Can play upon it. But what need I thus   20
My well-known body to anatomize
Among my household? Why is Rumour here?

I run before King Harry's victory,
Who in a bloody field by Shrewsbury
Hath beaten down young Hotspur and his troops,
Quenching the flame of bold rebellion
Even with the rebels' blood. But what mean I
To speak so true at first? My office is
To noise abroad that Harry Monmouth fell
Under the wrath of noble Hotspur's sword,
And that the King before the Douglas' rage
Stooped his anointed head as low as death.
This have I rumoured through the peasant towns
Between that royal field of Shrewsbury
And this worm-eaten hold of raggèd stone,
Where Hotspur's father, old Northumberland,
Lies crafty-sick. The posts come tiring on,
And not a man of them brings other news
Than they have learnt of me. From Rumour's tongues
They bring smooth comforts false, worse than true
          wrongs.   *Exit*

Enter the Lord Bardolph at one door

LORD BARDOLPH
  Who keeps the gate here, ho?
    Enter the Porter

                              Where is the Earl?

PORTER
  What shall I say you are?

LORD BARDOLPH   Tell thou the Earl
  That the Lord Bardolph doth attend him here.

PORTER
  His lordship is walked forth into the orchard.
  Please it your honour knock but at the gate,
  And he himself will answer.
    Enter Northumberland

LORD BARDOLPH   Here comes the Earl.
                                    Exit Porter

NORTHUMBERLAND
  What news, Lord Bardolph? Every minute now
  Should be the father of some stratagem.
  The times are wild; contention, like a horse
  Full of high feeding, madly hath broke loose   10
  And bears down all before him.

LORD BARDOLPH   Noble Earl,
  I bring you certain news from Shrewsbury.

NORTHUMBERLAND
  Good, an God will!
LORD BARDOLPH   As good as heart can wish.
  The King is almost wounded to the death,
  And, in the fortune of my lord your son,
  Prince Harry slain outright; and both the Blunts
  Killed by the hand of Douglas; young Prince John
  And Westmorland and Stafford fled the field;
  And Harry Monmouth's brawn, the hulk Sir John,
20 Is prisoner to your son. O, such a day,
  So fought, so followed, and so fairly won,
  Came not till now to dignify the times
  Since Caesar's fortunes!
NORTHUMBERLAND   How is this derived?
  Saw you the field? Came you from Shrewsbury?
LORD BARDOLPH
  I spake with one, my lord, that came from thence,
  A gentleman well bred, and of good name,
  That freely rendered me these news for true.
       Enter Travers
NORTHUMBERLAND
  Here comes my servant Travers, whom I sent
  On Tuesday last to listen after news.
LORD BARDOLPH
30 My lord, I over-rode him on the way,
  And he is furnished with no certainties
  More than he haply may retail from me.
NORTHUMBERLAND
  Now, Travers, what good tidings comes with you?
TRAVERS
  My lord, Sir John Umfrevile turned me back
  With joyful tidings, and, being better horsed,
  Out-rode me. After him came spurring hard
  A gentleman almost forspent with speed,

That stopped by me to breathe his bloodied horse.
He asked the way to Chester, and of him
I did demand what news from Shrewsbury.   40
He told me that rebellion had ill luck,
And that young Harry Percy's spur was cold.
With that he gave his able horse the head,
And bending forward struck his armèd heels
Against the panting sides of his poor jade
Up to the rowel-head; and starting so
He seemed in running to devour the way,
Staying no longer question.

NORTHUMBERLAND   Ha? Again!
Said he young Harry Percy's spur was cold?
Of Hotspur, Coldspur? That rebellion   50
Had met ill luck?

LORD BARDOLPH My lord, I'll tell you what.
If my young lord your son have not the day,
Upon mine honour, for a silken point
I'll give my barony – never talk of it.

NORTHUMBERLAND
Why should that gentleman that rode by Travers
Give then such instances of loss?

LORD BARDOLPH   Who, he?
He was some hilding fellow that had stolen
The horse he rode on, and, upon my life,
Spoke at a venture. Look, here comes more news.
    Enter Morton

NORTHUMBERLAND
Yea, this man's brow, like to a title-leaf,   60
Foretells the nature of a tragic volume.
So looks the strand whereon the imperious flood
Hath left a witnessed usurpation.
Say, Morton, didst thou come from Shrewsbury?

MORTON

   I ran from Shrewsbury, my noble lord,
   Where hateful death put on his ugliest mask
   To fright our party.

NORTHUMBERLAND How doth my son, and brother?
   Thou tremblest, and the whiteness in thy cheek
   Is apter than thy tongue to tell thy errand.
70   Even such a man, so faint, so spiritless,
   So dull, so dead in look, so woe-begone,
   Drew Priam's curtain in the dead of night
   And would have told him half his Troy was burnt;
   But Priam found the fire ere he his tongue,
   And I my Percy's death ere thou reportest it.
   This thou wouldst say, 'Your son did thus and thus;
   Your brother thus; so fought the noble Douglas',
   Stopping my greedy ear with their bold deeds.
   But in the end, to stop my ear indeed,
80   Thou hast a sigh to blow away this praise,
   Ending with 'Brother, son, and all are dead.'

MORTON

   Douglas is living, and your brother, yet;
   But, for my lord your son –

NORTHUMBERLAND   Why, he is dead!
   See what a ready tongue suspicion hath!
   He that but fears the thing he would not know
   Hath by instinct knowledge from others' eyes
   That what he feared is chanced. Yet speak, Morton;
   Tell thou an earl his divination lies,
   And I will take it as a sweet disgrace
90   And make thee rich for doing me such wrong.

MORTON

   You are too great to be by me gainsaid;
   Your spirit is too true, your fears too certain.

NORTHUMBERLAND

   Yet, for all this, say not that Percy's dead.
   I see a strange confession in thine eye.
   Thou shakest thy head, and holdest it fear or sin
   To speak a truth. If he be slain –
   The tongue offends not that reports his death;
   And he doth sin that doth belie the dead,
   Not he which says the dead is not alive.
   Yet the first bringer of unwelcome news   100
   Hath but a losing office, and his tongue
   Sounds ever after as a sullen bell
   Remembered tolling a departing friend.

LORD BARDOLPH

   I cannot think, my lord, your son is dead.

MORTON

   I am sorry I should force you to believe
   That which I would to God I had not seen;
   But these mine eyes saw him in bloody state,
   Rendering faint quittance, wearied and out-breathed,
   To Harry Monmouth, whose swift wrath beat down
   The never-daunted Percy to the earth,   110
   From whence with life he never more sprung up.
   In few, his death, whose spirit lent a fire
   Even to the dullest peasant in his camp,
   Being bruited once, took fire and heat away
   From the best-tempered courage in his troops;
   For from his metal was his party steeled,
   Which once in him abated, all the rest
   Turned on themselves, like dull and heavy lead;
   And as the thing that's heavy in itself
   Upon enforcement flies with greatest speed,   120
   So did our men, heavy in Hotspur's loss,
   Lend to this weight such lightness with their fear
   That arrows fled not swifter toward their aim

Than did our soldiers, aiming at their safety,
Fly from the field. Then was that noble Worcester
So soon ta'en prisoner, and that furious Scot,
The bloody Douglas, whose well-labouring sword
Had three times slain th'appearance of the King,
Gan vail his stomach, and did grace the shame
Of those that turned their backs, and in his flight,
Stumbling in fear, was took. The sum of all
Is that the King hath won, and hath sent out
A speedy power to encounter you, my lord,
Under the conduct of young Lancaster
And Westmorland. This is the news at full.

NORTHUMBERLAND
For this I shall have time enough to mourn.
In poison there is physic, and these news,
Having been well, that would have made me sick,
Being sick, have in some measure made me well.
And as the wretch whose fever-weakened joints,
Like strengthless hinges, buckle under life,
Impatient of his fit, breaks like a fire
Out of his keeper's arms, even so my limbs,
Weakened with grief, being now enraged with grief,
Are thrice themselves. Hence, therefore, thou nice crutch!
A scaly gauntlet now with joints of steel
Must glove this hand. And hence, thou sickly coif!
Thou art a guard too wanton for the head
Which princes, fleshed with conquest, aim to hit.
Now bind my brows with iron, and approach
The raggèd'st hour that time and spite dare bring
To frown upon th'enraged Northumberland!
Let heaven kiss earth! Now let not Nature's hand
Keep the wild flood confined! Let order die!
And let this world no longer be a stage
To feed contention in a lingering act;

But let one spirit of the first-born Cain
Reign in all bosoms, that, each heart being set
On bloody courses, the rude scene may end,
And darkness be the burier of the dead!   160

LORD BARDOLPH
This strainèd passion doth you wrong, my lord.

MORTON
Sweet Earl, divorce not wisdom from your honour;
The lives of all your loving complices
Lean on your health, the which, if you give o'er
To stormy passion, must perforce decay.
You cast th'event of war, my noble lord,
And summed the account of chance before you said
'Let us make head.' It was your presurmise
That in the dole of blows your son might drop.
You knew he walked o'er perils, on an edge,   170
More likely to fall in than to get o'er.
You were advised his flesh was capable
Of wounds and scars, and that his forward spirit
Would lift him where most trade of danger ranged.
Yet did you say 'Go forth'; and none of this,
Though strongly apprehended, could restrain
The stiff-borne action. What hath then befallen,
Or what hath this bold enterprise brought forth,
More than that being which was like to be?

LORD BARDOLPH
We all that are engagèd to this loss   180
Knew that we ventured on such dangerous seas
That if we wrought out life 'twas ten to one;
And yet we ventured for the gain proposed,
Choked the respect of likely peril feared,
And since we are o'erset, venture again.
Come, we will all put forth, body and goods.

MORTON

> 'Tis more than time. And, my most noble lord,
> I hear for certain, and dare speak the truth,
> The gentle Archbishop of York is up
190   With well-appointed powers. He is a man
> Who with a double surety binds his followers.
> My lord, your son had only but the corpse,
> But shadows and the shows of men, to fight;
> For that same word 'rebellion' did divide
> The action of their bodies from their souls.
> And they did fight with queasiness, constrained,
> As men drink potions, that their weapons only
> Seemed on our side; but, for their spirits and souls,
> This word – 'rebellion' – it had froze them up
200   As fish are in a pond. But now the Bishop
> Turns insurrection to religion;
> Supposed sincere and holy in his thoughts,
> He's followed both with body and with mind,
> And doth enlarge his rising with the blood
> Of fair King Richard, scraped from Pomfret stones;
> Derives from heaven his quarrel and his cause;
> Tells them he doth bestride a bleeding land,
> Gasping for life under great Bolingbroke;
> And more and less do flock to follow him.

NORTHUMBERLAND

210   I knew of this before, but, to speak truth,
> This present grief had wiped it from my mind.
> Go in with me, and counsel every man
> The aptest way for safety and revenge.
> Get posts and letters, and make friends with speed –
> Never so few, and never yet more need.   *Exeunt*

Enter Sir John Falstaff, followed by his Page bearing   I.2
    his sword and buckler

FALSTAFF Sirrah, you giant, what says the doctor to my
    water?

PAGE He said, sir, the water itself was a good healthy
    water; but, for the party that owed it, he might have
    more diseases than he knew for.

FALSTAFF Men of all sorts take a pride to gird at me. The
    brain of this foolish-compounded clay, man, is not able
    to invent anything that intends to laughter more than I
    invent, or is invented on me; I am not only witty in
    myself, but the cause that wit is in other men. I do here   10
    walk before thee like a sow that hath overwhelmed all
    her litter but one. If the Prince put thee into my service
    for any other reason than to set me off, why then I have
    no judgement. Thou whoreson mandrake, thou art
    fitter to be worn in my cap than to wait at my heels. I
    was never manned with an agate till now, but I will inset
    you neither in gold nor silver, but in vile apparel, and
    send you back again to your master for a jewel – the
    juvenal the Prince your master, whose chin is not yet
    fledge. I will sooner have a beard grow in the palm of   20
    my hand than he shall get one off his cheek; and yet he
    will not stick to say his face is a face-royal. God may
    finish it when He will, 'tis not a hair amiss yet. He may
    keep it still at a face-royal, for a barber shall never earn
    sixpence out of it. And yet he'll be crowing as if he had
    writ man ever since his father was a bachelor. He may
    keep his own grace, but he's almost out of mine, I can
    assure him. What said Master Dommelton about the
    satin for my short cloak and my slops?

PAGE He said, sir, you should procure him better assur-   30
    ance than Bardolph. He would not take his bond and
    yours; he liked not the security.

FALSTAFF Let him be damned like the glutton! Pray
God his tongue be hotter! A whoreson Achitophel! A
rascally yea-forsooth knave, to bear a gentleman in hand,
and then stand upon security! The whoreson smoothy-
pates do now wear nothing but high shoes and bunches
of keys at their girdles; and if a man is through with
them in honest taking up, then they must stand upon
40   security. I had as lief they would put ratsbane in my
mouth as offer to stop it with security. I looked 'a should
have sent me two-and-twenty yards of satin, as I am a
true knight, and he sends me 'security'! Well he may
sleep in security, for he hath the horn of abundance, and
the lightness of his wife shines through it – and yet
cannot he see, though he have his own lanthorn to light
him. Where's Bardolph?

PAGE He's gone in Smithfield to buy your worship a
horse.

50   FALSTAFF I bought him in Paul's, and he'll buy me a
horse in Smithfield. An I could get me but a wife in the
stews, I were manned, horsed, and wived.

Enter the Lord Chief Justice and his Servant

PAGE Sir, here comes the nobleman that committed the
Prince for striking him about Bardolph.

FALSTAFF Wait close; I will not see him.

LORD CHIEF JUSTICE What's he that goes there?

SERVANT Falstaff, an't please your lordship.

LORD CHIEF JUSTICE He that was in question for the
robbery?

60   SERVANT He, my lord – but he hath since done good
service at Shrewsbury, and, as I hear, is now going with
some charge to the Lord John of Lancaster.

LORD CHIEF JUSTICE What, to York? Call him back
again.

SERVANT Sir John Falstaff!

FALSTAFF Boy, tell him I am deaf.

PAGE You must speak louder; my master is deaf.

LORD CHIEF JUSTICE I am sure he is, to the hearing of
   anything good. Go pluck him by the elbow; I must
   speak with him.   70

SERVANT Sir John!

FALSTAFF What! A young knave, and begging! Is there
   not wars? Is there not employment? Doth not the King
   lack subjects? Do not the rebels need soldiers? Though
   it be a shame to be on any side but one, it is worse shame
   to beg than to be on the worst side, were it worse than
   the name of rebellion can tell how to make it.

SERVANT You mistake me, sir.

FALSTAFF Why, sir, did I say you were an honest man?
   Setting my knighthood and my soldiership aside, I had   80
   lied in my throat if I had said so.

SERVANT I pray you, sir, then set your knighthood and
   your soldiership aside, and give me leave to tell you
   you lie in your throat if you say I am any other than an
   honest man.

FALSTAFF I give thee leave to tell me so? I lay aside that
   which grows to me? If thou gettest any leave of me,
   hang me. If thou takest leave, thou wert better be
   hanged. You hunt counter. Hence! Avaunt!

SERVANT Sir, my lord would speak with you.   90

LORD CHIEF JUSTICE Sir John Falstaff, a word with
   you.

FALSTAFF My good lord! God give your lordship good
   time of day. I am glad to see your lordship abroad; I
   heard say your lordship was sick. I hope your lordship
   goes abroad by advice. Your lordship, though not clean
   past your youth, have yet some smack of age in you,
   some relish of the saltness of time; and I most humbly
   beseech your lordship to have a reverend care of your
   health.   100

LORD CHIEF JUSTICE Sir John, I sent for you — before
your expedition to Shrewsbury.

FALSTAFF An't please your lordship, I hear his majesty
is returned with some discomfort from Wales.

LORD CHIEF JUSTICE I talk not of his majesty. You
would not come when I sent for you.

FALSTAFF And I hear, moreover, his highness is fallen
into this same whoreson apoplexy.

LORD CHIEF JUSTICE Well, God mend him! I pray you
110 let me speak with you.

FALSTAFF This apoplexy, as I take it, is a kind of
lethargy, an't please your lordship, a kind of sleeping in
the blood, a whoreson tingling.

LORD CHIEF JUSTICE What tell you me of it? Be it as
it is.

FALSTAFF It hath it original from much grief, from study,
and perturbation of the brain. I have read the cause of
his effects in Galen; it is a kind of deafness.

LORD CHIEF JUSTICE I think you are fallen into the
120 disease, for you hear not what I say to you.

FALSTAFF Very well, my lord, very well. Rather, an't
please you, it is the disease of not listening, the malady
of not marking, that I am troubled withal.

LORD CHIEF JUSTICE To punish you by the heels
would amend the attention of your ears, and I care not
if I do become your physician.

FALSTAFF I am as poor as Job, my lord, but not so
patient. Your lordship may minister the potion of
imprisonment to me in respect of poverty; but how I
130 should be your patient to follow your prescriptions, the
wise may make some dram of a scruple, or indeed a
scruple itself.

LORD CHIEF JUSTICE I sent for you, when there were

matters against you for your life, to come speak with me.

FALSTAFF As I was then advised by my learned counsel
in the laws of this land-service, I did not come.

LORD CHIEF JUSTICE Well, the truth is, Sir John, you
live in great infamy.

FALSTAFF He that buckles himself in my belt cannot live
in less.   140

LORD CHIEF JUSTICE Your means are very slender, and
your waste is great.

FALSTAFF I would it were otherwise; I would my means
were greater and my waist slenderer.

LORD CHIEF JUSTICE You have misled the youthful
Prince.

FALSTAFF The young Prince hath misled me. I am the
fellow with the great belly, and he my dog.

LORD CHIEF JUSTICE Well, I am loath to gall a new-
healed wound. Your day's service at Shrewsbury hath a   150
little gilded over your night's exploit on Gad's Hill. You
may thank th'unquiet time for your quiet o'erposting
that action.

FALSTAFF My lord!

LORD CHIEF JUSTICE But since all is well, keep it so.
Wake not a sleeping wolf.

FALSTAFF To wake a wolf is as bad as smell a fox.

LORD CHIEF JUSTICE What! You are as a candle, the
better part burnt out.

FALSTAFF A wassail candle, my lord, all tallow – if I did   160
say of wax, my growth would approve the truth.

LORD CHIEF JUSTICE There is not a white hair in your
face but should have his effect of gravity.

FALSTAFF His effect of gravy, gravy, gravy.

LORD CHIEF JUSTICE You follow the young Prince up
and down, like his ill angel.

FALSTAFF Not so, my lord; your ill angel is light, but I
hope he that looks upon me will take me without
weighing. And yet in some respects, I grant, I cannot
170 go — I cannot tell. Virtue is of so little regard in these
costermongers' times that true valour is turned bearherd; pregnancy is made a tapster, and his quick wit
wasted in giving reckonings; all the other gifts appertinent to man, as the malice of this age shapes them, are
not worth a gooseberry. You that are old consider not
the capacities of us that are young; you do measure the
heat of our livers with the bitterness of your galls; and
we that are in the vaward of our youth, I must confess,
are wags too.

180 LORD CHIEF JUSTICE Do you set down your name in
the scroll of youth, that are written down old with all
the characters of age? Have you not a moist eye, a dry
hand, a yellow cheek, a white beard, a decreasing leg,
an increasing belly? Is not your voice broken, your wind
short, your chin double, your wit single, and every part
about you blasted with antiquity? And will you yet call
yourself young? Fie, fie, fie, Sir John!

FALSTAFF My lord, I was born about three of the clock
in the afternoon, with a white head, and something a
190 round belly. For my voice, I have lost it with hallooing,
and singing of anthems. To approve my youth further,
I will not. The truth is, I am only old in judgement and
understanding; and he that will caper with me for a
thousand marks, let him lend me the money, and have
at him! For the box of the ear that the Prince gave you,
he gave it like a rude prince, and you took it like a
sensible lord. I have checked him for it, and the young
lion repents — (*aside*) marry, not in ashes and sackcloth,
but in new silk and old sack.

200 LORD CHIEF JUSTICE Well, God send the Prince a
better companion!

FALSTAFF God send the companion a better prince! I
cannot rid my hands of him.

LORD CHIEF JUSTICE Well, the King hath severed you
and Prince Harry. I hear you are going with Lord John
of Lancaster against the Archbishop and the Earl of
Northumberland.

FALSTAFF Yea, I thank your pretty sweet wit for it. But
look you pray, all you that kiss my lady Peace at home,
that our armies join not in a hot day; for, by the Lord,   210
I take but two shirts out with me, and I mean not to
sweat extraordinarily. If it be a hot day, and I brandish
anything but a bottle – I would I might never spit white
again. There is not a dangerous action can peep out
his head but I am thrust upon it. Well, I cannot last
ever – but it was alway yet the trick of our English
nation, if they have a good thing, to make it too common.
If ye will needs say I am an old man, you should give
me rest. I would to God my name were not so terrible
to the enemy as it is. I were better to be eaten to death   220
with a rust than to be scoured to nothing with perpetual
motion.

LORD CHIEF JUSTICE Well, be honest, be honest, and
God bless your expedition!

FALSTAFF Will your lordship lend me a thousand pound
to furnish me forth?

LORD CHIEF JUSTICE Not a penny, not a penny! You
are too impatient to bear crosses. Fare you well. Commend me to my cousin Westmorland.

Exeunt Lord Chief Justice and Servant

FALSTAFF If I do, fillip me with a three-man beetle. A   230
man can no more separate age and covetousness than 'a
can part young limbs and lechery; but the gout galls the
one, and the pox pinches the other; and so both the
degrees prevent my curses. Boy!

PAGE Sir?

FALSTAFF What money is in my purse?

PAGE Seven groats and two pence.

FALSTAFF I can get no remedy against this consumption
of the purse; borrowing only lingers and lingers it out,
240 but the disease is incurable. Go bear this letter to my
lord of Lancaster; this to the Prince; this to the Earl
of Westmorland – and this to old mistress Ursula, whom
I have weekly sworn to marry since I perceived the first
white hair of my chin. About it! You know where to
find me.   *Exit Page*

A pox of this gout! Or a gout of this pox! For the one
or the other plays the rogue with my great toe. 'Tis no
matter if I do halt; I have the wars for my colour, and
my pension shall seem the more reasonable. A good wit
250 will make use of anything; I will turn diseases to commodity.   *Exit*

I.3   *Enter the Archbishop of York, Thomas Mowbray the*
             Earl Marshal, Lord Hastings, and Lord Bardolph

ARCHBISHOP
    Thus have you heard our cause and known our means,
    And, my most noble friends, I pray you all
    Speak plainly your opinions of our hopes.
    And first, Lord Marshal, what say you to it?

MOWBRAY
    I well allow the occasion of our arms,
    But gladly would be better satisfied
    How in our means we should advance ourselves
    To look with forehead bold and big enough
    Upon the power and puissance of the King.

HASTINGS
10 Our present musters grow upon the file

To five-and-twenty thousand men of choice;
And our supplies live largely in the hope
Of great Northumberland, whose bosom burns
With an incensèd fire of injuries.

LORD BARDOLPH

The question then, Lord Hastings, standeth thus –
Whether our present five-and-twenty thousand
May hold up head without Northumberland.

HASTINGS

With him we may.

LORD BARDOLPH   Yea, marry, there's the point;
But if without him we be thought too feeble,
My judgement is, we should not step too far   20
Till we had his assistance by the hand;
For in a theme so bloody-faced as this,
Conjecture, expectation, and surmise
Of aids incertain should not be admitted.

ARCHBISHOP

'Tis very true, Lord Bardolph, for indeed
It was young Hotspur's cause at Shrewsbury.

LORD BARDOLPH

It was, my lord; who lined himself with hope,
Eating the air and promise of supply,
Flattering himself in project of a power
Much smaller than the smallest of his thoughts,   30
And so, with great imagination
Proper to madmen, led his powers to death,
And winking leaped into destruction.

HASTINGS

But, by your leave, it never yet did hurt
To lay down likelihoods and forms of hope.

LORD BARDOLPH

Yes, if this present quality of war,
Indeed, the instant action, a cause on foot,

Lives so in hope – as in an early spring
We see th'appearing buds; which to prove fruit
40 Hope gives not so much warrant, as despair
That frosts will bite them. When we mean to build,
We first survey the plot, then draw the model,
And when we see the figure of the house,
Then must we rate the cost of the erection,
Which if we find outweighs ability,
What do we then but draw anew the model
In fewer offices, or at least desist
To build at all? Much more, in this great work –
Which is almost to pluck a kingdom down
50 And set another up – should we survey
The plot of situation and the model,
Consent upon a sure foundation,
Question surveyors, know our own estate,
How able such a work to undergo,
To weigh against his opposite; or else
We fortify in paper and in figures,
Using the names of men instead of men,
Like one that draws the model of an house
Beyond his power to build it, who, half-through,
60 Gives o'er, and leaves his part-created cost
A naked subject to the weeping clouds,
And waste for churlish winter's tyranny.

HASTINGS

Grant that our hopes, yet likely of fair birth,
Should be still-born, and that we now possessed
The utmost man of expectation,
I think we are so, body strong enough,
Even as we are, to equal with the King.

LORD BARDOLPH

What, is the King but five-and-twenty thousand?

HASTINGS

 To us no more, nay, not so much, Lord Bardolph;
 For his divisions, as the times do brawl,   70
 Are in three heads: one power against the French;
 And one against Glendower; perforce a third
 Must take up us. So is the unfirm King
 In three divided, and his coffers sound
 With hollow poverty and emptiness.

ARCHBISHOP

 That he should draw his several strengths together
 And come against us in full puissance
 Need not be dreaded.

HASTINGS   If he should do so,
 He leaves his back unarmed, the French and Welsh
 Baying him at the heels; never fear that.   80

LORD BARDOLPH

 Who is it like should lead his forces hither?

HASTINGS

 The Duke of Lancaster, and Westmorland;
 Against the Welsh, himself and Harry Monmouth;
 But who is substituted 'gainst the French
 I have no certain notice.

ARCHBISHOP   Let us on,
 And publish the occasion of our arms.
 The commonwealth is sick of their own choice;
 Their over-greedy love hath surfeited.
 An habitation giddy and unsure
 Hath he that buildeth on the vulgar heart.   90
 O thou fond many, with what loud applause
 Didst thou beat heaven with blessing Bolingbroke,
 Before he was what thou wouldst have him be!
 And being now trimmed in thine own desires,
 Thou, beastly feeder, art so full of him
 That thou provokest thyself to cast him up.

So, so, thou common dog, didst thou disgorge
Thy glutton bosom of the royal Richard –
And now thou wouldst eat thy dead vomit up,
100   And howlest to find it. What trust is in these times?
They that, when Richard lived, would have him die
Are now become enamoured on his grave.
Thou that threwest dust upon his goodly head,
When through proud London he came sighing on
After th'admirèd heels of Bolingbroke,
Cryest now 'O earth, yield us that king again,
And take thou this!' O thoughts of men accursed!
Past and to come seems best; things present, worst.

MOWBRAY
Shall we go draw our numbers and set on?

HASTINGS
110   We are time's subjects, and time bids be gone. *Exeunt*

*

II.I   *Enter the Hostess of the tavern with two Officers,*
            Fang and Snare

HOSTESS Master Fang, have you entered the action?

FANG It is entered.

HOSTESS Where's your yeoman? Is't a lusty yeoman?
    Will 'a stand to't?

FANG Sirrah – where's Snare?

HOSTESS O Lord, ay! Good Master Snare.

SNARE (*from behind them*) Here, here!

FANG Snare, we must arrest Sir John Falstaff.

HOSTESS Yea, good Master Snare, I have entered him and
10 all.

SNARE It may chance cost some of us our lives, for he will
    stab.

HOSTESS Alas the day, take heed of him – he stabbed me
    in mine own house, most beastly, in good faith. 'A cares
    not what mischief he does, if his weapon be out. He
    will foin like any devil; he will spare neither man,
    woman, nor child.

FANG If I can close with him, I care not for his thrust.

HOSTESS No, nor I neither; I'll be at your elbow.

FANG An I but fist him once, an 'a come but within my   20
    vice –

HOSTESS I am undone by his going, I warrant you, he's an
    infinitive thing upon my score. Good Master Fang,
    hold him sure; good Master Snare, let him not 'scape.
    'A comes continuantly to Pie Corner – saving your
    manhoods – to buy a saddle, and he is indited to dinner
    to the Lubber's Head in Lumbert Street to Master
    Smooth's the silkman. I pray you, since my exion is
    entered, and my case so openly known to the world, let
    him be brought in to his answer. A hundred mark is a long   30
    one for a poor lone woman to bear, and I have borne,
    and borne, and borne, and have been fubbed off, and
    fubbed off, and fubbed off, from this day to that day,
    that it is a shame to be thought on. There is no honesty
    in such dealing, unless a woman should be made an ass,
    and a beast, to bear every knave's wrong.

    Enter Falstaff, Bardolph, and the Page
    Yonder he comes, and that arrant malmsey-nose knave
    Bardolph with him. Do your offices, do your offices,
    Master Fang and Master Snare, do me, do me, do me
    your offices.   40

FALSTAFF How now, whose mare's dead? What's the
    matter?

FANG I arrest you at the suit of Mistress Quickly.

FALSTAFF Away, varlets! Draw, Bardolph! Cut me off
    the villain's head! Throw the quean in the channel!

HOSTESS Throw me in the channel? I'll throw thee in
the channel! Wilt thou, wilt thou, thou bastardly rogue?
Murder! Murder! Ah, thou honeysuckle villain, wilt
thou kill God's officers and the King's? Ah, thou
50   honeyseed rogue! Thou art a honeyseed, a man-queller
– and a woman-queller.

FALSTAFF Keep them off, Bardolph!

FANG A rescue! A rescue!

HOSTESS Good people, bring a rescue or two. Thou wot,
wot thou, thou wot, wot ta? Do, do, thou rogue! Do,
thou hempseed!

PAGE Away, you scullion! You rampallian! You fustilarian! I'll tickle your catastrophe!

Enter the Lord Chief Justice and his men

LORD CHIEF JUSTICE What is the matter? Keep the
60   peace here, ho!

HOSTESS Good my lord, be good to me; I beseech you,
stand to me.

LORD CHIEF JUSTICE
How now, Sir John? What are you brawling here?
Doth this become your place, your time, and business?
You should have been well on your way to York.
Stand from him, fellow; wherefore hangest thou upon
him?

HOSTESS O my most worshipful lord, an't please your
grace, I am a poor widow of Eastcheap, and he is
arrested at my suit.

70   LORD CHIEF JUSTICE For what sum?

HOSTESS It is more than for some, my lord, it is for all I
have. He hath eaten me out of house and home; he hath
put all my substance into that fat belly of his – but I
will have some of it out again, or I will ride thee a-nights
like the mare.

FALSTAFF I think I am as like to ride the mare if I have
     any vantage of ground to get up.

LORD CHIEF JUSTICE How comes this, Sir John? What
     man of good temper would endure this tempest of
     exclamation? Are you not ashamed to enforce a poor   80
     widow to so rough a course to come by her own?

FALSTAFF What is the gross sum that I owe thee?

HOSTESS Marry, if thou wert an honest man, thyself and
     the money too. Thou didst swear to me upon a parcel-
     gilt goblet, sitting in my Dolphin chamber, at the
     round table, by a sea-coal fire, upon Wednesday in
     Wheeson week, when the Prince broke thy head for
     liking his father to a singing-man of Windsor, thou
     didst swear to me then, as I was washing thy wound,
     to marry me, and make me my lady thy wife. Canst   90
     thou deny it? Did not goodwife Keech the butcher's
     wife come in then and call me gossip Quickly? – coming
     in to borrow a mess of vinegar, telling us she had a good
     dish of prawns, whereby thou didst desire to eat some,
     whereby I told thee they were ill for a green wound?
     And didst thou not, when she was gone downstairs,
     desire me to be no more so familiarity with such poor
     people, saying that ere long they should call me madam?
     And didst thou not kiss me, and bid me fetch thee thirty
     shillings? I put thee now to thy book oath. Deny it if   100
     thou canst.

FALSTAFF My lord, this is a poor mad soul, and she says
     up and down the town that her eldest son is like you.
     She hath been in good case, and the truth is, poverty
     hath distracted her. But, for these foolish officers, I
     beseech you I may have redress against them.

LORD CHIEF JUSTICE Sir John, Sir John, I am well
     acquainted with your manner of wrenching the true

cause the false way. It is not a confident brow, nor the
throng of words that come with such more than
impudent sauciness from you, can thrust me from a
level consideration. You have, as it appears to me,
practised upon the easy-yielding spirit of this woman,
and made her serve your uses both in purse and in
person.

HOSTESS Yea, in truth, my lord.

LORD CHIEF JUSTICE Pray thee, peace. Pay her the
debt you owe her, and unpay the villainy you have done
with her; the one you may do with sterling money and
the other with current repentance.

FALSTAFF My lord, I will not undergo this sneap without
reply. You call honourable boldness impudent sauciness; if a man will make curtsy and say nothing, he is
virtuous. No, my lord, my humble duty remembered,
I will not be your suitor. I say to you I do desire
deliverance from these officers, being upon hasty
employment in the King's affairs.

LORD CHIEF JUSTICE You speak as having power to do
wrong; but answer in the effect of your reputation, and
satisfy the poor woman.

FALSTAFF Come hither, hostess.

    He takes her aside
    Enter Gower

LORD CHIEF JUSTICE Now, Master Gower, what news?

GOWER
  The King, my lord, and Harry Prince of Wales
  Are near at hand; the rest the paper tells.

    He gives him a letter

FALSTAFF As I am a gentleman!

HOSTESS Faith, you said so before.

FALSTAFF As I am a gentleman! Come, no more words
of it.

HOSTESS By this heavenly ground I tread on, I must be
    fain to pawn both my plate and the tapestry of my   140
    dining-chambers.

FALSTAFF Glasses, glasses, is the only drinking; and for
    thy walls, a pretty slight drollery, or the story of the
    Prodigal, or the German hunting, in waterwork, is
    worth a thousand of these bed-hangers and these fly-
    bitten tapestries. Let it be ten pound if thou canst.
    Come, an 'twere not for thy humours, there's not a
    better wench in England! Go, wash thy face, and draw
    the action. Come, thou must not be in this humour with
    me; dost not know me? Come, come, I know thou wast   150
    set on to this.

HOSTESS Pray thee, Sir John, let it be but twenty nobles;
    i'faith, I am loath to pawn my plate, so God save me,
    la!

FALSTAFF Let it alone; I'll make other shift – you'll be a
    fool still.

HOSTESS Well, you shall have it, though I pawn my
    gown. I hope you'll come to supper. You'll pay me all
    together?

FALSTAFF Will I live? (*To Bardolph*) Go, with her, with   160
    her! Hook on, hook on!

HOSTESS Will you have Doll Tearsheet meet you at
    supper?

FALSTAFF No more words; let's have her.

    Exeunt Hostess, Fang, Snare, Bardolph, and Page

LORD CHIEF JUSTICE I have heard better news.

FALSTAFF What's the news, my lord?

LORD CHIEF JUSTICE Where lay the King tonight?

GOWER At Basingstoke, my lord.

FALSTAFF I hope, my lord, all's well. What is the news,
    my lord?   170

LORD CHIEF JUSTICE Come all his forces back?

GOWER
>No, fifteen hundred foot, five hundred horse
>Are marched up to my lord of Lancaster,
>Against Northumberland and the Archbishop.

FALSTAFF Comes the King back from Wales, my noble
lord?

LORD CHIEF JUSTICE
>You shall have letters of me presently.
>Come, go along with me, good Master Gower.

FALSTAFF My lord!

180 LORD CHIEF JUSTICE What's the matter?

FALSTAFF Master Gower, shall I entreat you with me to
dinner?

GOWER I must wait upon my good lord here, I thank you,
good Sir John.

LORD CHIEF JUSTICE Sir John, you loiter here too long,
being you are to take soldiers up in counties as you go.

FALSTAFF Will you sup with me, Master Gower?

LORD CHIEF JUSTICE What foolish master taught you
these manners, Sir John?

190 FALSTAFF Master Gower, if they become me not, he was
a fool that taught them me. This is the right fencing
grace, my lord: tap for tap, and so part fair.

LORD CHIEF JUSTICE Now the Lord lighten thee, thou
art a great fool.   *Exeunt*

II.2   *Enter Prince Henry and Poins*

PRINCE HENRY Before God, I am exceeding weary.

POINS Is't come to that? I had thought weariness durst
not have attached one of so high blood.

PRINCE HENRY Faith, it does me, though it discolours
the complexion of my greatness to acknowledge it. Doth
it not show vilely in me to desire small beer?

POINS Why, a prince should not be so loosely studied as
    to remember so weak a composition.
PRINCE HENRY Belike then my appetite was not princely
    got, for, by my troth, I do now remember the poor   10
    creature small beer. But indeed, these humble consider-
    ations make me out of love with my greatness. What a
    disgrace is it to me to remember thy name! Or to know
    thy face tomorrow! Or to take note how many pair of
    silk stockings thou hast – viz. these, and those that were
    thy peach-coloured once! Or to bear the inventory of
    thy shirts, as, one for superfluity, and another for use!
    But that the tennis-court keeper knows better than I,
    for it is a low ebb of linen with thee when thou keepest
    not racket there – as thou hast not done a great while,   20
    because the rest of thy low countries have made a shift
    to eat up thy holland. And God knows whether those
    that bawl out the ruins of thy linen shall inherit His
    kingdom – but the midwives say the children are not in
    the fault. Whereupon the world increases, and kindreds
    are mightily strengthened.
POINS How ill it follows, after you have laboured so hard,
    you should talk so idly! Tell me, how many good young
    princes would do so, their fathers being so sick as yours
    at this time is?   30
PRINCE HENRY Shall I tell thee one thing, Poins?
POINS Yes, faith, and let it be an excellent good thing.
PRINCE HENRY It shall serve, among wits of no higher
    breeding than thine.
POINS Go to, I stand the push of your one thing that you
    will tell.
PRINCE HENRY Marry, I tell thee it is not meet that I
    should be sad now my father is sick. Albeit I could tell
    to thee, as to one it pleases me for fault of a better to
    call my friend, I could be sad, and sad indeed too.   40

POINS Very hardly, upon such a subject.

PRINCE HENRY By this hand, thou thinkest me as far in
the devil's book as thou and Falstaff, for obduracy and
persistency. Let the end try the man. But I tell thee,
my heart bleeds inwardly that my father is so sick; and
keeping such vile company as thou art hath in reason
taken from me all ostentation of sorrow.

POINS The reason?

PRINCE HENRY What wouldst thou think of me if I
50   should weep?

POINS I would think thee a most princely hypocrite.

PRINCE HENRY It would be every man's thought, and
thou art a blessed fellow, to think as every man thinks.
Never a man's thought in the world keeps the roadway
better than thine. Every man would think me an
hypocrite indeed. And what accites your most worshipful thought to think so?

POINS Why, because you have been so lewd, and so much
engraffed to Falstaff.

60   PRINCE HENRY And to thee.

POINS By this light, I am well spoke on; I can hear it
with mine own ears. The worst that they can say of me
is that I am a second brother, and that I am a proper
fellow of my hands, and those two things I confess I
cannot help. By the mass, here comes Bardolph.

Enter Bardolph and the Page

PRINCE HENRY And the boy that I gave Falstaff – 'a had
him from me Christian, and look if the fat villain have
not transformed him ape.

BARDOLPH God save your grace!

70   PRINCE HENRY And yours, most noble Bardolph!

POINS (*to Bardolph*) Come, you virtuous ass, you bashful
fool, must you be blushing? Wherefore blush you now?
What a maidenly man-at-arms are you become! Is't

such a matter to get a pottle-pot's maidenhead?

PAGE 'A calls me e'en now, my lord, through a red lattice,
and I could discern no part of his face from the window.
At last I spied his eyes, and methought he had made
two holes in the ale-wife's petticoat, and so peeped
through.

PRINCE HENRY Has not the boy profited?   80

BARDOLPH Away, you whoreson upright rabbit, away!

PAGE Away, you rascally Althaea's dream, away!

PRINCE HENRY Instruct us, boy! What dream, boy?

PAGE Marry, my lord, Althaea dreamt she was delivered
of a firebrand; and therefore I call him her dream.

PRINCE HENRY A crown's-worth of good interpretation!
There 'tis, boy.

POINS O that this blossom could be kept from cankers!
Well, there is sixpence to preserve thee.

BARDOLPH An you do not make him be hanged among   90
you, the gallows shall have wrong.

PRINCE HENRY And how doth thy master, Bardolph?

BARDOLPH Well, my lord. He heard of your grace's
coming to town. There's a letter for you.

POINS Delivered with good respect. And how doth the
martlemas your master?

BARDOLPH In bodily health, sir.

POINS Marry, the immortal part needs a physician, but
that moves not him. Though that be sick, it dies not.

PRINCE HENRY I do allow this wen to be as familiar   100
with me as my dog, and he holds his place, for look you
how he writes —

POINS (*reading the letter*) *John Falstaff, knight* — every
man must know that as oft as he has occasion to name
himself, even like those that are kin to the king, for
they never prick their finger but they say 'There's some
of the King's blood spilt.' 'How comes that?' says he

that takes upon him not to conceive. The answer is as
ready as a borrower's cap: 'I am the King's poor
cousin, sir.'

PRINCE HENRY Nay, they will be kin to us, or they will
fetch it from Japhet. But the letter: *Sir John Falstaff,*
knight, to the son of the King nearest his father, Harry
Prince of Wales, greeting.

POINS Why, this is a certificate!

PRINCE HENRY Peace! *I will imitate the honourable*
Romans in brevity.

POINS He sure means brevity in breath, short-winded.

PRINCE HENRY *I commend me to thee, I commend thee,*
and I leave thee. Be not too familiar with Poins, for he
misuses thy favours so much that he swears thou art to
marry his sister Nell. Repent at idle times as thou mayst,
and so farewell.

> *Thine by yea and no — which is as much as to*
> *say, as thou usest him — Jack Falstaff with*
> *my familiars, John with my brothers and*
> *sisters, and Sir John with all Europe.*

POINS My lord, I'll steep this letter in sack and make
him eat it.

PRINCE HENRY That's to make him eat twenty of his
words. But do you use me thus, Ned? Must I marry
your sister?

POINS God send the wench no worse fortune! But I never
said so.

PRINCE HENRY Well, thus we play the fools with the
time, and the spirits of the wise sit in the clouds and
mock us. – Is your master here in London?

BARDOLPH Yea, my lord.

PRINCE HENRY Where sups he? Doth the old boar feed
in the old frank?

BARDOLPH At the old place, my lord, in Eastcheap.

PRINCE HENRY What company?

PAGE Ephesians, my lord, of the old church.

PRINCE HENRY Sup any women with him?

PAGE None, my lord, but old Mistress Quickly, and
Mistress Doll Tearsheet.

PRINCE HENRY What pagan may that be?

PAGE A proper gentlewoman, sir, and a kinswoman of my
master's.

PRINCE HENRY Even such kin as the parish heifers are   150
to the town bull. Shall we steal upon them, Ned, at
supper?

POINS I am your shadow, my lord; I'll follow you.

PRINCE HENRY Sirrah, you boy, and Bardolph, no word
to your master that I am yet come to town. There's for
your silence.

BARDOLPH I have no tongue, sir.

PAGE And for mine, sir, I will govern it.

PRINCE HENRY Fare you well; go.

Exeunt Bardolph and Page

This Doll Tearsheet should be some road.   160

POINS I warrant you, as common as the way between
Saint Albans and London.

PRINCE HENRY How might we see Falstaff bestow
himself tonight in his true colours, and not ourselves
be seen?

POINS Put on two leathern jerkins and aprons, and wait
upon him at his table as drawers.

PRINCE HENRY From a god to a bull? A heavy descension! It was Jove's case. From a prince to a prentice?
A low transformation, that shall be mine; for in every-   170
thing the purpose must weigh with the folly. Follow
me, Ned.   *Exeunt*

II.3   *Enter Northumberland, Lady Northumberland, and*
            Lady Percy

NORTHUMBERLAND

    I pray thee, loving wife, and gentle daughter,
    Give even way unto my rough affairs;
    Put not you on the visage of the times
    And be like them to Percy troublesome.

LADY NORTHUMBERLAND

    I have given over; I will speak no more.
    Do what you will; your wisdom be your guide.

NORTHUMBERLAND

    Alas, sweet wife, my honour is at pawn,
    And but my going, nothing can redeem it.

LADY PERCY

    O, yet, for God's sake, go not to these wars!
10   The time was, father, that you broke your word
    When you were more endeared to it than now,
    When your own Percy, when my heart's dear Harry,
    Threw many a northward look to see his father
    Bring up his powers. But he did long in vain.
    Who then persuaded you to stay at home?
    There were two honours lost, yours and your son's.
    For yours, the God of heaven brighten it!
    For his, it stuck upon him as the sun
    In the grey vault of heaven, and by his light
20   Did all the chivalry of England move
    To do brave acts. He was indeed the glass
    Wherein the noble youth did dress themselves.
    He had no legs that practised not his gait;
    And speaking thick, which nature made his blemish,
    Became the accents of the valiant;
    For those that could speak low and tardily
    Would turn their own perfection to abuse,
    To seem like him. So that in speech, in gait,

In diet, in affections of delight,
In military rules, humours of blood,   30
He was the mark and glass, copy and book,
That fashioned others. And him – O wondrous him!
O miracle of men! – him did you leave,
Second to none, unseconded by you,
To look upon the hideous god of war
In disadvantage, to abide a field
Where nothing but the sound of Hotspur's name
Did seem defensible. So you left him.
Never, O never, do his ghost the wrong
To hold your honour more precise and nice   40
With others than with him! Let them alone.
The Marshal and the Archbishop are strong;
Had my sweet Harry had but half their numbers,
Today might I, hanging on Hotspur's neck,
Have talked of Monmouth's grave.

NORTHUMBERLAND   Beshrew your heart,
Fair daughter, you do draw my spirits from me
With new lamenting ancient oversights.
But I must go and meet with danger there,
Or it will seek me in another place
And find me worse provided.

LADY NORTHUMBERLAND   O, fly to Scotland,   50
Till that the nobles and the armèd commons
Have of their puissance made a little taste.

LADY PERCY
If they get ground and vantage of the King,
Then join you with them like a rib of steel,
To make strength stronger; but, for all our loves,
First let them try themselves. So did your son;
He was so suffered; so came I a widow,
And never shall have length of life enough
To rain upon remembrance with mine eyes,

60   That it may grow and sprout as high as heaven
        For recordation to my noble husband.

NORTHUMBERLAND
        Come, come, go in with me. 'Tis with my mind
        As with the tide swelled up unto his height,
        That makes a still-stand, running neither way.
        Fain would I go to meet the Archbishop,
        But many thousand reasons hold me back.
        I will resolve for Scotland. There am I,
        Till time and vantage crave my company.   *Exeunt*

II.4   *Enter Francis and another Drawer*

    FRANCIS What the devil hast thou brought there – apple-
        johns? Thou knowest Sir John cannot endure an apple-
        john.

    DRAWER Mass, thou sayst true. The Prince once set a
        dish of apple-johns before him, and told him there were
        five more Sir Johns, and, putting off his hat, said 'I will
        now take my leave of these six dry, round, old, withered
        knights.' It angered him to the heart. But he hath forgot
        that.

10 FRANCIS Why then, cover, and set them down, and see
        if thou canst find out Sneak's noise. Mistress Tearsheet
        would fain hear some music.

    DRAWER (*preparing to leave*) Dispatch! The room where
        they supped is too hot; they'll come in straight.

        Enter Will

    WILL Sirrah, here will be the Prince and Master Poins
        anon, and they will put on two of our jerkins and aprons,
        and Sir John must not know of it. Bardolph hath
        brought word.

    FRANCIS By the mass, here will be old utis. It will be an
20   excellent stratagem.

DRAWER I'll see if I can find out Sneak.

Exeunt Francis and Drawer
Enter Hostess and Doll Tearsheet

HOSTESS I'faith, sweetheart, methinks now you are in an
excellent good temperality. Your pulsidge beats as
extraordinarily as heart would desire, and your colour,
I warrant you, is as red as any rose, in good truth, la!
But, i'faith, you have drunk too much canaries, and
that's a marvellous searching wine, and it perfumes the
blood ere one can say 'What's this?' How do you now?

DOLL Better than I was – hem!

HOSTESS Why, that's well said – a good heart's worth   30
gold. Lo, here comes Sir John.

Enter Falstaff, singing

FALSTAFF

   When Arthur first in court –
empty the jordan –   *Exit Will*
   And was a worthy king –
how now, Mistress Doll?

HOSTESS Sick of a calm, yea, good faith.

FALSTAFF So is all her sect; an they be once in a calm
they are sick.

DOLL A pox damn you, you muddy rascal, is that all the
comfort you give me?   40

FALSTAFF You make fat rascals, Mistress Doll.

DOLL I make them? Gluttony and diseases make them;
I make them not.

FALSTAFF If the cook help to make the gluttony, you
help to make the diseases, Doll. We catch of you, Doll,
we catch of you. Grant that, my poor virtue, grant that.

DOLL Yea, Mary's joys, our chains and our jewels –

FALSTAFF – your brooches, pearls, and ouches – for to
serve bravely is to come halting off, you know; to come
off the breach, with his pike bent bravely; and to   50

surgery bravely; to venture upon the charged chambers
bravely –

DOLL Hang yourself, you muddy conger, hang yourself!

HOSTESS By my troth, this is the old fashion; you two
never meet but you fall to some discord. You are both,
i'good truth, as rheumatic as two dry toasts; you cannot
one bear with another's confirmities. What the goodyear! One must bear, and that (*to Doll*) must be you;
you are the weaker vessel, as they say, the emptier
60   vessel.

DOLL Can a weak empty vessel bear such a huge full
hogshead? There's a whole merchant's venture of
Bordeaux stuff in him. You have not seen a hulk better
stuffed in the hold. Come, I'll be friends with thee,
Jack; thou art going to the wars, and whether I shall
ever see thee again or no there is nobody cares.

    Enter the Drawer

DRAWER Sir, Ancient Pistol's below, and would speak
with you.

DOLL Hang him, swaggering rascal. Let him not come
70   hither. It is the foul-mouthed'st rogue in England.

HOSTESS If he swagger, let him not come here. No, by
my faith! I must live among my neighbours; I'll no
swaggerers. I am in good name and fame with the very
best. Shut the door. There comes no swaggerers here. I
have not lived all this while to have swaggering now.
Shut the door, I pray you.

FALSTAFF Dost thou hear, hostess?

HOSTESS Pray ye, pacify yourself, Sir John; there comes
no swaggerers here.

80   FALSTAFF Dost thou hear? It is mine ancient.

HOSTESS Tilly-fally, Sir John, ne'er tell me; an your
ancient swagger, 'a comes not in my doors. I was before
Master Tisick the debuty t'other day, and, as he said

to me – 'twas no longer ago than Wednesday last, i'good
faith – 'Neighbour Quickly,' says he – Master Dumb
our minister was by then – 'Neighbour Quickly,' says
he, 'receive those that are civil, for,' said he, 'you are in
an ill name' – now 'a said so, I can tell whereupon.
'For,' says he, 'you are an honest woman, and well
thought on; therefore take heed what guests you receive;   90
receive,' says he, 'no swaggering companions.' There
comes none here. You would bless you to hear what he
said. No, I'll no swaggerers.

FALSTAFF He's no swaggerer, hostess, a tame cheater,
i'faith. You may stroke him as gently as a puppy grey-
hound. He'll not swagger with a Barbary hen, if her
feathers turn back in any show of resistance. Call him
up, drawer.   *Exit Drawer*

HOSTESS Cheater, call you him? I will bar no honest man
my house, nor no cheater, but I do not love swaggering;   100
by my troth, I am the worse when one says 'swagger'.
Feel, masters, how I shake, look you, I warrant you.

DOLL So you do, hostess.

HOSTESS Do I? Yea, in very truth, do I, an 'twere an
aspen leaf. I cannot abide swaggerers.

   Enter Ancient Pistol, Bardolph, and the Page

PISTOL God save you, Sir John!

FALSTAFF Welcome, Ancient Pistol! Here, Pistol, I
charge you with a cup of sack – do you discharge upon
mine hostess.

PISTOL I will discharge upon her, Sir John, with two   110
bullets.

FALSTAFF She is pistol-proof, sir; you shall not hardly
offend her.

HOSTESS Come, I'll drink no proofs, nor no bullets. I'll
drink no more than will do me good, for no man's
pleasure, I.

PISTOL Then to you, Mistress Dorothy! I will charge
   you.

DOLL Charge me? I scorn you, scurvy companion. What,
120   you poor, base, rascally, cheating, lack-linen mate!
   Away, you mouldy rogue, away! I am meat for your
   master.

PISTOL I know you, Mistress Dorothy.

DOLL Away, you cutpurse rascal, you filthy bung, away!
   By this wine, I'll thrust my knife in your mouldy chaps
   an your play the saucy cuttle with me. Away, you bottle-
   ale rascal, you basket-hilt stale juggler, you! Since when,
   I pray you, sir? God's light, with two points on your
   shoulder? Much!

130 PISTOL God let me not live but I will murder your ruff
   for this.

FALSTAFF No more, Pistol! I would not have you go off
   here. Discharge yourself of our company, Pistol.

HOSTESS No, good Captain Pistol, not here, sweet captain!

DOLL Captain! Thou abominable damned cheater, art
   thou not ashamed to be called captain? An captains
   were of my mind, they would truncheon you out, for
   taking their names upon you before you have earned
140   them. You a captain? You slave! For what? For tearing
   a poor whore's ruff in a bawdy-house? He a captain!
   Hang him, rogue, he lives upon mouldy stewed prunes
   and dried cakes. A captain? God's light, these villains
   will make the word as odious as the word 'occupy',
   which was an excellent good word before it was ill-
   sorted. Therefore captains had need look to't.

BARDOLPH Pray thee go down, good ancient.

FALSTAFF Hark thee hither, Mistress Doll.

PISTOL Not I; I tell thee what, Corporal Bardolph, I
150   could tear her! I'll be revenged of her.

PAGE Pray thee go down.

PISTOL I'll see her damned first! To Pluto's damnèd
lake, by this hand, to th'infernal deep, with Erebus and
tortures vile also! Hold hook and line, say I! Down,
down, dogs! Down, faitours! Have we not Hiren here?
  He brandishes his sword

HOSTESS Good Captain Peesel, be quiet; 'tis very late,
i'faith. I beseek you now, aggravate your choler.

PISTOL

These be good humours indeed! Shall pack-horses,
And hollow pampered jades of Asia,
Which cannot go but thirty mile a day,   160
Compare with Caesars and with Cannibals,
And Troyant Greeks? Nay, rather damn them with
King Cerberus, and let the welkin roar!
Shall we fall foul for toys?

HOSTESS By my troth, captain, these are very bitter
words.

BARDOLPH Be gone, good ancient; this will grow to a
brawl anon.

PISTOL Die men like dogs! Give crowns like pins! Have
we not Hiren here?   170

HOSTESS O' my word, captain, there's none such here.
What the goodyear, do you think I would deny her?
For God's sake, be quiet.

PISTOL

Then feed and be fat, my fair Calipolis!
Come, give's some sack.
Si fortune me tormente sperato me contento.
Fear we broadsides? No, let the fiend give fire!
Give me some sack. And, sweetheart, lie thou there!
  (*He lays down his sword*)
Come we to full points here? And are etceteras noth-
  ings?

180   FALSTAFF Pistol, I would be quiet.

PISTOL Sweet knight, I kiss thy neaf. What! We have
    seen the seven stars!

DOLL For God's sake, thrust him downstairs; I cannot
    endure such a fustian rascal.

PISTOL Thrust him downstairs? Know we not Gal-
    loway nags?

FALSTAFF Quoit him down, Bardolph, like a shove-groat
    shilling. Nay, an 'a do nothing but speak nothing, 'a
    shall be nothing here.

190   BARDOLPH Come, get you downstairs.

PISTOL
    What! Shall we have incision? Shall we imbrue?
        (*He snatches up his sword*)
    Then death rock me asleep, abridge my doleful days!
    Why then, let grievous, ghastly, gaping wounds
    Untwind the Sisters Three! Come, Atropos, I say!

HOSTESS Here's goodly stuff toward!

FALSTAFF Give me my rapier, boy.

DOLL I pray thee, Jack, I pray thee do not draw.

FALSTAFF (*drawing*) Get you downstairs.

HOSTESS Here's a goodly tumult! I'll forswear keeping

200   house afore I'll be in these tirrits and frights! So!
        (*Falstaff thrusts at Pistol*)
    Murder, I warrant now! Alas, alas, put up your naked
    weapons, put up your naked weapons.
                    Exit Bardolph, driving Pistol out

DOLL I pray thee, Jack, be quiet; the rascal's gone. Ah,
    you whoreson little valiant villain, you!

HOSTESS Are you not hurt i'th'groin? Methought 'a made
    a shrewd thrust at your belly.
        Enter Bardolph

FALSTAFF Have you turned him out o'doors?

BARDOLPH Yea, sir, the rascal's drunk. You have hurt

him, sir, i'th'shoulder.

FALSTAFF A rascal, to brave me!   210

DOLL Ah, you sweet little rogue, you! Alas, poor ape,
how thou sweatest! Come, let me wipe thy face. Come
on, you whoreson chops! Ah, rogue, i'faith, I love thee.
Thou art as valorous as Hector of Troy, worth five of
Agamemnon, and ten times better than the Nine
Worthies. Ah, villain!

FALSTAFF A rascally slave! I will toss the rogue in a
blanket.

DOLL Do, an thou darest for thy heart. An thou dost, I'll
canvass thee between a pair of sheets.   220

      Enter musicians

PAGE The music is come, sir.

FALSTAFF Let them play. Play, sirs!

      (*Music*)

Sit on my knee, Doll. A rascal bragging slave! The
rogue fled from me like quicksilver.

DOLL I'faith, and thou followed'st him like a church.
Thou whoreson little tidy Bartholomew boar-pig, when
wilt thou leave fighting a-days, and foining a-nights,
and begin to patch up thine old body for heaven?

      Enter, behind, the Prince and Poins disguised as
      drawers

FALSTAFF Peace, good Doll, do not speak like a death's-
head; do not bid me remember mine end.   230

DOLL Sirrah, what humour's the Prince of?

FALSTAFF A good shallow young fellow. 'A would have
made a good pantler; 'a would ha' chipped bread well.

DOLL They say Poins has a good wit.

FALSTAFF He a good wit? Hang him, baboon! His wit's
as thick as Tewkesbury mustard. There's no more conceit in him than is in a mallet.

DOLL Why does the Prince love him so, then?

FALSTAFF Because their legs are both of a bigness, and 'a
240   plays at quoits well, and eats conger and fennel, and
drinks off candles' ends for flap-dragons, and rides the
wild mare with the boys, and jumps upon joint-stools,
and swears with a good grace, and wears his boots very
smooth like unto the sign of the leg, and breeds no bate
with telling of discreet stories, and such other gambol
faculties 'a has that show a weak mind and an able
body, for the which the Prince admits him. For the
Prince himself is such another – the weight of a hair
will turn the scales between their avoirdupois.

250 PRINCE HENRY Would not this nave of a wheel have his
ears cut off?

POINS Let's beat him before his whore.

PRINCE HENRY Look whe'er the withered elder hath not
his poll clawed like a parrot.

POINS Is it not strange that desire should so many years
outlive performance?

FALSTAFF Kiss me, Doll.

PRINCE HENRY Saturn and Venus this year in conjunction! What says th'almanac to that?

260 POINS And look whether the fiery trigon his man be not
lisping to his master's old tables, his note-book, his
counsel-keeper.

FALSTAFF Thou dost give me flattering busses.

DOLL By my troth, I kiss thee with a most constant heart.

FALSTAFF I am old, I am old.

DOLL I love thee better than I love e'er a scurvy young
boy of them all.

FALSTAFF What stuff wilt have a kirtle of? I shall receive
money a-Thursday; shalt have a cap tomorrow. A
270 merry song! Come, it grows late; we'll to bed. Thou'lt
forget me when I am gone.

DOLL By my troth, thou'lt set me a-weeping an thou

sayst so. Prove that ever I dress myself handsome till
thy return. Well, hearken a'th'end.

FALSTAFF Some sack, Francis.

PRINCE HENRY *and* POINS (*coming forward*) Anon, anon,
sir.

FALSTAFF Ha! A bastard son of the King's? And art not
thou Poins his brother?

PRINCE HENRY Why, thou globe of sinful continents,   280
what a life dost thou lead!

FALSTAFF A better than thou – I am a gentleman; thou
art a drawer.

PRINCE HENRY Very true, sir, and I come to draw you
out by the ears.

HOSTESS O, the Lord preserve thy grace! By my troth,
welcome to London! Now the Lord bless that sweet
face of thine! O Jesu, are you come from Wales?

FALSTAFF Thou whoreson mad compound of majesty,
by this light – flesh and corrupt blood (*laying his hand*   290
upon Doll), thou art welcome.

DOLL How! You fat fool, I scorn you.

POINS My lord, he will drive you out of your revenge
and turn all to a merriment, if you take not the heat.

PRINCE HENRY You whoreson candle-mine you, how
vilely did you speak of me now, before this honest,
virtuous, civil gentlewoman!

HOSTESS God's blessing of your good heart, and so she
is, by my troth!

FALSTAFF Didst thou hear me?   300

PRINCE HENRY Yea, and you knew me, as you did when
you ran away by Gad's Hill; you knew I was at your
back, and spoke it on purpose to try my patience.

FALSTAFF No, no, no, not so; I did not think thou wast
within hearing.

PRINCE HENRY I shall drive you then to confess the

wilful abuse, and then I know how to handle you.

FALSTAFF No abuse, Hal, o' mine honour, no abuse.

PRINCE HENRY Not? To dispraise me, and call me
pantler, and bread-chipper, and I know not what?

FALSTAFF No abuse, Hal.

POINS No abuse?

FALSTAFF No abuse, Ned, i'th'world, honest Ned, none.
I dispraised him before the wicked that the wicked
might not fall in love with (*turning to Prince Henry*) thee
– in which doing, I have done the part of a careful friend
and a true subject, and thy father is to give me thanks
for it. No abuse, Hal; none, Ned, none; no, faith, boys,
none.

PRINCE HENRY See now whether pure fear and entire
cowardice doth not make thee wrong this virtuous
gentlewoman to close with us. Is she of the wicked? Is
thine hostess here of the wicked? Or is thy boy of the
wicked? Or honest Bardolph, whose zeal burns in his
nose, of the wicked?

POINS Answer, thou dead elm, answer.

FALSTAFF The fiend hath pricked down Bardolph irrecoverable, and his face in Lucifer's privy-kitchen,
where he doth nothing but roast malt-worms. For the
boy, there is a good angel about him, but the devil binds
him too.

PRINCE HENRY For the women?

FALSTAFF For one of them, she's in hell already, and
burns poor souls. For th'other, I owe her money, and
whether she be damned for that I know not.

HOSTESS No, I warrant you.

FALSTAFF No, I think thou art not; I think thou art quit
for that. Marry, there is another indictment upon thee,
for suffering flesh to be eaten in thy house, contrary to
the law, for the which I think thou wilt howl.

HOSTESS All victuallers do so. What's a joint of mutton
  or two in a whole Lent?

PRINCE HENRY You, gentlewoman –

DOLL What says your grace?

FALSTAFF His grace says that which his flesh rebels
  against.

  Peto knocks at door

HOSTESS Who knocks so loud at door? Look to th'door
  there, Francis.

  Enter Peto

PRINCE HENRY

  Peto, how now, what news?

PETO

  The King your father is at Westminster,   350
  And there are twenty weak and wearied posts
  Come from the north; and as I came along
  I met and overtook a dozen captains,
  Bare-headed, sweating, knocking at the taverns,
  And asking every one for Sir John Falstaff.

PRINCE HENRY

  By heaven, Poins, I feel me much to blame,
  So idly to profane the precious time
  When tempest of commotion, like the south
  Borne with black vapour, doth begin to melt
  And drop upon our bare unarmèd heads.   360
  Give me my sword and cloak. Falstaff, good night.

                          Exeunt Prince and Poins

FALSTAFF Now comes in the sweetest morsel of the
  night, and we must hence and leave it unpicked.

  Knocking within   *Exit Bardolph*

  More knocking at the door?

  Enter Bardolph

  How now, what's the matter?

BARDOLPH
　　You must away to court, sir, presently.
　　A dozen captains stay at door for you.
FALSTAFF (*to Page*) Pay the musicians, sirrah. Farewell
　　hostess; farewell, Doll. You see, my good wenches, how
370　men of merit are sought after; the undeserver may sleep
　　when the man of action is called on. Farewell, good
　　wenches. If I be not sent away post, I will see you again
　　ere I go.
DOLL I cannot speak; if my heart be not ready to burst –
　　well, sweet Jack, have a care of thyself.
FALSTAFF Farewell, farewell.
　　　　　　Exit with Bardolph, Peto, Page, and musicians
HOSTESS Well, fare thee well. I have known thee these
　　twenty-nine years, come peascod-time, but an honester
　　and truer-hearted man – well, fare thee well.
380 BARDOLPH (*at the door*) Mistress Tearsheet!
HOSTESS What's the matter?
BARDOLPH Bid Mistress Tearsheet come to my master.
HOSTESS O, run, Doll, run! Run, good Doll! Come! –
　　She comes blubbered. – Yea, will you come, Doll?
　　　　　　　　　　　　　　　　　　　　　　　　　Exeunt

　　　　　　　　　　　　　　　*

III.1　　　　　*Enter the King in his nightgown, followed by a page*
KING HENRY IV
　　Go call the Earls of Surrey and of Warwick –
　　But, ere they come, bid them o'er-read these letters
　　And well consider of them. Make good speed.
　　　　　　　　　　　　　　　　　　　　　　　　　Exit page
　　How many thousand of my poorest subjects
　　Are at this hour asleep! O sleep, O gentle sleep,

Nature's soft nurse, how have I frighted thee,
That thou no more wilt weigh my eyelids down
And steep my senses in forgetfulness?
Why rather, sleep, liest thou in smoky cribs,
Upon uneasy pallets stretching thee,   10
And hushed with buzzing night-flies to thy slumber,
Than in the perfumed chambers of the great,
Under the canopies of costly state,
And lulled with sound of sweetest melody?
O thou dull god, why liest thou with the vile
In loathsome beds, and leavest the kingly couch
A watch-case, or a common 'larum-bell?
Wilt thou upon the high and giddy mast
Seal up the ship-boy's eyes, and rock his brains
In cradle of the rude imperious surge,   20
And in the visitation of the winds,
Who take the ruffian billows by the top,
Curling their monstrous heads, and hanging them
With deafing clamour in the slippery clouds,
That with the hurly death itself awakes?
Canst thou, O partial sleep, give thy repose
To the wet sea-son in an hour so rude,
And in the calmest and most stillest night,
With all appliances and means to boot,
Deny it to a king? Then happy low, lie down!   30
Uneasy lies the head that wears a crown.
      Enter Warwick and Surrey

WARWICK

   Many good morrows to your majesty!

KING HENRY IV

   Is it good morrow, lords?

WARWICK

   'Tis one o'clock, and past.

KING HENRY IV

    Why then, good morrow to you all, my lords.

    Have you read o'er the letters that I sent you?

WARWICK

    We have, my liege.

KING HENRY IV

    Then you perceive the body of our kingdom

    How foul it is, what rank diseases grow,

40   And with what danger, near the heart of it.

WARWICK

    It is but as a body yet distempered,

    Which to his former strength may be restored

    With good advice and little medicine.

    My lord Northumberland will soon be cooled.

KING HENRY IV

    O God, that one might read the book of fate,

    And see the revolution of the times

    Make mountains level, and the continent,

    Weary of solid firmness, melt itself

    Into the sea; and other times to see

50   The beachy girdle of the ocean

    Too wide for Neptune's hips; how chance's mocks

    And changes fill the cup of alteration

    With divers liquors! 'Tis not ten years gone

    Since Richard and Northumberland, great friends,

    Did feast together, and in two years after

    Were they at wars. It is but eight years since

    This Percy was the man nearest my soul,

    Who like a brother toiled in my affairs

    And laid his love and life under my foot;

60   Yea, for my sake, even to the eyes of Richard

    Gave him defiance. But which of you was by –

    (*To Warwick*) You, cousin Nevil, as I may remember –

    When Richard, with his eye brimful of tears,

Then checked and rated by Northumberland,
Did speak these words, now proved a prophecy?
'Northumberland, thou ladder by the which
My cousin Bolingbroke ascends my throne' –
Though then, God knows, I had no such intent
But that necessity so bowed the state
That I and greatness were compelled to kiss –   70
'The time shall come' – thus did he follow it –
'The time will come that foul sin, gathering head,
Shall break into corruption' – so went on,
Foretelling this same time's condition,
And the division of our amity.

WARWICK
There is a history in all men's lives
Figuring the natures of the times deceased,
The which observed, a man may prophesy,
With a near aim, of the main chance of things
As yet not come to life, who in their seeds   80
And weak beginning lie intreasurèd.
Such things become the hatch and brood of time,
And by the necessary form of this
King Richard might create a perfect guess
That great Northumberland, then false to him,
Would of that seed grow to a greater falseness,
Which should not find a ground to root upon
Unless on you.

KING HENRY IV Are these things then necessities?
Then let us meet them like necessities,
And that same word even now cries out on us.   90
They say the Bishop and Northumberland
Are fifty thousand strong.

WARWICK   It cannot be, my lord.
Rumour doth double, like the voice and echo,
The numbers of the feared. Please it your grace

To go to bed. Upon my soul, my lord,
The powers that you already have sent forth
Shall bring this prize in very easily.
To comfort you the more, I have received
A certain instance that Glendower is dead.
100   Your majesty hath been this fortnight ill,
And these unseasoned hours perforce must add
Unto your sickness.
KING HENRY IV   I will take your counsel.
And were these inward wars once out of hand,
We would, dear lords, unto the Holy Land.   *Exeunt*

III.2   *Enter Justice Shallow and Justice Silence*

SHALLOW Come on, come on, come on! Give me your
hand, sir, give me your hand, sir! An early stirrer, by
the rood! And how doth my good cousin Silence?

SILENCE Good morrow, good cousin Shallow.

SHALLOW And how doth my cousin your bedfellow? And
your fairest daughter and mine, my god-daughter Ellen?

SILENCE Alas, a black woosel, cousin Shallow!

SHALLOW By yea and no, sir. I dare say my cousin
William is become a good scholar – he is at Oxford still
10   is he not?

SILENCE Indeed, sir, to my cost.

SHALLOW 'A must then to the Inns o'Court shortly. I
was once of Clement's Inn, where I think they will talk
of mad Shallow yet.

SILENCE You were called 'lusty Shallow' then, cousin.

SHALLOW By the mass, I was called anything, and I
would have done anything indeed too, and roundly too.
There was I, and little John Doit of Staffordshire, and
black George Barnes, and Francis Pickbone, and Will
20   Squele, a Cotsole man – you had not four such swinge-

bucklers in all the Inns o'Court again. And I may say
to you, we knew where the bona-robas were, and had
the best of them all at commandment. Then was Jack
Falstaff, now Sir John, a boy, and page to Thomas
Mowbray, Duke of Norfolk.

SILENCE This Sir John, cousin, that comes hither anon
about soldiers?

SHALLOW The same Sir John, the very same. I see him
break Scoggin's head at the court gate, when 'a was a
crack, not thus high; and the very same day did I fight   30
with one Samson Stockfish, a fruiterer, behind Gray's
Inn. Jesu, Jesu, the mad days that I have spent! And to
see how many of my old acquaintance are dead!

SILENCE We shall all follow, cousin.

SHALLOW Certain, 'tis certain, very sure, very sure.
Death, as the Psalmist saith, is certain to all; all shall
die. How a good yoke of bullocks at Stamford fair?

SILENCE By my troth, I was not there.

SHALLOW Death is certain. Is old Double of your town
living yet?   40

SILENCE Dead, sir.

SHALLOW Jesu, Jesu, dead! 'A drew a good bow, and
dead! 'A shot a fine shoot. John o'Gaunt loved him well,
and betted much money on his head. Dead! 'A would
have clapped i'th'clout at twelve score, and carried you
a forehand shaft a fourteen and fourteen and a half,
that it would have done a man's heart good to see. How
a score of ewes now?

SILENCE Thereafter as they be; a score of good ewes may
be worth ten pounds.   50

SHALLOW And is old Double dead?

SILENCE Here come two of Sir John Falstaff's men, as I
think.

    Enter Bardolph and one with him

SHALLOW Good morrow, honest gentlemen.

BARDOLPH I beseech you, which is Justice Shallow?

SHALLOW I am Robert Shallow, sir, a poor esquire of
this county, and one of the King's justices of the peace.
What is your good pleasure with me?

BARDOLPH My captain, sir, commends him to you, my
captain Sir John Falstaff, a tall gentleman, by heaven,
and a most gallant leader.

SHALLOW He greets me well, sir; I knew him a good
backsword man. How doth the good knight? May I ask
how my lady his wife doth?

BARDOLPH Sir, pardon; a soldier is better accommodated
than with a wife.

SHALLOW It is well said, in faith, sir, and it is well said
indeed too. 'Better accommodated'! It is good, yea
indeed is it. Good phrases are surely, and ever were,
very commendable. 'Accommodated': it comes of
accommodo. Very good, a good phrase.

BARDOLPH Pardon, sir, I have heard the word – phrase
call you it? By this day, I know not the phrase, but I
will maintain the word with my sword to be a soldier-
like word, and a word of exceeding good command, by
heaven. Accommodated: that is, when a man is, as they
say, accommodated, or when a man is being whereby 'a
may be thought to be accommodated; which is an
excellent thing.

SHALLOW It is very just.

Enter Falstaff

Look, here comes good Sir John. Give me your good
hand, give me your worship's good hand. By my troth,
you like well, and bear your years very well. Welcome,
good Sir John.

FALSTAFF I am glad to see you well, good Master Robert
Shallow. Master Surecard, as I think?

SHALLOW No, Sir John, it is my cousin Silence, in commission with me.

FALSTAFF Good Master Silence, it well befits you should be of the peace.   90

SILENCE Your good worship is welcome.

FALSTAFF Fie, this is hot weather, gentlemen. Have you provided me here half a dozen sufficient men?

SHALLOW Marry, have we, sir. Will you sit?

FALSTAFF Let me see them, I beseech you.

SHALLOW Where's the roll? Where's the roll? Where's the roll? Let me see, let me see, let me see. So, so, so, so, so, so, so. Yea, marry, sir. Rafe Mouldy! Let them appear as I call, let them do so, let them do so. Let me see – where is Mouldy?   100

Enter Mouldy

MOULDY Here, an't please you.

SHALLOW What think you, Sir John? A good-limbed fellow, young, strong, and of good friends.

FALSTAFF Is thy name Mouldy?

MOULDY Yea, an't please you.

FALSTAFF 'Tis the more time thou wert used.

SHALLOW Ha, ha, ha! Most excellent, i'faith! Things that are mouldy lack use! Very singular good, in faith, well said, Sir John, very well said.

FALSTAFF Prick him.   110

MOULDY I was pricked well enough before, an you could have let me alone. My old dame will be undone now for one to do her husbandry and her drudgery. You need not to have pricked me; there are other men fitter to go out than I.

FALSTAFF Go to! Peace, Mouldy; you shall go, Mouldy; it is time you were spent.

MOULDY Spent?

SHALLOW Peace, fellow, peace – stand aside. Know you

120   where you are? For th'other, Sir John – let me see.
    Simon Shadow!
       Enter Shadow

FALSTAFF Yea, marry, let me have him to sit under. He's
    like to be a cold soldier.

SHALLOW Where's Shadow?

SHADOW Here, sir.

FALSTAFF Shadow, whose son art thou?

SHADOW My mother's son, sir.

FALSTAFF Thy mother's son! Like enough, and thy
    father's shadow. So the son of the female is the shadow
130   of the male; it is often so, indeed – but much of the
    father's substance!

SHALLOW Do you like him, Sir John?

FALSTAFF Shadow will serve for summer. Prick him, for
    we have a number of shadows fill up the muster-book.

SHALLOW Thomas Wart!
       Enter Wart

FALSTAFF Where's he?

WART Here, sir.

FALSTAFF Is thy name Wart?

WART Yea, sir.

140 FALSTAFF Thou art a very ragged Wart.

SHALLOW Shall I prick him, Sir John?

FALSTAFF It were superfluous, for his apparel is built
    upon his back, and the whole frame stands upon pins.
    Prick him no more.

SHALLOW Ha, ha, ha! You can do it, sir, you can do it;
    I commend you well. Francis Feeble!
       Enter Feeble

FEEBLE Here, sir.

SHALLOW What trade art thou, Feeble?

FEEBLE A woman's tailor, sir.

150 SHALLOW Shall I prick him, sir?

FALSTAFF You may; but if he had been a man's tailor
he'd ha' pricked you. Wilt thou make as many holes in
an enemy's battle as thou hast done in a woman's
petticoat?

FEEBLE I will do my good will, sir; you can have no more.

FALSTAFF Well, said, good woman's tailor! Well said,
courageous Feeble! Thou wilt be as valiant as the
wrathful dove, or most magnanimous mouse. Prick the
woman's tailor well, Master Shallow; deep, Master
Shallow.   160

FEEBLE I would Wart might have gone, sir.

FALSTAFF I would thou wert a man's tailor, that thou
mightst mend him and make him fit to go. I cannot put
him to a private soldier, that is the leader of so many
thousands. Let that suffice, most forcible Feeble.

FEEBLE It shall suffice, sir.

FALSTAFF I am bound to thee, reverend Feeble. Who is
next?

SHALLOW Peter Bullcalf o'th'green!
     Enter Bullcalf

FALSTAFF Yea, marry, let's see Bullcalf.   170

BULLCALF Here, sir.

FALSTAFF 'Fore God, a likely fellow! Come, prick Bullcalf till he roar again.

BULLCALF O Lord, good my lord captain –

FALSTAFF What, dost thou roar before thou art pricked?

BULLCALF O Lord, sir, I am a diseased man.

FALSTAFF What disease hast thou?

BULLCALF A whoreson cold, sir, a cough, sir, which I
caught with ringing in the King's affairs upon his
coronation day, sir.   180

FALSTAFF Come, thou shalt go to the wars in a gown.
We will have away thy cold, and I will take such order
that thy friends shall ring for thee. Is here all?

SHALLOW Here is two more called than your number.
You must have but four here, sir; and so, I pray you,
go in with me to dinner.

FALSTAFF Come, I will go drink with you, but I cannot
tarry dinner. I am glad to see you, by my troth, Master
Shallow.

190 SHALLOW O, Sir John, do you remember since we lay all
night in the Windmill in Saint George's Field?

FALSTAFF No more of that, Master Shallow.

SHALLOW Ha, 'twas a merry night! And is Jane Nightwork alive?

FALSTAFF She lives, Master Shallow.

SHALLOW She never could away with me.

FALSTAFF Never, never. She would always say she could
not abide Master Shallow.

SHALLOW By the mass, I could anger her to th'heart. She
200 was then a bona-roba. Doth she hold her own well?

FALSTAFF Old, old, Master Shallow.

SHALLOW Nay, she must be old, she cannot choose but
be old, certain she's old, and had Robin Nightwork by
old Nightwork before I came to Clement's Inn.

SILENCE That's fifty-five year ago.

SHALLOW Ha, cousin Silence, that thou hadst seen that
that this knight and I have seen! Ha, Sir John, said I
well?

FALSTAFF We have heard the chimes at midnight, Master
210 Shallow.

SHALLOW That we have, that we have, that we have! In
faith, Sir John, we have. Our watchword was 'Hem,
boys!' Come, let's to dinner; come, let's to dinner.
Jesus, the days that we have seen! Come, come.

Exeunt Falstaff, Shallow, and Silence

BULLCALF Good Master Corporate Bardolph, stand my
friend – and here's four Harry ten shillings in French

crowns for you. In very truth, sir, I had as lief be
hanged, sir, as go. And yet for mine own part, sir, I do
not care, but rather because I am unwilling, and, for
mine own part, have a desire to stay with my friends;   220
else, sir, I did not care, for mine own part, so much.

BARDOLPH Go to; stand aside.

MOULDY And, good Master Corporal Captain, for my old
dame's sake stand my friend. She has nobody to do
anything about her when I am gone, and she is old and
cannot help herself. You shall have forty, sir.

BARDOLPH Go to; stand aside.

FEEBLE By my troth, I care not; a man can die but once;
we owe God a death. I'll ne'er bear a base mind. An't
be my destiny, so; an't be not, so. No man's too good   230
to serve's prince; and, let it go which way it will, he
that dies this year is quit for the next.

BARDOLPH Well said; th'art a good fellow.

FEEBLE Faith, I'll bear no base mind.

    Enter Falstaff and the Justices

FALSTAFF Come, sir, which men shall I have?

SHALLOW Four of which you please.

BARDOLPH (*aside to Falstaff*) Sir, a word with you. I have
three pound to free Mouldy and Bullcalf.

FALSTAFF Go to, well.

SHALLOW Come, Sir John, which four will you have?   240

FALSTAFF Do you choose for me.

SHALLOW Marry, then, Mouldy, Bullcalf, Feeble, and
Shadow.

FALSTAFF Mouldy and Bullcalf: for you, Mouldy, stay at
home till you are past service; and for your part,
Bullcalf, grow till you come unto it. I will none of you.

SHALLOW Sir John, Sir John, do not yourself wrong;
they are your likeliest men, and I would have you served
with the best.

250 FALSTAFF Will you tell me, Master Shallow, how to
choose a man? Care I for the limb, the thews, the
stature, bulk, and big assemblance of a man? Give me
the spirit, Master Shallow. Here's Wart; you see what
a ragged appearance it is. 'A shall charge you, and
discharge you, with the motion of a pewterer's hammer,
come off and on swifter than he that gibbets on the
brewer's bucket. And this same half-faced fellow
Shadow; give me this man; he presents no mark to the
enemy – the foeman may with as great aim level at the
260 edge of a penknife. And for a retreat, how swiftly will
this Feeble the woman's tailor run off! O, give me the
spare men, and spare me the great ones. Put me a caliver
into Wart's hand, Bardolph.

BARDOLPH Hold, Wart, traverse. Thas! Thas! Thas!

FALSTAFF Come, manage me your caliver. So, very well!
Go to, very good! Exceeding good! O, give me always
a little, lean, old, chopped, bald shot. Well said, i'faith!
Wart, th'art a good scab. Hold, there's a tester for thee.

SHALLOW He is not his craft's master; he doth not do it
270 right. I remember at Mile End Green, when I lay at
Clement's Inn – I was then Sir Dagonet in Arthur's
show – there was a little quiver fellow, and 'a would
manage you his piece thus, and 'a would about, and
about, and come you in, and come you in. 'Rah, tah,
tah!' would 'a say. 'Bounce!' would 'a say. And away
again would 'a go, and again would 'a come. I shall
ne'er see such a fellow.

FALSTAFF These fellows will do well, Master Shallow.
God keep you, Master Silence; I will not use many
280 words with you. Fare you well, gentlemen both; I thank
you. I must a dozen mile tonight. Bardolph, give the
soldiers coats.

SHALLOW Sir John, the Lord bless you! God prosper

your affairs! God send us peace! At your return, visit
my house; let our old acquaintance be renewed. Per-
adventure I will with ye to the court.

FALSTAFF 'Fore God, would you would.

SHALLOW Go to; I have spoke at a word. God keep you!

FALSTAFF Fare you well, gentle gentlemen.

Exeunt Shallow and Silence

On, Bardolph, lead the men away.   290

Exeunt Bardolph and the recruits

As I return, I will fetch off these justices. I do see the
bottom of Justice Shallow. Lord, Lord, how subject we
old men are to this vice of lying! This same starved
justice hath done nothing but prate to me of the wildness
of his youth, and the feats he hath done about Turnbull
Street, and every third word a lie, duer paid to the
hearer than the Turk's tribute. I do remember him at
Clement's Inn, like a man made after supper of a
cheese-paring. When 'a was naked, he was for all the
world like a forked radish, with a head fantastically   300
carved upon it with a knife. 'A was so forlorn that his
dimensions to any thick sight were invincible. 'A was
the very genius of famine, yet lecherous as a monkey,
and the whores called him mandrake. 'A came ever in
the rearward of the fashion, and sung those tunes to the
overscutched housewives that he heard the carmen
whistle, and sware they were his fancies or his good-
nights. And now is this Vice's dagger become a squire,
and talks as familiarly of John o'Gaunt as if he had
been sworn brother to him, and I'll be sworn 'a ne'er   310
saw him but once in the tilt-yard, and then he burst his
head for crowding among the marshal's men. I saw it
and told John o'Gaunt he beat his own name, for you
might have thrust him and all his apparel into an eel-
skin – the case of a treble hautboy was a mansion for

him, a court. And now has he land and beefs. Well, I'll
be acquainted with him if I return, and't shall go hard
but I'll make him a philosopher's two stones to me. If
the young dace be a bait for the old pike, I see no
320   reason in the law of nature but I may snap at him. Let
time shape, and there an end.   *Exit*

*

IV. I   *Enter the Archbishop, Mowbray, and Hastings, with*
        their forces, within the Forest of Gaultree

ARCHBISHOP
  What is this forest called?

HASTINGS
  'Tis Gaultree Forest, an't shall please your grace.

ARCHBISHOP
  Here stand, my lords, and send discoverers forth
  To know the numbers of our enemies.

HASTINGS
  We have sent forth already.

ARCHBISHOP   'Tis well done.
  My friends and brethren in these great affairs,
  I must acquaint you that I have received
  New-dated letters from Northumberland,
  Their cold intent, tenor, and substance, thus:
10   Here doth he wish his person, with such powers
  As might hold sortance with his quality,
  The which he could not levy; whereupon
  He is retired to ripe his growing fortunes
  To Scotland, and concludes in hearty prayers
  That your attempts may overlive the hazard
  And fearful meeting of their opposite.

MOWBRAY

Thus do the hopes we have in him touch ground
And dash themselves to pieces.

Enter a Messenger

HASTINGS   Now, what news?

MESSENGER

West of this forest, scarcely off a mile,
In goodly form comes on the enemy,   20
And, by the ground they hide, I judge their number
Upon or near the rate of thirty thousand.

MOWBRAY

The just proportion that we gave them out.
Let us sway on and face them in the field.

Enter Westmorland

ARCHBISHOP

What well-appointed leader fronts us here?

MOWBRAY

I think it is my lord of Westmorland.

WESTMORLAND

Health and fair greeting from our general,
The Prince, Lord John and Duke of Lancaster.

ARCHBISHOP

Say on, my lord of Westmorland, in peace,
What doth concern your coming.

WESTMORLAND   Then, my lord,   30
Unto your grace do I in chief address
The substance of my speech. If that rebellion
Came like itself, in base and abject routs,
Led on by bloody youth, guarded with rage,
And countenanced by boys and beggary;
I say, if damned commotion so appeared
In his true, native, and most proper shape,
You, reverend father, and these noble lords
Had not been here to dress the ugly form

40 Of base and bloody insurrection
With your fair honours. You, Lord Archbishop,
Whose see is by a civil peace maintained,
Whose beard the silver hand of peace hath touched,
Whose learning and good letters peace hath tutored,
Whose white investments figure innocence,
The dove and very blessèd spirit of peace,
Wherefore do you so ill translate yourself
Out of the speech of peace that bears such grace
Into the harsh and boisterous tongue of war,
50 Turning your books to graves, your ink to blood,
Your pens to lances, and your tongue divine
To a loud trumpet and a point of war?

ARCHBISHOP
Wherefore do I this? So the question stands.
Briefly, to this end: we are all diseased,
And with our surfeiting and wanton hours
Have brought ourselves into a burning fever,
And we must bleed for it; of which disease
Our late King Richard being infected died.
But, my most noble lord of Westmorland,
60 I take not on me here as a physician,
Nor do I as an enemy to peace
Troop in the throngs of military men,
But rather show awhile like fearful war
To diet rank minds sick of happiness,
And purge th'obstructions which begin to stop
Our very veins of life. Hear me more plainly.
I have in equal balance justly weighed
What wrongs our arms may do, what wrongs we suffer,
And find our griefs heavier than our offences.
70 We see which way the stream of time doth run
And are enforced from our most quiet there
By the rough torrent of occasion,

And have the summary of all our griefs,
When time shall serve, to show in articles,
Which long ere this we offered to the King,
And might by no suit gain our audience.
When we are wronged, and would unfold our griefs,
We are denied access unto his person
Even by those men that most have done us wrong.
The dangers of the days but newly gone,   80
Whose memory is written on the earth
With yet-appearing blood, and the examples
Of every minute's instance, present now,
Hath put us in these ill-beseeming arms,
Not to break peace, or any branch of it,
But to establish here a peace indeed,
Concurring both in name and quality.

WESTMORLAND

Whenever yet was your appeal denied?
Wherein have you been gallèd by the King?
What peer hath been suborned to grate on you,   90
That you should seal this lawless bloody book
Of forged rebellion with a seal divine?

ARCHBISHOP

My brother general, the commonwealth,
I make my quarrel in particular.

WESTMORLAND

There is no need of any such redress,
Or if there were, it not belongs to you.

MOWBRAY

Why not to him in part, and to us all
That feel the bruises of the days before,
And suffer the condition of these times
To lay a heavy and unequal hand   100
Upon our honours?

WESTMORLAND   O, my good lord Mowbray,

Construe the times to their necessities,
And you shall say, indeed, it is the time,
And not the King, that doth you injuries.
Yet for your part, it not appears to me
Either from the King or in the present time
That you should have an inch of any ground
To build a grief on. Were you not restored
To all the Duke of Norfolk's signories,
110   Your noble and right well-remembered father's?

MOWBRAY

What thing, in honour, had my father lost
That need to be revived and breathed in me?
The King that loved him, as the state stood then,
Was force perforce compelled to banish him,
And then that Henry Bolingbroke and he,
Being mounted and both rousèd in their seats,
Their neighing coursers daring of the spur,
Their armèd staves in charge, their beavers down,
Their eyes of fire sparkling through sights of steel,
120   And the loud trumpet blowing them together,
Then, then, when there was nothing could have stayed
My father from the breast of Bolingbroke,
O, when the King did throw his warder down,
His own life hung upon the staff he threw.
Then threw he down himself and all their lives
That by indictment and by dint of sword
Have since miscarried under Bolingbroke.

WESTMORLAND

You speak, Lord Mowbray, now you know not what.
The Earl of Hereford was reputed then
130   In England the most valiant gentleman.
Who knows on whom fortune would then have smiled?
But if your father had been victor there,
He ne'er had borne it out of Coventry;

For all the country, in a general voice,
Cried hate upon him, and all their prayers and love
Were set on Herford, whom they doted on,
And blessed, and graced, indeed more than the King.
But this is mere digression from my purpose.
Here come I from our princely general
To know your griefs, to tell you from his grace   140
That he will give you audience; and wherein
It shall appear that your demands are just,
You shall enjoy them, everything set off
That might so much as think you enemies.

MOWBRAY

But he hath forced us to compel this offer,
And it proceeds from policy, not love.

WESTMORLAND

Mowbray, you overween to take it so.
This offer comes from mercy, not from fear;
For lo, within a ken our army lies,
Upon mine honour, all too confident   150
To give admittance to a thought of fear.
Our battle is more full of names than yours,
Our men more perfect in the use of arms,
Our armour all as strong, our cause the best;
Then reason will our hearts should be as good.
Say you not then our offer is compelled.

MOWBRAY

Well, by my will we shall admit no parley.

WESTMORLAND

That argues but the shame of your offence;
A rotten case abides no handling.

HASTINGS

Hath the Prince John a full commission,   160
In very ample virtue of his father,
To hear and absolutely to determine

Of what conditions we shall stand upon?

WESTMORLAND

That is intended in the general's name.
I muse you make so slight a question.

ARCHBISHOP

Then take, my lord of Westmorland, this schedule,
For this contains our general grievances.
Each several article herein redressed,
All members of our cause, both here and hence,
170   That are ensinewed to this action
Acquitted by a true substantial form
And present execution of our wills –
To us and to our purposes confined
We come within our awful banks again,
And knit our powers to the arm of peace.

WESTMORLAND

This will I show the general. Please you, lords,
In sight of both our battles we may meet,
At either end in peace – which God so frame! –
Or to the place of difference call the swords
180   Which must decide it.

ARCHBISHOP   My lord, we will do so.

Exit Westmorland

MOWBRAY

There is a thing within my bosom tells me
That no conditions of our peace can stand.

HASTINGS

Fear you not that. If we can make our peace
Upon such large terms, and so absolute,
As our conditions shall consist upon,
Our peace shall stand as firm as rocky mountains.

MOWBRAY

Yea, but our valuation shall be such
That every slight and false-derivèd cause,

Yea, every idle, nice, and wanton reason,
Shall to the King taste of this action;   190
That, were our royal faiths martyrs in love,
We shall be winnowed with so rough a wind
That even our corn shall seem as light as chaff,
And good from bad find no partition.

ARCHBISHOP

No, no, my lord. Note this: the King is weary
Of dainty and such picking grievances,
For he hath found to end one doubt by death
Revives two greater in the heirs of life;
And therefore will he wipe his tables clean,
And keep no tell-tale to his memory   200
That may repeat and history his loss
To new remembrance. For full well he knows
He cannot so precisely weed this land
As his misdoubts present occasion.
His foes are so enrooted with his friends
That, plucking to unfix an enemy,
He doth unfasten so and shake a friend.
So that this land, like an offensive wife
That hath enraged him on to offer strokes,
As he is striking, holds his infant up,   210
And hangs resolved correction in the arm
That was upreared to execution.

HASTINGS

Besides, the King hath wasted all his rods
On late offenders, that he now doth lack
The very instruments of chastisement,
So that his power, like to a fangless lion,
May offer, but not hold.

ARCHBISHOP   'Tis very true;
And therefore be assured, my good Lord Marshal,
If we do now make our atonement well,

220   Our peace will, like a broken limb united,
        Grow stronger for the breaking.
MOWBRAY   Be it so.
        Here is returned my lord of Westmorland.
            Enter Westmorland
WESTMORLAND
        The Prince is here at hand. Pleaseth your lordship
        To meet his grace just distance 'tween our armies?
MOWBRAY
        Your grace of York, in God's name then, set forward.
ARCHBISHOP
        Before, and greet his grace! My lord, we come.
            They go forward

IV.2   *Enter Prince John of Lancaster and his army*
PRINCE JOHN
        You are well encountered here, my cousin Mowbray;
        Good day to you, gentle Lord Archbishop;
        And so to you, Lord Hastings, and to all.
        My lord of York, it better showed with you
        When that your flock, assembled by the bell,
        Encircled you to hear with reverence
        Your exposition on the holy text,
        Than now to see you here an iron man,
        Cheering a rout of rebels with your drum,
10   Turning the word to sword, and life to death.
        That man that sits within a monarch's heart
        And ripens in the sunshine of his favour,
        Would he abuse the countenance of the king?
        Alack, what mischiefs might he set abroach
        In shadow of such greatness! With you, Lord Bishop,
        It is even so. Who hath not heard it spoken
        How deep you were within the books of God?

To us the speaker in His parliament,
To us th'imagined voice of God himself,
The very opener and intelligencer   20
Between the grace, the sanctities, of heaven
And our dull workings. O, who shall believe
But you misuse the reverence of your place,
Imply the countenance and grace of heaven
As a false favourite doth his prince's name,
In deeds dishonourable? You have taken up,
Under the counterfeited zeal of God,
The subjects of His substitute, my father,
And both against the peace of heaven and him
Have here up-swarmed them.

ARCHBISHOP   Good my lord of Lancaster,   30
I am not here against your father's peace,
But, as I told my lord of Westmorland,
The time misordered doth, in common sense,
Crowd us and crush us to this monstrous form
To hold our safety up. I sent your grace
The parcels and particulars of our grief,
The which hath been with scorn shoved from the court,
Whereon this Hydra son of war is born,
Whose dangerous eyes may well be charmed asleep
With grant of our most just and right desires,   40
And true obedience, of this madness cured,
Stoop tamely to the foot of majesty.

MOWBRAY
If not, we ready are to try our fortunes
To the last man.

HASTINGS   And though we here fall down,
We have supplies to second our attempt.
If they miscarry, theirs shall second them,
And so success of mischief shall be born,
And heir from heir shall hold this quarrel up

Whiles England shall have generation.

PRINCE JOHN

50 You are too shallow, Hastings, much too shallow,
To sound the bottom of the after-times.

WESTMORLAND

Pleaseth your grace to answer them directly
How far forth you do like their articles.

PRINCE JOHN

I like them all, and do allow them well,
And swear here, by the honour of my blood,
My father's purposes have been mistook,
And some about him have too lavishly
Wrested his meaning and authority.
My lord, these griefs shall be with speed redressed,

60 Upon my soul, they shall. If this may please you,
Discharge your powers unto their several counties,
As we will ours; and here, between the armies,
Let's drink together friendly and embrace,
That all their eyes may bear those tokens home
Of our restorèd love and amity.

ARCHBISHOP

I take your princely word for these redresses.

PRINCE JOHN

I give it you, and will maintain my word;
And thereupon I drink unto your grace.

HASTINGS

Go, captain, and deliver to the army

70 This news of peace. Let them have pay, and part.
I know it will well please them. Hie thee, captain!

Exit a captain

ARCHBISHOP

To you, my noble lord of Westmorland!

WESTMORLAND

I pledge your grace – and if you knew what pains

I have bestowed to breed this present peace
You would drink freely; but my love to ye
Shall show itself more openly hereafter.

ARCHBISHOP

I do not doubt you.

WESTMORLAND   I am glad of it.
Health to my lord and gentle cousin, Mowbray.

MOWBRAY

You wish me health in very happy season,
For I am on the sudden something ill.   80

ARCHBISHOP

Against ill chances men are ever merry,
But heaviness foreruns the good event.

WESTMORLAND

Therefore be merry, coz, since sudden sorrow
Serves to say thus, 'Some good thing comes tomorrow.'

ARCHBISHOP

Believe me, I am passing light in spirit.

MOWBRAY

So much the worse, if your own rule be true.
    Shouts within

PRINCE JOHN

The word of peace is rendered. Hark how they shout!

MOWBRAY

This had been cheerful after victory.

ARCHBISHOP

A peace is of the nature of a conquest,
For then both parties nobly are subdued,   90
And neither party loser.

PRINCE JOHN   Go, my lord,
And let our army be dischargèd too. *Exit Westmorland*
And, good my lord, so please you, let our trains
March by us, that we may peruse the men
We should have coped withal.

ARCHBISHOP   Go, good Lord Hastings
    And, ere they be dismissed, let them march by.
                                            Exit Hastings

PRINCE JOHN
    I trust, lords, we shall lie tonight together.
        Enter Westmorland
    Now, cousin, wherefore stands our army still?

WESTMORLAND
    The leaders, having charge from you to stand,
100   Will not go off until they hear you speak.

PRINCE JOHN
    They know their duties.
        Enter Hastings

HASTINGS
    My lord, our army is dispersed already.
    Like youthful steers unyoked they take their courses
    East, west, north, south; or like a school broke up,
    Each hurries toward his home and sporting-place.

WESTMORLAND
    Good tidings, my lord Hastings – for the which
    I do arrest thee, traitor, of high treason;
    And you, Lord Archbishop, and you, Lord Mowbray,
    Of capital treason I attach you both.

MOWBRAY
110   Is this proceeding just and honourable?

WESTMORLAND
    Is your assembly so?

ARCHBISHOP
    Will you thus break your faith?

PRINCE JOHN   I pawned thee none.
    I promised you redress of these same grievances
    Whereof you did complain, which, by mine honour,
    I will perform with a most Christian care.
    But, for you rebels, look to taste the due

Meet for rebellion and such acts as yours.
Most shallowly did you these arms commence,
Fondly brought here, and foolishly sent hence.
Strike up our drums, pursue the scattered stray;   120
God, and not we, hath safely fought today.
Some guard these traitors to the block of death,
Treason's true bed and yielder-up of breath.   *Exeunt*

Alarum. Excursions. Enter Falstaff and Sir John   IV.3
   Colevile

FALSTAFF What's your name, sir? Of what condition are
   you, and of what place?
COLEVILE I am a knight, sir, and my name is Colevile
   of the Dale.
FALSTAFF Well then, Colevile is your name, a knight is
   your degree, and your place the Dale. Colevile shall be
   still your name, a traitor your degree, and the dungeon
   your place – a place deep enough; so shall you be still
   Colevile of the Dale.
COLEVILE Are not you Sir John Falstaff?   10
FALSTAFF As good a man as he, sir, whoe'er I am. Do
   ye yield, sir, or shall I sweat for you? If I do sweat,
   they are the drops of thy lovers, and they weep for thy
   death. Therefore rouse up fear and trembling, and do
   observance to my mercy.
COLEVILE I think you are Sir John Falstaff, and in that
   thought yield me.
   He kneels
FALSTAFF I have a whole school of tongues in this belly
   of mine, and not a tongue of them all speaks any other
   word but my name. An I had but a belly of any indif-   20
   ferency, I were simply the most active fellow in Europe;

my womb, my womb, my womb undoes me. Here
comes our general.

   Retreat sounded
   Enter Prince John, Westmorland, and Blunt, with
   soldiers

PRINCE JOHN
   The heat is past; follow no further now.
   Call in the powers, good cousin Westmorland.

                        Exit Westmorland

   Now, Falstaff, where have you been all this while?
   When everything is ended, then you come.
   These tardy tricks of yours will, on my life,
   One time or other break some gallows' back.

30 FALSTAFF I would be sorry, my lord, but it should be
   thus. I never knew yet but rebuke and check was the
   reward of valour. Do you think me a swallow, an arrow,
   or a bullet? Have I in my poor and old motion the
   expedition of thought? I have speeded hither with the
   very extremest inch of possibility; I have foundered nine
   score and odd posts; and here, travel-tainted as I am,
   have in my pure and immaculate valour taken Sir John
   Colevile of the Dale, a most furious knight and valorous
   enemy. But what of that? He saw me, and yielded;
40 that I may justly say, with the hook-nosed fellow of
   Rome, three words, 'I came, saw, and overcame.'

PRINCE JOHN It was more of his courtesy than your
   deserving.

FALSTAFF I know not. Here he is, and here I yield him.
   And I beseech your grace, let it be booked with the rest
   of this day's deeds, or by the Lord I will have it in a
   particular ballad else, with mine own picture on the
   top on't, Colevile kissing my foot – to the which course
   if I be enforced, if you do not all show like gilt two-
50 pences to me, and I in the clear sky of fame o'ershine

you as much as the full moon doth the cinders of the
element, which show like pins' heads to her, believe not
the word of the noble. Therefore let me have right, and
let desert mount.

PRINCE JOHN Thine's too heavy to mount.

FALSTAFF Let it shine, then.

PRINCE JOHN Thine's too thick to shine.

FALSTAFF Let it do something, my good lord, that may
do me good, and call it what you will.

PRINCE JOHN Is thy name Colevile?　　　　　　　　60

COLEVILE It is, my lord.

PRINCE JOHN A famous rebel art thou, Colevile.

FALSTAFF And a famous true subject took him.

COLEVILE
I am, my lord, but as my betters are
That led me hither. Had they been ruled by me,
You should have won them dearer than you have.

FALSTAFF I know not how they sold themselves, but
thou like a kind fellow gavest thyself away gratis, and I
thank thee for thee.

　　　Enter Westmorland

PRINCE JOHN
Now, have you left pursuit?　　　　　　　　70

WESTMORLAND
Retreat is made and execution stayed.

PRINCE JOHN
Send Colevile with his confederates
To York, to present execution.
Blunt, lead him hence, and see you guard him sure.

　　　　　　　　　Exit Blunt with Colevile

And now dispatch we toward the court, my lords.
I hear the King my father is sore sick.
Our news shall go before us to his majesty,
Which, cousin, you shall bear to comfort him,

And we with sober speed will follow you.

80 FALSTAFF My lord, I beseech you give me leave to go
through Gloucestershire, and when you come to court,
stand my good lord in your good report.

PRINCE JOHN

Fare you well, Falstaff. I, in my condition,
Shall better speak of you than you deserve.

Exeunt all but Falstaff

FALSTAFF I would you had the wit; 'twere better than
your dukedom. Good faith, this same young sober-
blooded boy doth not love me, nor a man cannot make
him laugh – but that's no marvel, he drinks no wine.
There's never none of these demure boys come to any
90 proof, for thin drink doth so over-cool their blood, and
making many fish meals, that they fall into a kind of
male green-sickness; and then when they marry they
get wenches. They are generally fools and cowards –
which some of us should be too, but for inflammation.
A good sherris-sack hath a twofold operation in it. It
ascends me into the brain, dries me there all the foolish
and dull and crudy vapours which environ it, makes it
apprehensive, quick, forgetive, full of nimble, fiery, and
delectable shapes, which delivered o'er to the voice, the
100 tongue, which is the birth, becomes excellent wit. The
second property of your excellent sherris is the warming
of the blood, which before, cold and settled, left the
liver white and pale, which is the badge of pusillanimity
and cowardice; but the sherris warms it, and makes it
course from the inwards to the parts' extremes. It
illumineth the face, which, as a beacon, gives warning
to all the rest of this little kingdom, man, to arm; and
then the vital commoners, and inland petty spirits,
muster me all to their captain, the heart, who, great and
110 puffed up with this retinue, doth any deed of courage;

and this valour comes of sherris. So that skill in the
weapon is nothing without sack, for that sets it a-work,
and learning a mere hoard of gold kept by a devil, till
sack commences it and sets it in act and use. Hereof
comes it that Prince Harry is valiant; for the cold blood
he did naturally inherit of his father he hath like lean,
sterile, and bare land manured, husbanded, and tilled,
with excellent endeavour of drinking good and good
store of fertile sherris, that he is become very hot and
valiant. If I had a thousand sons, the first human   120
principle I would teach them should be to forswear
thin potations, and to addict themselves to sack.

    Enter Bardolph

How now, Bardolph?

BARDOLPH The army is discharged all and gone.

FALSTAFF Let them go. I'll through Gloucestershire, and
    there will I visit Master Robert Shallow, Esquire. I
    have him already tempering between my finger and my
    thumb, and shortly will I seal with him. Come away.

                                Exeunt

    Enter the King, carried in a chair, Warwick, Thomas   IV.4
    Duke of Clarence, Humphrey Duke of Gloucester,
    and attendant lords

KING HENRY IV

    Now, lords, if God doth give successful end
    To this debate that bleedeth at our doors,
    We will our youth lead on to higher fields,
    And draw no swords but what are sanctified.
    Our navy is addressed, our power collected,
    Our substitutes in absence well invested,
    And everything lies level to our wish;
    Only we want a little personal strength,

And pause us till these rebels now afoot
10   Come underneath the yoke of government.

WARWICK
Both which we doubt not but your majesty
Shall soon enjoy.

KING HENRY IV   Humphrey, my son of Gloucester,
Where is the Prince your brother?

GLOUCESTER
I think he's gone to hunt, my lord, at Windsor.

KING HENRY IV
And how accompanied?

GLOUCESTER   I do not know, my lord.

KING HENRY IV
Is not his brother Thomas of Clarence with him?

GLOUCESTER
No, my good lord, he is in presence here.

CLARENCE
What would my lord and father?

KING HENRY IV
Nothing but well to thee, Thomas of Clarence.
20   How chance thou art not with the Prince thy brother?
He loves thee, and thou dost neglect him, Thomas.
Thou hast a better place in his affection
Than all thy brothers; cherish it, my boy,
And noble offices thou mayst effect
Of mediation, after I am dead,
Between his greatness and thy other brethren.
Therefore omit him not; blunt not his love,
Nor lose the good advantage of his grace
By seeming cold, or careless of his will.
30   For he is gracious, if he be observed;
He hath a tear for pity, and a hand
Open as day for melting charity;
Yet notwithstanding, being incensed, he is flint,

As humorous as winter, and as sudden
As flaws congealèd in the spring of day.
His temper therefore must be well observed.
Chide him for faults, and do it reverently,
When you perceive his blood inclined to mirth;
But, being moody, give him time and scope,
Till that his passions, like a whale on ground,   40
Confound themselves with working. Learn this, Thomas,
And thou shalt prove a shelter to thy friends,
A hoop of gold to bind thy brothers in,
That the united vessel of their blood,
Mingled with venom of suggestion,
As force perforce the age will pour it in,
Shall never leak, though it do work as strong
As aconitum or rash gunpowder.

CLARENCE

I shall observe him with all care and love.

KING HENRY IV

Why art thou not at Windsor with him, Thomas?   50

CLARENCE

He is not there today; he dines in London.

KING HENRY IV

And how accompanied? Canst thou tell that?

CLARENCE

With Poins, and other his continual followers.

KING HENRY IV

Most subject is the fattest soil to weeds,
And he, the noble image of my youth,
Is overspread with them; therefore my grief
Stretches itself beyond the hour of death.
The blood weeps from my heart when I do shape
In forms imaginary th'unguided days
And rotten times that you shall look upon   60
When I am sleeping with my ancestors.

For when his headstrong riot hath no curb,
When rage and hot blood are his counsellors,
When means and lavish manners meet together,
O, with what wings shall his affections fly
Towards fronting peril and opposed decay!

WARWICK

My gracious lord, you look beyond him quite.
The Prince but studies his companions
Like a strange tongue, wherein, to gain the language
'Tis needful that the most immodest word
Be looked upon and learnt, which, once attained,
Your highness knows, comes to no further use
But to be known and hated. So, like gross terms,
The Prince will, in the perfectness of time,
Cast off his followers, and their memory
Shall as a pattern or a measure live
By which his grace must mete the lives of other,
Turning past evils to advantages.

KING HENRY IV

'Tis seldom when the bee doth leave her comb
In the dead carrion.

Enter Westmorland

                         Who's here? Westmorland?

WESTMORLAND

Health to my sovereign, and new happiness
Added to that that I am to deliver!
Prince John your son doth kiss your grace's hand.
Mowbray, the Bishop Scroop, Hastings, and all
Are brought to the correction of your law.
There is not now a rebel's sword unsheathed,
But Peace puts forth her olive everywhere.
The manner how this action hath been borne
Here at more leisure may your highness read,
With every course in his particular.

KING HENRY IV

 O Westmorland, thou art a summer bird,
 Which ever in the haunch of winter sings
 The lifting up of day.

  Enter Harcourt

      Look, here's more news.

HARCOURT

 From enemies heaven keep your majesty,
 And, when they stand against you, may they fall
 As those that I am come to tell you of!
 The Earl Northumberland and the Lord Bardolph,
 With a great power of English and of Scots,
 Are by the shrieve of Yorkshire overthrown.
 The manner and true order of the fight   100
 This packet, please it you, contains at large.

KING HENRY IV

 And wherefore should these good news make me sick?
 Will Fortune never come with both hands full,
 But wet her fair words still in foulest terms?
 She either gives a stomach and no food –
 Such are the poor, in health – or else a feast
 And takes away the stomach – such are the rich
 That have abundance and enjoy it not.
 I should rejoice now at this happy news,
 And now my sight fails, and my brain is giddy. 110
 O me! Come near me. Now I am much ill.

GLOUCESTER

 Comfort, your majesty!

CLARENCE   O my royal father!

WESTMORLAND

 My sovereign lord, cheer up yourself, look up.

WARWICK

 Be patient, Princes. You do know these fits
 Are with his highness very ordinary.

Stand from him, give him air; he'll straight be well.

CLARENCE
No, no, he cannot long hold out these pangs.
Th'incessant care and labour of his mind
Hath wrought the mure that should confine it in
120 So thin that life looks through and will break out.

GLOUCESTER
The people fear me, for they do observe
Unfathered heirs and loathly births of nature.
The seasons change their manners, as the year
Had found some months asleep and leaped them over

CLARENCE
The river hath thrice flowed, no ebb between,
And the old folk, time's doting chronicles,
Say it did so a little time before
That our great-grandsire, Edward, sicked and died.

WARWICK
Speak lower, Princes, for the King recovers.

GLOUCESTER
130 This apoplexy will certain be his end.

KING HENRY IV
I pray you take me up, and bear me hence
Into some other chamber. Softly, pray.

IV.5   *They take up the King and lay him on a bed*
Let there be no noise made, my gentle friends,
Unless some dull and favourable hand
Will whisper music to my weary spirit.

WARWICK
Call for the music in the other room.

KING HENRY IV
Set me the crown upon my pillow here.

CLARENCE

His eye is hollow, and he changes much.

WARWICK

Less noise, less noise!

Enter Prince Henry

PRINCE HENRY Who saw the Duke of Clarence?

CLARENCE I am here, brother, full of heaviness.

PRINCE HENRY How now, rain within doors, and none   10
abroad? How doth the King?

GLOUCESTER Exceeding ill.

PRINCE HENRY Heard he the good news yet? Tell it him.

GLOUCESTER

He altered much upon hearing it.

PRINCE HENRY If he be sick with joy, he'll recover
without physic.

WARWICK

Not so much noise, my lords. Sweet Prince, speak low;
The King your father is disposed to sleep.

CLARENCE

Let us withdraw into the other room.

WARWICK

Will't please your grace to go along with us?   20

PRINCE HENRY

No, I will sit and watch here by the King.

Exeunt all but Prince Henry

Why doth the crown lie there upon his pillow,
Being so troublesome a bedfellow?
O polished perturbation! Golden care!
That keepest the ports of slumber open wide
To many a watchful night! Sleep with it now!
Yet not so sound, and half so deeply sweet,
As he whose brow with homely biggen bound
Snores out the watch of night. O majesty!
When thou dost pinch thy bearer, thou dost sit   30

Like a rich armour worn in heat of day,
That scaldest with safety. By his gates of breath
There lies a downy feather which stirs not;
Did he suspire, that light and weightless down
Perforce must move. My gracious lord! My father!
This sleep is sound indeed; this is a sleep
That from this golden rigol hath divorced
So many English kings. Thy due from me
Is tears and heavy sorrows of the blood,
40   Which nature, love, and filial tenderness
Shall, O dear father, pay thee plenteously.
My due from thee is this imperial crown,
Which, as immediate from thy place and blood,
Derives itself to me.

    He puts the crown on his head

                   Lo where it sits,
Which God shall guard, and put the world's whole
     strength
Into one giant arm, it shall not force
This lineal honour from me. This from thee
Will I to mine leave, as 'tis left to me.   *Ex*

KING HENRY IV
Warwick! Gloucester! Clarence!

    Enter Warwick, Gloucester, Clarence, and attendant
    lords

CLARENCE
50   Doth the King call?

WARWICK   What would your majesty?

KING HENRY IV
Why did you leave me here alone, my lords?

CLARENCE
We left the Prince my brother here, my liege,
Who undertook to sit and watch by you.

KING HENRY IV The Prince of Wales? Where is he

Let me see him. He is not here.

WARWICK

This door is open; he is gone this way.

GLOUCESTER

He came not through the chamber where we stayed.

KING HENRY IV Where is the crown? Who took it from
my pillow?

WARWICK

When we withdrew, my liege, we left it here.   60

KING HENRY IV

The Prince hath ta'en it hence. Go, seek him out.
Is he so hasty that he doth suppose
My sleep my death?
Find him, my lord of Warwick; chide him hither.
                                        Exit Warwick
This part of his conjoins with my disease,
And helps to end me. See, sons, what things you are.
How quickly nature falls into revolt
When gold becomes her object!
For this the foolish over-careful fathers
Have broke their sleep with thoughts,   70
Their brains with care, their bones with industry;
For this they have engrossed and pillèd up
The cankered heaps of strange-achievèd gold;
For this they have been thoughtful to invest
Their sons with arts and martial exercises;
When, like the bee tolling from every flower,
Our thighs packed with wax, our mouths with honey,
We bring it to the hive; and like the bees
Are murdered for our pains. This bitter taste
Yields his engrossments to the ending father.   80
    Enter Warwick
Now where is he that will not stay so long
Till his friend sickness have determined me?

WARWICK
    My lord, I found the Prince in the next room,
    Washing with kindly tears his gentle cheeks,
    With such a deep demeanour in great sorrow,
    That tyranny, which never quaffed but blood,
    Would, by beholding him, have washed his knife
    With gentle eye-drops. He is coming hither.

KING HENRY IV
    But wherefore did he take away the crown?
      Enter Prince Henry

90   Lo where he comes. Come hither to me, Harry. –
    Depart the chamber, leave us here alone.
      Exeunt all except King Henry IV and Prince Henry

PRINCE HENRY
    I never thought to hear you speak again.

KING HENRY IV
    Thy wish was father, Harry, to that thought.
    I stay too long by thee, I weary thee.
    Dost thou so hunger for mine empty chair
    That thou wilt needs invest thee with my honours
    Before thy hour be ripe? O foolish youth!
    Thou seekest the greatness that will overwhelm thee.
    Stay but a little, for my cloud of dignity
100   Is held from falling with so weak a wind
    That it will quickly drop; my day is dim.
    Thou hast stolen that which after some few hours
    Were thine without offence, and at my death
    Thou hast sealed up my expectation.
    Thy life did manifest thou lovedst me not,
    And thou wilt have me die assured of it.
    Thou hidest a thousand daggers in thy thoughts,
    Which thou hast whetted on thy stony heart,
    To stab at half an hour of my life.
110   What, canst thou not forbear me half an hour?

Then get thee gone, and dig my grave thyself,
And bid the merry bells ring to thine ear
That thou art crownèd, not that I am dead.
Let all the tears that should bedew my hearse
Be drops of balm to sanctify thy head;
Only compound me with forgotten dust.
Give that which gave thee life unto the worms.
Pluck down my officers, break my decrees;
For now a time is come to mock at form —
Harry the Fifth is crowned! Up, vanity!   120
Down, royal state! All you sage counsellors, hence!
And to the English court assemble now,
From every region, apes of idleness!
Now, neighbour confines, purge you of your scum!
Have you a ruffian that will swear, drink, dance,
Revel the night, rob, murder, and commit
The oldest sins the newest kind of ways?
Be happy, he will trouble you no more.
England shall double gild his treble guilt;   130
England shall give him office, honour, might;
For the fifth Harry from curbed licence plucks
The muzzle of restraint, and the wild dog
Shall flesh his tooth on every innocent.
O my poor kingdom, sick with civil blows!
When that my care could not withhold thy riots,
What wilt thou do when riot is thy care?
O, thou wilt be a wilderness again,
Peopled with wolves, thy old inhabitants!

PRINCE HENRY (*kneels*)

O, pardon me, my liege! But for my tears,
The moist impediments unto my speech,   140
I had forestalled this dear and deep rebuke
Ere you with grief had spoke and I had heard
The course of it so far. There is your crown,

And He that wears the crown immortally
Long guard it yours! If I affect it more
Than as your honour and as your renown,
Let me no more from this obedience rise,
Which my most inward true and duteous spirit
Teacheth this prostrate and exterior bending.
150 God witness with me, when I here came in
And found no course of breath within your majesty,
How cold it struck my heart! If I do feign,
O, let me in my present wildness die,
And never live to show th'incredulous world
The noble change that I have purposèd!
Coming to look on you, thinking you dead,
And dead almost, my liege, to think you were,
I spake unto this crown as having sense,
And thus upbraided it: 'The care on thee depending
160 Hath fed upon the body of my father;
Therefore thou best of gold art worse than gold.
Other, less fine in carat, is more precious,
Preserving life in medicine potable;
But thou, most fine, most honoured, most renowned,
Hast eat thy bearer up.' Thus, my most royal liege,
Accusing it, I put it on my head,
To try with it, as with an enemy
That had before my face murdered my father,
The quarrel of a true inheritor.
170 But if it did infect my blood with joy
Or swell my thoughts to any strain of pride,
If any rebel or vain spirit of mine
Did with the least affection of a welcome
Give entertainment to the might of it,
Let God for ever keep it from my head,
And make me as the poorest vassal is
That doth with awe and terror kneel to it!

KING HENRY IV

    God put it in thy mind to take it hence,
    That thou mightst win the more thy father's love,
    Pleading so wisely in excuse of it!   180
    Come hither, Harry; sit thou by my bed,
    And hear, I think, the very latest counsel
    That ever I shall breathe. God knows, my son,
    By what by-paths and indirect crooked ways
    I met this crown, and I myself know well
    How troublesome it sat upon my head.
    To thee it shall descend with better quiet,
    Better opinion, better confirmation,
    For all the soil of the achievement goes
    With me into the earth. It seemed in me   190
    But as an honour snatched with boisterous hand,
    And I had many living to upbraid
    My gain of it by their assistances,
    Which daily grew to quarrel and to bloodshed,
    Wounding supposèd peace. All these bold fears
    Thou seest with peril I have answerèd,
    For all my reign hath been but as a scene
    Acting that argument. And now my death
    Changes the mood, for what in me was purchased
    Falls upon thee in a more fairer sort,   200
    So thou the garland wearest successively.
    Yet though thou standest more sure than I could do,
    Thou art not firm enough, since griefs are green;
    And all my friends, which thou must make thy friends,
    Have but their stings and teeth newly ta'en out,
    By whose fell working I was first advanced,
    And by whose power I well might lodge a fear
    To be again displaced; which to avoid,
    I cut them off, and had a purpose now
    To lead out many to the Holy Land,   210

Lest rest and lying still might make them look
Too near unto my state. Therefore, my Harry,
Be it thy course to busy giddy minds
With foreign quarrels, that action hence borne out
May waste the memory of the former days.
More would I, but my lungs are wasted so
That strength of speech is utterly denied me.
How I came by the crown, O God forgive,
And grant it may with thee in true peace live!

PRINCE HENRY

220   You won it, wore it, kept it, gave it me;
Then plain and right must my possession be,
Which I with more than with a common pain
'Gainst all the world will rightfully maintain.

Enter Prince John of Lancaster, Warwick, and
attendant lords

KING HENRY IV

Look, look, here comes my John of Lancaster.

PRINCE JOHN

Health, peace, and happiness to my royal father!

KING HENRY IV

Thou bringest me happiness and peace, son John,
But health, alack, with youthful wings is flown
From this bare withered trunk. Upon thy sight
My worldly business makes a period.

230   Where is my lord of Warwick?

PRINCE HENRY   My lord of Warwick!

KING HENRY IV

Doth any name particular belong
Unto the lodging where I first did swoon?

WARWICK

'Tis called Jerusalem, my noble lord.

KING HENRY IV

Laud be to God! Even there my life must end.

It hath been prophesied to me, many years,
I should not die but in Jerusalem,
Which vainly I supposed the Holy Land.
But bear me to that chamber; there I'll lie;
In that Jerusalem shall Harry die.   *Exeunt*

*

Enter Shallow, Falstaff, Bardolph, and the Page   **V.I**

SHALLOW By cock and pie, sir; you shall not away to-
    night. What, Davy, I say!

FALSTAFF You must excuse me, Master Robert Shallow.

SHALLOW I will not excuse you; you shall not be excused;
    excuses shall not be admitted; there is no excuse shall
    serve; you shall not be excused. Why, Davy!

    Enter Davy

DAVY Here, sir.

SHALLOW Davy, Davy, Davy, Davy! Let me see, Davy;
    let me see, Davy; let me see – yea, marry, William cook,
    bid him come hither. Sir John, you shall not be excused. 10

DAVY Marry, sir, thus: those precepts cannot be served;
    and again, sir – shall we sow the hade land with wheat?

SHALLOW With red wheat, Davy. But for William cook
    – are there no young pigeons?

DAVY Yes, sir. Here is now the smith's note for shoeing
    and plough-irons.

SHALLOW Let it be cast and paid. Sir John, you shall not
    be excused.

DAVY Now, sir, a new link to the bucket must needs be
    had. And, sir, do you mean to stop any of William's   20
    wages, about the sack he lost at Hinckley fair?

SHALLOW 'A shall answer it. Some pigeons, Davy, a
    couple of short-legged hens, a joint of mutton, and any

pretty little tiny kickshaws, tell William cook.

DAVY Doth the man of war stay all night, sir?

SHALLOW Yea, Davy. I will use him well; a friend
i'th'court is better than a penny in purse. Use his men
well, Davy, for they are arrant knaves, and will backbite.

DAVY No worse than they are backbitten, sir, for they have
marvellous foul linen.

SHALLOW Well conceited, Davy – about thy business,
Davy.

DAVY I beseech you, sir, to countenance William Visor of
Woncot against Clement Perkes o'th'Hill.

SHALLOW There is many complaints, Davy, against that
Visor; that Visor is an arrant knave, on my knowledge.

DAVY I grant your worship that he is a knave, sir; but yet
God forbid, sir, but a knave should have some countenance at his friend's request. An honest man, sir, is able
to speak for himself, when a knave is not. I have served
your worship truly, sir, this eight years, and if I cannot
once or twice in a quarter bear out a knave against an
honest man, I have little credit with your worship. The
knave is mine honest friend, sir; therefore, I beseech
you, let him be countenanced.

SHALLOW Go to; I say he shall have no wrong. Look
about, Davy.

Exit Davy

Where are you, Sir John? Come, come, come, off with
your boots. Give me your hand, Master Bardolph.

BARDOLPH I am glad to see your worship.

SHALLOW I thank thee with all my heart, kind Master
Bardolph; (*to the Page*) and welcome, my tall fellow.
Come, Sir John.

FALSTAFF I'll follow you, good Master Robert Shallow.

Exit Shallow

Bardolph, look to our horses.

Exeunt Bardolph and Page

If I were sawed into quantities, I should make four
dozen of such bearded hermits' staves as Master Shallow. It is a wonderful thing to see the semblable
coherence of his men's spirits and his. They, by
observing him, do bear themselves like foolish justices;   60
he, by conversing with them, is turned into a justice-like
servingman. Their spirits are so married in conjunction,
with the participation of society, that they flock together
in consent, like so many wild geese. If I had a suit to
Master Shallow, I would humour his men with the
imputation of being near their master; if to his men, I
would curry with Master Shallow that no man could
better command his servants. It is certain that either
wise bearing or ignorant carriage is caught, as men take
diseases, one of another; therefore let men take heed   70
of their company. I will devise matter enough out of
this Shallow to keep Prince Harry in continual laughter
the wearing out of six fashions, which is four terms, or
two actions, and 'a shall laugh without intervallums. O,
it is much that a lie with a slight oath, and a jest with a
sad brow, will do with a fellow that never had the ache
in his shoulders! O, you shall see him laugh till his face
be like a wet cloak ill laid up!

SHALLOW (*within*) Sir John!

FALSTAFF I come, Master Shallow, I come, Master   80
  Shallow.   *Exit*

Enter Warwick and the Lord Chief Justice   **V.2**

WARWICK
  How now, my Lord Chief Justice, whither away?
LORD CHIEF JUSTICE
  How doth the King?

WARWICK

  Exceeding well; his cares are now all ended.

LORD CHIEF JUSTICE

  I hope, not dead.

WARWICK   He's walked the way of nature,

  And to our purposes he lives no more.

LORD CHIEF JUSTICE

  I would his majesty had called me with him.

  The service that I truly did his life

  Hath left me open to all injuries.

WARWICK

  Indeed I think the young King loves you not.

LORD CHIEF JUSTICE

10 I know he doth not, and do arm myself

  To welcome the condition of the time,

  Which cannot look more hideously upon me

  Than I have drawn it in my fantasy.

    Enter Prince John of Lancaster, Clarence,

    Gloucester, and attendant lords

WARWICK

  Here come the heavy issue of dead Harry.

  O that the living Harry had the temper

  Of he, the worst of these three gentlemen!

  How many nobles then should hold their places

  That must strike sail to spirits of vile sort!

LORD CHIEF JUSTICE

  O God, I fear all will be overturned.

PRINCE JOHN

20 Good morrow, cousin Warwick, good morrow.

GLOUCESTER *and* CLARENCE

  Good morrow, cousin.

PRINCE JOHN

  We meet like men that had forgot to speak.

WARWICK

We do remember, but our argument
Is all too heavy to admit much talk.

PRINCE JOHN

Well, peace be with him that hath made us heavy.

LORD CHIEF JUSTICE

Peace be with us, lest we be heavier.

GLOUCESTER

O, good my lord, you have lost a friend indeed,
And I dare swear you borrow not that face
Of seeming sorrow – it is sure your own.

PRINCE JOHN

Though no man be assured what grace to find,   30
You stand in coldest expectation.
I am the sorrier; would 'twere otherwise.

CLARENCE

Well, you must now speak Sir John Falstaff fair,
Which swims against your stream of quality.

LORD CHIEF JUSTICE

Sweet Princes, what I did I did in honour,
Led by th'impartial conduct of my soul.
And never shall you see that I will beg
A raggèd and forestalled remission.
If truth and upright innocency fail me,
I'll to the King my master that is dead,   40
And tell him who hath sent me after him.

WARWICK

Here comes the Prince.

Enter King Henry V, attended by Blunt and others

LORD CHIEF JUSTICE

Good morrow, and God save your majesty!

KING HENRY V

This new and gorgeous garment, majesty,
Sits not so easy on me as you think.

Brothers, you mix your sadness with some fear.
This is the English, not the Turkish court;
Not Amurath an Amurath succeeds,
But Harry Harry. Yet be sad, good brothers,
50 For, by my faith, it very well becomes you.
Sorrow so royally in you appears
That I will deeply put the fashion on
And wear it in my heart. Why then, be sad;
But entertain no more of it, good brothers,
Than a joint burden laid upon us all.
For me, by heaven, I bid you be assured,
I'll be your father and your brother too.
Let me but bear your love, I'll bear your cares.
Yet weep that Harry's dead, and so will I;
60 But Harry lives, that shall convert those tears
By number into hours of happiness.

PRINCES
We hope no otherwise from your majesty.

KING HENRY V
You all look strangely on me – and (*to Lord Chief Justice*)
    you most;
You are, I think, assured I love you not.

LORD CHIEF JUSTICE
I am assured, if I be measured rightly,
Your majesty hath no just cause to hate me.

KING HENRY V
No?
How might a prince of my great hopes forget
So great indignities you laid upon me?
70 What! Rate, rebuke, and roughly send to prison
Th'immediate heir of England? Was this easy?
May this be washed in Lethe and forgotten?

LORD CHIEF JUSTICE
I then did use the person of your father;

The image of his power lay then in me
And in th'administration of his law.
Whiles I was busy for the commonwealth,
Your highness pleasèd to forget my place,
The majesty and power of law and justice,
The image of the King whom I presented,
And struck me in my very seat of judgement;   80
Whereon, as an offender to your father,
I gave bold way to my authority
And did commit you. If the deed were ill,
Be you contented, wearing now the garland,
To have a son set your decrees at naught?
To pluck down justice from your awful bench?
To trip the course of law, and blunt the sword
That guards the peace and safety of your person?
Nay, more, to spurn at your most royal image,
And mock your workings in a second body?   90
Question your royal thoughts, make the case yours;
Be now the father and propose a son,
Hear your own dignity so much profaned,
See your most dreadful laws so loosely slighted,
Behold yourself so by a son disdained;
And then imagine me taking your part,
And in your power soft silencing your son.
After this cold considerance sentence me,
And, as you are a king, speak in your state
What I have done that misbecame my place,   100
My person, or my liege's sovereignty.

KING HENRY V

You are right justice, and you weigh this well.
Therefore still bear the balance and the sword,
And I do wish your honours may increase
Till you do live to see a son of mine
Offend you and obey you, as I did.

So shall I live to speak my father's words:
'Happy am I, that have a man so bold
That dares do justice on my proper son;
And not less happy, having such a son
That would deliver up his greatness so
Into the hands of justice.' You did commit me –
For which I do commit into your hand
Th'unstained sword that you have used to bear,
With this remembrance: that you use the same
With the like bold, just, and impartial spirit
As you have done 'gainst me. There is my hand.
You shall be as a father to my youth;
My voice shall sound as you do prompt mine ear,
And I will stoop and humble my intents
To your well-practised wise directions.
And, Princes all, believe me, I beseech you,
My father is gone wild into his grave,
For in his tomb lie my affections;
And with his spirits sadly I survive
To mock the expectation of the world,
To frustrate prophecies, and to raze out
Rotten opinion, who hath writ me down
After my seeming. The tide of blood in me
Hath proudly flowed in vanity till now.
Now doth it turn, and ebb back to the sea,
Where it shall mingle with the state of floods,
And flow henceforth in formal majesty.
Now call we our high court of parliament,
And let us choose such limbs of noble counsel
That the great body of our state may go
In equal rank with the best-governed nation;
That war, or peace, or both at once, may be
As things acquainted and familiar to us;
In which you, father, shall have foremost hand.

Our coronation done, we will accite,
As I before remembered, all our state.
And, God consigning to my good intents,
No prince nor peer shall have just cause to say,
God shorten Harry's happy life one day!   *Exeunt*

Enter Falstaff, Shallow, Silence, Davy, Bardolph,   V.3
and the Page

SHALLOW Nay, you shall see my orchard, where, in an
arbour, we will eat a last year's pippin of mine own
graffing, with a dish of caraways, and so forth – come,
cousin Silence – and then to bed.

FALSTAFF 'Fore God, you have here a goodly dwelling,
and a rich.

SHALLOW Barren, barren, barren; beggars all, beggars
all, Sir John – marry, good air. Spread, Davy, spread,
Davy, well said, Davy.

FALSTAFF This Davy serves you for good uses – he is   10
your servingman and your husband.

SHALLOW A good varlet, a good varlet, a very good
varlet, Sir John – by the mass, I have drunk too much
sack at supper – a good varlet. Now sit down, now sit
down – come, cousin.

SILENCE Ah, sirrah! quoth 'a, we shall
(*sings*) Do nothing but eat, and make good cheer,
         And praise God for the merry year,
         When flesh is cheap and females dear,
         And lusty lads roam here and there,   20
            So merrily,
         And ever among so merrily.

FALSTAFF There's a merry heart, good Master Silence!
I'll give you a health for that anon.

SHALLOW Give Master Bardolph some wine, Davy.

DAVY Sweet sir, sit – I'll be with you anon. Most sweet
   sir, sit; master page, good master page, sit. Proface!
   What you want in meat, we'll have in drink; but you
   must bear; the heart's all.   *Exit*

30 SHALLOW Be merry, Master Bardolph; and, my little
   soldier there, be merry.

SILENCE (*sings*)
      Be merry, be merry, my wife has all,
      For women are shrews, both short and tall.
      'Tis merry in hall, when beards wags all,
      And welcome merry Shrovetide! Be merry, be merry.

FALSTAFF I did not think Master Silence had been a man
   of this mettle.

SILENCE Who, I? I have been merry twice and once ere
   now.

      Enter Davy

40 DAVY (*to Bardolph*) There's a dish of leather-coats for
   you.

SHALLOW Davy!

DAVY Your worship? I'll be with you straight. (*To Bardolph*) A cup of wine, sir?

SILENCE (*sings*)
         A cup of wine that's brisk and fine,
         And drink unto thee, leman mine,
         And a merry heart lives long-a.

FALSTAFF Well said, Master Silence.

SILENCE An we shall be merry, now comes in the sweet
50 o'th'night.

FALSTAFF Health and long life to you, Master Silence.

SILENCE (*sings*)
         Fill the cup, and let it come,
         I'll pledge you a mile to th'bottom.

SHALLOW Honest Bardolph, welcome! If thou wantest
   anything and wilt not call, beshrew thy heart. (*To the*

Page) Welcome, my little tiny thief, and welcome indeed, too! I'll drink to Master Bardolph, and to all the cabileros about London.

DAVY I hope to see London once ere I die.

BARDOLPH An I might see you there, Davy –   60

SHALLOW By the mass, you'll crack a quart together – ha! will you not, Master Bardolph?

BARDOLPH Yea, sir, in a pottle-pot.

SHALLOW By God's liggens, I thank thee. The knave will stick by thee, I can assure thee that; 'a will not out, 'a; 'tis true bred!

BARDOLPH And I'll stick by him, sir.

SHALLOW Why, there spoke a king. Lack nothing! Be merry!

One knocks at door

Look who's at door there, ho! Who knocks?   70

Exit Davy

FALSTAFF (*to Silence, seeing him drink*) Why, now you have done me right.

SILENCE (*sings*)

          Do me right,
          And dub me knight:
          Samingo.

Is't not so?

FALSTAFF 'Tis so.

SILENCE Is't so? Why then, say an old man can do somewhat.

Enter Davy

DAVY An't please your worship, there's one Pistol come   80
from the court with news.

FALSTAFF From the court? Let him come in.

Enter Pistol

How now, Pistol?

PISTOL Sir John, God save you!

FALSTAFF What wind blew you hither, Pistol?

PISTOL Not the ill wind which blows no man to good
Sweet knight, thou art now one of the greatest men i
this realm.

SILENCE By'r lady, I think 'a be, but goodman Puff o
90   Barson.

PISTOL

Puff?

Puff i'thy teeth, most recreant coward base!

Sir John, I am thy Pistol and thy friend,

And helter-skelter have I rode to thee,

And tidings do I bring, and lucky joys,

And golden times, and happy news of price.

FALSTAFF I pray thee now, deliver them like a man o
this world.

PISTOL

A foutre for the world and worldlings base!

100   I speak of Africa and golden joys.

FALSTAFF

O base Assyrian knight, what is thy news?

Let King Cophetua know the truth thereof.

SILENCE (sings)

And Robin Hood, Scarlet, and John.

PISTOL

Shall dunghill curs confront the Helicons?

And shall good news be baffled?

Then, Pistol, lay thy head in Furies' lap.

SHALLOW Honest gentleman, I know not your breeding

PISTOL Why then, lament therefor.

SHALLOW Give me pardon, sir. If, sir, you come wit
110   news from the court, I take it there's but two ways
either to utter them or conceal them. I am, sir, unde
the King, in some authority.

PISTOL

    Under which king, Besonian? Speak, or die.

SHALLOW

    Under King Harry.

PISTOL   Harry the Fourth, or Fifth?

SHALLOW

    Harry the Fourth.

PISTOL   A foutre for thine office!

    Sir John, thy tender lambkin now is King;

    Harry the Fifth's the man. I speak the truth –

    When Pistol lies, do this, and fig me, like

    The bragging Spaniard.

FALSTAFF   What, is the old King dead?

PISTOL

    As nail in door! The things I speak are just.   120

FALSTAFF Away, Bardolph, saddle my horse! Master
    Robert Shallow, choose what office thou wilt in the land,
    'tis thine. Pistol, I will double-charge thee with dignities.

BARDOLPH O joyful day! I would not take a knighthood
    for my fortune.

PISTOL What, I do bring good news?

FALSTAFF Carry Master Silence to bed. Master Shallow,
    my lord Shallow – be what thou wilt – I am fortune's
    steward! Get on thy boots; we'll ride all night. O sweet
    Pistol! Away, Bardolph!   *Exit Bardolph* 130
    Come, Pistol, utter more to me, and withal devise
    something to do thyself good. Boot, boot, Master
    Shallow! I know the young King is sick for me. Let us
    take any man's horses – the laws of England are at my
    commandment. Blessed are they that have been my
    friends, and woe to my Lord Chief Justice!

PISTOL

    Let vultures vile seize on his lungs also!

'Where is the life that late I led?' say they;
Why, here it is. Welcome these pleasant days! *Exeunt*

V.4   *Enter Beadles dragging in Hostess Quickly and Doll*
       Tearsheet

HOSTESS No, thou arrant knave! I would to God that I
   might die, that I might have thee hanged. Thou hast
   drawn my shoulder out of joint.

FIRST BEADLE The constables have delivered her over
   to me, and she shall have whipping-cheer, I warrant
   her; there hath been a man or two killed about her.

DOLL Nut-hook, nut-hook, you lie! Come on, I'll tell
   thee what, thou damned tripe-visaged rascal, an the
   child I go with do miscarry, thou wert better thou hadst
10   struck thy mother, thou paper-faced villain.

HOSTESS O the Lord, that Sir John were come! I would
   make this a bloody day to somebody. But I pray God
   the fruit of her womb miscarry!

FIRST BEADLE If it do, you shall have a dozen of cushions
   again – you have but eleven now. Come, I charge you
   both, go with me, for the man is dead that you and
   Pistol beat amongst you.

DOLL I'll tell you what, you thin man in a censer, I will
   have you as soundly swinged for this – you bluebottle
20   rogue, you filthy famished correctioner, if you be not
   swinged I'll forswear half-kirtles.

FIRST BEADLE Come, come, you she knight-errant,
   come!

HOSTESS O God, that right should thus overcome might!
   Well, of sufferance comes ease.

DOLL Come, you rogue, come, bring me to a justice.

HOSTESS Ay, come, you starved bloodhound.

DOLL Goodman death, goodman bones!

HOSTESS Thou atomy, thou!

DOLL Come, you thin thing, come, you rascal!   30

FIRST BEADLE Very well.   *Exeunt*

Enter three Grooms, strewers of rushes   V.5

FIRST GROOM More rushes, more rushes!

SECOND GROOM The trumpets have sounded twice.

THIRD GROOM 'Twill be two o'clock ere they come from
   the coronation. Dispatch, dispatch!

                                        Exeunt
   *Trumpets sound, and the King and his train pass over
   the stage. After them enter Falstaff, Shallow, Pistol,
   Bardolph, and the Page*

FALSTAFF Stand here by me, Master Shallow; I will
   make the King do you grace. I will leer upon him as 'a
   comes by, and do but mark the countenance that he
   will give me.

PISTOL God bless thy lungs, good knight!

FALSTAFF Come here, Pistol, stand behind me. (*To*   10
   Shallow) O, if I had had time to have made new
   liveries, I would have bestowed the thousand pound I
   borrowed of you. But 'tis no matter; this poor show doth
   better; this doth infer the zeal I had to see him.

SHALLOW It doth so.

FALSTAFF It shows my earnestness of affection –

PISTOL It doth so.

FALSTAFF My devotion –

PISTOL It doth, it doth, it doth!

FALSTAFF As it were, to ride day and night, and not to   20
   deliberate, not to remember, not to have patience to
   shift me –

SHALLOW It is best, certain.

FALSTAFF But to stand stained with travel, and sweating

with desire to see him, thinking of nothing else, putting
all affairs else in oblivion, as if there were nothing else
to be done but to see him.

PISTOL 'Tis *semper idem*, for *obsque hoc nihil est*; 'tis all in
every part.

30 SHALLOW 'Tis so, indeed.

PISTOL

My knight, I will inflame thy noble liver,
And make thee rage.
Thy Doll, and Helen of thy noble thoughts,
Is in base durance and contagious prison,
Haled thither
By most mechanical and dirty hand.
Rouse up Revenge from ebon den with fell Alecto's
snake,
For Doll is in. Pistol speaks naught but truth.

FALSTAFF I will deliver her.

The trumpets sound

PISTOL

40 There roared the sea, and trumpet-clangour sounds.

Enter the King and his train, the Lord Chief Justice
among them

FALSTAFF God save thy grace, King Hal, my royal Hal!

PISTOL The heavens thee guard and keep, most royal
imp of fame!

FALSTAFF God save thee, my sweet boy!

KING HENRY V My Lord Chief Justice, speak to that
vain man.

LORD CHIEF JUSTICE Have you your wits? Know you
what 'tis you speak?

FALSTAFF

My King! My Jove! I speak to thee, my heart!

KING HENRY V

50 I know thee not, old man. Fall to thy prayers.

How ill white hairs becomes a fool and jester.
I have long dreamt of such a kind of man,
So surfeit-swelled, so old, and so profane,
But being awaked I do despise my dream.
Make less thy body hence, and more thy grace;
Leave gormandizing; know the grave doth gape
For thee thrice wider than for other men.
Reply not to me with a fool-born jest.
Presume not that I am the thing I was,
For God doth know, so shall the world perceive,   60
That I have turned away my former self;
So will I those that kept me company.
When thou dost hear I am as I have been,
Approach me, and thou shalt be as thou wast,
The tutor and the feeder of my riots;
Till then I banish thee, on pain of death,
As I have done the rest of my misleaders,
Not to come near our person by ten mile.
For competence of life I will allow you,
That lack of means enforce you not to evils;   70
And as we hear you do reform yourselves,
We will, according to your strengths and qualities,
Give you advancement. (*To the Lord Chief Justice*) Be
    it your charge, my lord,
To see performed the tenor of my word.
Set on.   *Exeunt King and his train*
FALSTAFF Master Shallow, I owe you a thousand pound.
SHALLOW Yea, marry, Sir John, which I beseech you to
    let me have home with me.
FALSTAFF That can hardly be, Master Shallow. Do not
    you grieve at this. I shall be sent for in private to him. 80
    Look you, he must seem thus to the world. Fear not
    your advancements; I will be the man yet that shall
    make you great.

SHALLOW I cannot perceive how, unless you give me
  your doublet, and stuff me out with straw. I beseech
  you, good Sir John, let me have five hundred of my
  thousand.

FALSTAFF Sir, I will be as good as my word. This that
  you heard was but a colour.

90 SHALLOW A colour that I fear you will die in, Sir John.

FALSTAFF Fear no colours. Go with me to dinner. Come,
  Lieutenant Pistol; come, Bardolph. I shall be sent for
  soon at night.

  *Enter the Lord Chief Justice and Prince John, with
  officers*

LORD CHIEF JUSTICE
  Go, carry Sir John Falstaff to the Fleet.
  Take all his company along with him.

FALSTAFF
  My lord, my lord –

LORD CHIEF JUSTICE
  I cannot now speak; I will hear you soon.
  Take them away.

PISTOL
  Si fortuna me tormenta, spero me contenta.
                          *Exeunt all but Prince John and
                             the Lord Chief Justice*

PRINCE JOHN
100 I like this fair proceeding of the King's.
  He hath intent his wonted followers
  Shall all be very well provided for,
  But all are banished till their conversations
  Appear more wise and modest to the world.

LORD CHIEF JUSTICE
  And so they are.

PRINCE JOHN
  The King hath called his parliament, my lord.

LORD CHIEF JUSTICE
    He hath.
PRINCE JOHN
    I will lay odds that, ere this year expire,
    We bear our civil swords and native fire
    As far as France. I heard a bird so sing,   110
    Whose music, to my thinking, pleased the King.
    Come, will you hence?   *Exeunt*

Epilogue

First, my fear; then, my curtsy; last, my speech.

My fear is your displeasure; my curtsy, my duty; and my speech, to beg your pardons. If you look for a good speech now, you undo me, for what I have to say is of mine own making; and what indeed I should say will, I doubt, prove mine own marring. But to the purpose, and so to the venture. Be it known to you, as it is very well, I was lately here in the end of a displeasing play, to pray your patience for it, and to promise you a better. I meant indeed to pay you with this, which, if like an ill venture it come unluckily home, I break, and you, my gentle creditors, lose. Here I promised you I would be, and here I commit my body to your mercies. Bate me some, and I will pay you some, and, as most debtors do, promise you infinitely. And so I kneel down before you – but, indeed, to pray for the Queen.

If my tongue cannot entreat you to acquit me, will you command me to use my legs? And yet that were but light payment, to dance out of your debt. But a good conscience will make any possible satisfaction, and so would I. All the gentlewomen here have forgiven me. If the gentlemen will not, then the gentlemen do not agree with the gentlewomen, which was never seen in such an assembly.

One word more, I beseech you. If you be not too much cloyed with fat meat, our humble author will continue the story, with Sir John in it, and make you merry with fair Katherine of France – where, for anything I know, Falstaff shall die of a sweat, unless already 'a be killed with your hard opinions; for Oldcastle died 30 martyr, and this is not the man. My tongue is weary; when my legs are too, I will bid you good night.

An Account of the Text

Henry IV, Part II presents an editor with difficult textual problems, and it would be foolish to pretend that they can be answered with certainty. One might well remember the words of Sir Francis Bacon in *The Advancement of Learning* (1605): 'If a man will begin with certainties, he shall end in doubts; but if he will be content to begin with doubts, he shall end in certainties.' Alas, the problems posed by *Henry IV, Part II* are such that, though an editor must begin with many doubts, he will feel fortunate if he ends by resolving any of them.

Modern editors of Elizabethan plays try to get as near as they can to what the author would have authorized as the fair copy of the finished work. This presents a number of difficulties. Authorial fair copies are few and far between (and there are none in Shakespeare's hand), so there is little to guide us in deciding what one of Shakespeare's 'authorized fair copies' looked like. Often we cannot be sure what kind of manuscript the printer used when setting an edition in type – it could vary from an unrevised rough draft to a presentation scribal copy of a manuscript modified from the stage version used in the author's lifetime – and we may doubt the accuracy with which the compositor set his manuscript in type.

For *Henry IV, Part II* we have two printed editions, the Quarto (Q) printed by Valentine Simmes in 1600 ('quarto' describes a book where the sheets of paper are each printed on both sides and folded twice to produce eight pages per 'gathering' or quire) and the text published in 1623 in the first Folio (in a folio text the sheet of paper is folded only once). The Folio (F) contains thirty-six of Shakespeare's plays and seems to have been a project initiated by John Heminges and Henry Condell, two members of Shakespeare's company.

An editor must ask three questions of these two texts. What was the copy from which they were set? What is their relationship one to the other? And to what extent do they represent Shakespeare's intentions? In trying to answer these questions we must try to find out all we can of what happened in the printing-houses where the Quarto and Folio versions were set.

The Quarto seems to be derived from what editors call 'foul papers', a term used in Shakespeare's day by the dramatist Daborne to describe the rough draft or drafts which preceded the fair copy. The Q text, though almost complete, lacks eight passages (see the first list of collations below); some of these are inessential, but some make the action clear. It has been suggested that four of these passages may have been excised from Q because they included references to the deposition of Richard II, a dangerous subject in the last years of the sixteenth century. The stage directions of Q are often vague and frequently inadequate for performance, some of the characters are not consistently designated, and at one point (V.4.0) an actor, John Sincklo, is referred to by his own name instead of that of his role. There are also references to several mutes (characters who have nothing to say and no clear part in the play): Sir John Umfrevile (see note to I.1.161), Fauconbridge (see headnote to I.3), Sir John Russell (see headnote to II.2), and Kent (see headnote to IV.4). Presumably during the course of revision these names were dropped, for they do not appear in F. Two characters, Sir John Blunt and the Earl of Surrey, also have no lines to speak; F retains them where they are called for (Surrey's entry at III.1.31 and Blunt's escorting of Sir John Colevile at IV.3.74) but omits the other entries for Blunt given in Q (III.1.31 and V.2.42), presumably because no action is demanded of him and he is not addressed by name in those scenes. Even Falstaff's original name, Oldcastle, makes a fleeting appearance in Q as a speech-prefix at I.2.121 (and see note to Epilogue 30). There is little doubt that what the compositor had before him in 1600 was a version of the play written before a fair copy had been produced.

The Quarto is unusual in that it exists in two versions. One gathering, E, has four leaves in some copies and six in others. It seems that, when the play was being set into type, III.1 was missed out, probably by mistake, and some copies of the play were made up and distributed before the omission was made good. In adding the scene to the remaining copies the printer had to reset parts of II.4 and III.2, and, although the same man seems to have done the work, he did not follow exactly what he had set the first time. There are differences of spelling and occasionally of words: for example, he omitted *good* in III.2.58, but added it at 73. From this and other evidence of this man's work (he is identified as Simmes's Compositor 'A') it is possible to list the kind of changes and mistakes he makes – and they are many and varied

Henry IV, Part II, unlike *Part I*, was not reprinted until it appeared in the Folio in 1623. The publication of F was a highly speculative venture (this was only the second time that an English dramatist's plays had been collected together: Jonson's *Works* had appeared in 1616, the year Shakespeare died), and it presented the printer with many problems. The printing of the Histories section clearly ran into all sorts of difficulties. By identifying the appearance and reappearance of individual pieces of type, it has been shown that the histories were not printed in the order in which they appear in F. Thus *Henry IV, Parts I* and *II* were printed later than *Henry V, Henry VI, Parts I* and *II* and part of *Part III*. The printing of *Henry IV, Part II* may have been delayed because of difficulties in obtaining permission to print *Henry IV, Part I*, the publisher not wanting to print *Part II* if *Part I* was to be refused him by the owners of its copyright. The delay could also have been caused because the copy for *Part II* was not ready. Meanwhile space had to be left for both parts of *Henry IV*, and it was miscalculated. In *Part II* there is also a curious error in the page numbering, and, quite exceptionally in the printing of F (which is based on six-leaf quires – three sheets being folded together once to produce twelve pages), an eight-leaf quire had to be used. Furthermore the type for this quire was set in a strange order not found elsewhere in F. The play is one of only seven in the Folio to be provided with a list of 'The

Actors Names' (see p.130); and the Epilogue is given a page
to itself and printed in a larger type than usual. In a short
account of the text it is not possible to go into every possibility that might explain these circumstances; what follows is
a description of the basis on which this edition has been
prepared. It must be stressed that it can only be conjectural
– informed guesswork.

The texts of the Quarto and the Folio differ considerably.
Although Q omits eight passages, it contains many lines
and part-lines that do not appear in F. F drops the names
of characters in Q who are not required by the action; and
a few speeches are reallocated. F has some additional stage
directions but omits many that are given in Q, and even when
all the stage directions of Q and F are assembled they are
still short of what is needed to make the play actable. F offers
a much more literary text, removing colloquialisms, rusticisms,
archaisms and profanities (though occasionally a colloquialism
is added).

Many editors have argued that F shows some signs of stage
practice – for example, the reallocation of speeches at the
beginning of II.2 and possibly at III.2.54, and the entry of
the prospective recruits at the beginning of III.2 (see note at
each point, especially headnote to III.2) – and that it must
therefore be based either on a copy of Q annotated by reference to a manuscript which had been used in the theatre, or
on a new transcript of the prompt book itself. Both theories
have provoked much dispute and neither seems to me tenable.
The crux of the problem is the excision, wholly or in part,
of some twenty-five Q stage directions that are superior to
those remaining in F. Annotation of Q would not necessarily
have caused these to be obscured (to check that possibility I,
like some other editors, have marked a photocopy of Q to
bring it into line with the F text); and a transcript based on
the prompt book, far from losing so many essential stage
directions, would be expected to supplement them with others
necessary for a production. The absence of so many essential
entries and exits and of several of Q's directions for sound
effects does anything but suggest that F was based on a manuscript that had been prepared for use in the theatre. Furthermore,

all the directions added in F are ones that a reasonably intel-
ligent scribe could have supplied (many are final exeunts).
F also omits the first coronation procession (see headnote to
V.5) and three inessential but telling phrases: in Q Rumour is
described as *painted full of tongues*, the Page is said to bear
Falstaff's sword and buckler at the beginning of I.2, and
Henry IV to enter in his nightgown in III.1. Were there no
Q, editors could be excused for imagining that F was based
on a transcript of the author's foul papers, styled in a literary
manner by a pedantic but rather careless scribe.

How can one explain the absence from F of stage directions
available in Q, the tidying up of Q's text (for example, the
omission of mutes), the inclusion of eight passages not in
Q but the absence of many short passages, the literary style
and omission of profanities, and the divergences of action and
dialogue that might reflect stage practice? (There are other
problems, particularly associated with the printing of F, the
use of capitals, the miscalculation of space for *Henry IV, Part
II*, and the need for an eight-leaf gathering; these are more
readily explicable, but as they are specialized and have little
bearing on the edition printed here, they will not be discussed.)

Recently it has been suggested that some F texts were based
on fair copies which scribes made from Shakespeare's foul
papers before the production of a prompt book. This seems
to me unlikely in this case. The absence of important stage
directions which appear in the text being copied is at least as
odd in a fair copy as it is in a prompt book, though oddness
is not the same as impossibility, of course. It would not be
beyond a scribe making a fair copy, especially if he were experienced (as some scribes were) in copying play documents, to
provide exeunts that had been missed from what he was copying,
to remove mutes, and simultaneously to omit one or two lines
or phrases in error. He might also rearrange some prose as
verse and some verse as prose. But the F text of *Henry IV,
Part II* does not give the impression that it is based on a fair
copy. There are changes which seem to be outside the juris-
diction of a scribe: for instance, the reduction in the numbers
of Grooms (see note to V.5.3–4) and of Drawers, with a
reallocation of the Drawers' speeches that is no improvement

on Q (see note to II.4.1–21), and the omission of the first coronation procession. Of course, the scribe might have been instructed to make such changes, but if fair copy *is* involved, then these changes cannot be among those which, as some scholars have thought, reflect stage practice. Indications of stage practice would be expected to originate from the prompt book, as originally prepared or as amended. We know of fair copies that became prompt books, but that cannot have happened in this case because the basic stage directions are so inadequate. It is hardly possible that the same manuscript could simultaneously be a fair copy inadequate for performance and a manuscript reflecting stage practice.

A scribal fair copy of *Henry IV, Part II* made before its first performance would be very unlikely to reveal censorship of the profanities found in Q, since this practice was not legally required until 1606. Nor would one expect a fair copy to be so literary and so to reduce the colloquialisms which are a feature of the play. Again, it is possible that a fair copy made before the end of the sixteenth century was later amended to accord with the Act of 1606 (although strictly speaking that did not apply to the written word) and to remove colloquialisms and the like. But that still would not explain the absence of stage directions found in Q.

If neither the prompt book nor a fair copy were the basis for the F text, what was used? It seems likely to have been a transcript of something, since it is consistent in style, for instance in the frequent use of capital letters, which demonstrably originates from the copy, not from compositorial practice, since it occurs throughout and we know that the play was set by more than one compositor. It seems to reflect some stage practice, though we cannot be certain of that, and whatever theory is proposed must take account of the absence of some important stage directions. Finally, in the opinion of many scholars (particularly those who argue that the copy for F was an annotated version of Q) it should be possible for the theory proposed to allow for the influence of Q on the F text. How influential Q was is a matter of dispute, but the two opposing theories would be reconciled if what is proposed now enabled a transcript to form the basis of F and yet allowed the influence of

Q to show through. As there was already a fairly good Quarto available, the material used for making a transcript must have *seemed* to the publishers of F capable of providing a better text than was obtainable from Q – otherwise they might have simply reprinted Q, tidying up as common sense dictated (for example, omitting mutes and providing some exeunts) – and it must have been produced without recourse to the prompt book, because if the prompt book was available it would be far simpler to print from that, or, if it could not be released to the printer, to make a transcript of it. It is possible that the prompt book was unobtainable, for we know from a slip of paper surviving from about 1620 that *Henry IV, Part II* had not been performed in the preceding seven years.

Although the proposition is unorthodox, it seems to me worth considering whether, in the peculiar case of *Henry IV, Part II*, in order to produce what was thought to be a more reliable text a transcript was made with the aid of actors' parts, despite the trouble and expense this would mean. The objection to such a guess (it can be no more) is not so much its inherent improbability – for we have an improbable situation to contend with – as the practical difficulties that scholars have always assumed would obstruct the process of reconstructing the relationship of isolated lines from different parts, especially in scenes with several speakers. The one Elizabethan example we have of an actor's part shows that cues were brief and the name of the speaker of the cue was not given. It has also been assumed that the loss of a prompt book would mean the loss of the actors' parts too. It might be difficult to relate lines from parts, especially if they had been modified in performance (and the opening of II.4 might demonstrate that difficulty), but it is not impossible; and there is no certainty at all that the loss of a prompt book *must* mean the loss of the parts, even though they were probably intended to be kept together. Indeed one of the greatest authorities on the Elizabethan theatre, Sir Edmund Chambers, though arguing against assembling a text in this manner (and his authority is often quoted by others in deciding the issue), also said, 'I do not think assembling is inconceivable, as a last resort for recovering a text, when no original or foul papers or transcript was available. But surely it would be a very laborious and difficult business' (*William Shakespeare*, 1930, vol. 1, p. 155). We may continue to wonder why a new text was desired though the Q was available; but desired – and produced – it was. With the Q at hand, an excellent guide to the order of speeches was available. If a scribe were writing up a manuscript from actors' parts with the aid of the Q, it would be fairly easy for him to miss entries that were in Q if, in the main, he were using Q only as a guide to the order of speeches; and it would be particularly easy for him to miss the instructions for sound effects given in Q, especially if these did not appear in the actors' parts (as presumably they would not). It is noticeable that the only sound effect that F indicates is the trumpets at the second coronation procession (the only procession it gives). Q, however, has an indication for shouting at IV.2.86, for alarum and excursions at IV.3.0 and for a retreat to be sounded after IV.3.23; it indicates trumpets for the first procession but not the second, which is not so much a procession as a straightforward entry of the King and his train.

Were a scribe working from parts, this might also explain the number of composite entries in F. Thus at IV.1.0 it indicates that Westmorland and Colevile enter at the beginning of the scene, but the former is not required until line 24 (where F has a second direction that he should enter) and Colevile does not appear until IV.3. At V.1.0 F provides an entry for Silence (who does not appear in this scene), caused, perhaps, by an automatic association of Silence with Shallow, and brings on Davy a few lines too early. In V.3 F brings on Pistol at the beginning of the scene as well as at line 82 but omits to include an entry for Davy. The differences at the beginning of III.2 (where Q brings on only Shallow and Silence – presumably indicating that the prospective recruits enter separately as their names are called – and F brings them all on at once; see headnote) may, as has been suggested, reflect stage practice; alternatively there might have been some grouping by whoever prepared the manuscript for F. This was not complete, however, since the entries for *Bardolph and one with him* (III.2.53) and Falstaff (III.2.80) were not gathered in.

The use of actors' parts might also explain the inclusion in F of certain phrases, not in Q, that might be actors' interpolations: for example, at IV.5.50, and the two half-lines referred to in the note to IV.5.178 (though not that discussed in the note to IV.5.76–7). F's version of II.1.71–2, expanding *it is for all I have* to *it is for all: all I have*, also has the ring of an actor's rhetorical embellishment, as has F's addition of *Fy* a few lines later. There are further suspicious intensificatives in F which could conceivably reflect either a scribe or performance: for example, *good* is unnecessarily added at II.1.166, II.2.88 and 93, II.4.286, and III.2.192; *new* is added at II.2.78; *even* at II.4.286; *but a very* at V.1.43; and *your worship* (instead of 'you'), duplicating the same words in the previous sentence, at V.1.45. (For other cases where the influence of actors' parts is at least a possibility, see notes to I.1.161 and II.2.103; and see the notes to III.2.54 and 148 and V.5.15, 17, 19 for possible applications of the theory.)

Editors have usually relied on the Q for their texts of *Henry IV, Part II* but have often used F very freely as a source of readings and for the arrangement of III.2. In the light of what I take to be the way the F text was produced, I have tended to base my text much more on Q than has been customary. Though Q is not based on a fair copy, it does seem to have been set from a manuscript in Shakespeare's hand (see notes to III.2.87, IV.2.8 and IV.5.33); and many of its faults (such as mutes and lack of exeunts) can be put right by the common sense that the scribe who wrote out the copy for F applied intermittently. In making amendments I have used Alan E. Craven's study of the work of the compositor who set Q (*Studies in Bibliography* XXVI (1973)), and this, though not wholly reliable, has suggested some errors which that compositor might have made (see notes to I.1.41, II.4.47 and 330, but cf. IV.5.204). In adopting readings from F I have tried to avoid those that seem more likely to derive from an actor than from Shakespeare. The literary language of F has not been used, but F has, of course, been the source of the passages not printed in Q. As well as omitting what I take to be actors' interpolations (see notes to I.1.96, IV.5.50 and 178), I have in three places omitted passages which may represent Shakespeare's first thoughts.

These are discussed (and the passages given) in the notes to III.1.53, IV.1.92–4 and IV.5.76–7.

Trying to restore the author's intention in a text with so complex a history is fraught with difficulties and uncertainties. Many scholars have worked on these problems, and though at times I differ from them I am deeply in their debt. No edition of this play can hope to be definitive. Mine is no more than a fresh attempt to reproduce in modern spelling and punctuation what Shakespeare's fair copy of *Henry IV, Part II* might have been like had he himself seen it through the press.

POSTSCRIPT 1995

John Jowett and his scrutinizer, Stanley Wells, provide a detailed analysis of the origins of Q and F in *A Textual Companion* to the Oxford Shakespeare (1987). Q is, they say, 'a good example of a text printed directly from the author's papers' before Shakespeare reworked his material as a fair copy. Jowett believes F to be 'a heavily sophisticated scribal transcript' (*The Complete Works*, old-spelling edition (1986), p. 573), the scribe copying from the prompt book with a copy of Q available 'as a secondary document at which he occasionally glanced' (*A Textual Companion*, p. 353). Eleanor Prosser, in an important study (because it reflects on more than its immediate subject), *Shakespeare's Anonymous Editors: Scribe and Compositor in the Folio Text of '2 Henry IV'* (1981), argued that F's compositor worked from a transcript of Q that had no authority except for certain added passages, and that the scribe and compositor were responsible for many of the small differences between what Shakespeare wrote and F. She maintains that eighty-six F readings that editors tend to accept should be rejected.

A few years after editing this edition I suggested how printing techniques might have been transferred from Valentine Simmes's printing house to Peter Short's, in particular the use of two-skeleton forme printing used in setting *Henry IV, Part I*, Q1 ('The Selection and Presentation of Bibliographical Evidence', *Analytical & Enumerative Bibliography*, 1 (1977), pp. 101–36). In 'The Use of Headlines: Peter Short's

Shakespearian Quartos, *1 Henry IV* and *Richard III*', Susan
Zimmerman argued (convincingly, I think) against automati-
cally establishing correlations between compositors and press-
work in general and in Peter Short's house in particular (*The
Library* VI, 7 (1985), pp. 217–55). Fredson Bowers discussed
'Establishing Shakespeare's Text: Poins and Peto in *1 Henry
IV*' in *Studies in Bibliography* 34 (1981), pp. 189–98; and Gilian
West considered '"Titan", "Onyers", and Other Difficulties
in the Text of *1 Henry IV*' in *Shakespeare Quarterly* 34 (1983),
pp. 330–33.

COLLATIONS

The following lists are selective; the differences between the
Quarto, the Folio, and the many later editions are manifold,
and minor variants have been excluded here. List 1 shows
the more important readings adopted for this edition from the
Folio, with the rejected Quarto readings. List 2 is a selection
of the more important readings adopted from Q, with the
rejected F readings. List 3 shows the major emendations incorporated in this edition. Stage directions are treated in list 4.
List 5 notes some of the emendations suggested elsewhere but
not adopted here. List 6 refers to notes in the Commentary
about textual matters not included in the collation lists. Many
of the readings in the other lists are also discussed in the
Account of the Text and in the Commentary.

Readings of this edition are printed to the left of the square
brackets. Quotations from Q and F are given in their original
spelling, except that 'long s' (ſ) has been replaced by 's'.

1

Readings adopted from F, with rejected Q readings. F's
readings (as given in this edition) are printed first, followed,
to the right of the square bracket, by what appears in Q. The
list is selective, and cases where the text is differently arranged
as verse or prose in Q and F are not included.

The Characters in the Play] *(see Commentary) not in* Q; *the list of* THE ACTORS NAMES *printed at the end of the text in* F *reads as follows*:

RVMOVR the Presentor.
King *Henry* the Fourth.
Prince *Henry*, afterwards Crowned King *Henrie* the Fift.
Prince *Iohn* of Lancaster. ⎫
Humphrey of Gloucester.   ⎬ Sonnes to *Henry* the Fourth,
Thomas of Clarence.   ⎭ & brethren to *Henry* 5.

Northumberland.   ⎫
The Arch Byshop of Yorke. ⎪
Mowbray.   ⎪
Hastings.   ⎬ Opposites against King
Lord Bardolfe.   ⎪ *Henrie* the Fourth.
Trauers.   ⎪
Morton.   ⎪
Coleuile.   ⎭

Warwicke.   ⎫   Pointz.   ⎫
Westmerland.   ⎪   Falstaffe.   ⎪
Surrey.   ⎬ Of the   Bardolphe.   ⎬ Irregular
Gowre.   ⎪ Kings   Pistoll.   ⎪ Humorists.
Harecourt.   ⎪ Partie.   Peto.   ⎪
Lord Chiefe Iustice. ⎭   Page.   ⎭

Shallow. ⎫ Both Country
Silence. ⎭ Iustices.
Dauie, Seruant to Shallow.   Drawers   Northumberlands Wife.
Phang, and Snare, 2. Seriants   Beadles. Percies Widdow.
Mouldie. ⎫   Groomes   Hostesse Quickly.
Shadow.   ⎪   Doll Teare-sheete.
Wart.   ⎬ Country   Epilogue.
Feeble.   ⎪ Soldiers
Bullcalfe.⎭

Induction

     36 Where] When

I.1

     28 whom] who
     41 ill] bad
   164 Lean on your] Leaue on you
166–79 You cast ... to be?] *not in* Q
   186 forth, body] forth body
189–209 The gentle ... follow him.] *not in* Q

I.2

    35 rascally yea-forsooth] rascall yea forsooth
    47 Where's Bardolph] *follows* it *at* 45 *in* Q
    86 me so?] me, so
    97 age] an ague
    98 time] time in you
   144 slenderer] slender
   172 and] and hath
   174 this] his
       them, are] the one
   205 and Prince Harry] *not in* Q

I.3

 21–4 Till we ... admitted.] *not in* Q
 36–55 Yes ... or else] *not in* Q
    58 one] on
    71 Are] And
    78 be] to be
 79–80 He ... Baying] French and Welch he leaues his back
       vnarmde, they baying
85–108 ARCHBISHOP Let us ... worst.] *not in* Q
   109 MOWBRAY] *Bish.*

II.1

    21 vice] view
    25 continuantly] continually
   102 mad] made
   168 Basingstoke] Billingsgate

II.2

    15 viz.] with
    21 thy] the
 21–2 made a shift to] *not in* Q

   81 rabbit] rabble
   90 be] *not in* Q
  126 *familiars*] family

II.3

   11 endeared] endeere
 23–45 He had ... grave.] *not in* Q

II.4

  42–3 them; I] I
  169 Die ... crowns] Men like dogges giue crownes
  249 the] *not in* Q

III.1

   18 mast] masse *in corrected* Q (*the whole of* III.1 *was
     initially omitted from* Q; *see p.* 121)
   22 billows] pillowes *in some copies of corrected* Q
   26 thy] them *in corrected* Q
   30 happy low, lie] (happy) low lie *in corrected* Q
   36 letters] letter *in corrected* Q
   53 liquors. 'Tis not ten years gone |] liquors! O, if
     this were seene, | The happiest youth viewing his
     progresse through, | What perills past, what crosses
     to ensue? | Would shut the booke and sit him downe
     and die: | Tis not ten yeeres gone, | *in corrected* Q

III.2

   37 Stamford] Samforth
   54 SHALLOW] *not in corrected* Q *as originally printed,
     nor as reset; Bardolfe. in uncorrected* Q
   65 accommodated] accommodate
   86 Surecard] Soccard
  110 FALSTAFF Prick him.] *Iohn prickes him.*
 120–21 see. Simon] see Simon
  142 for his] for
  285 my house] our house
  290 On] *Shal.* On
  304 ever] ouer
  320 him. Let] F, *uncorrected* Q; him, till *in corrected* Q

IV.1

 55–79 And with ... wrong.] *not in* Q
   92 divine? |] F, *corrected* Q; divine, | And consecrate
     commotions bitter edge. | *in uncorrected* Q

93 commonwealth, |] F, *corrected* Q – *the latter omitting the comma*; commonwealth | To brother borne an houshold cruelty, | *in uncorrected* Q

101–37 O ... the King.] *not in* Q

173 to our] our

224 armies?] armies

IV.2

8 Than] That

man] man talking

26 taken] ta'en

48 this] his

69 HASTINGS] *Prince*

117 and such acts as yours] *not in* Q

122 these traitors] this traitour

IV.4

32 melting] meeting

52 Canst thou tell that?] *not in* Q

94 heaven] heauens

120 and will break out] *not in* Q

132 Softly, pray.] *not in* Q

IV.5

77 thighs] thigh,

108 Which] Whom

178 put it] put

V.1

21 Hinckley] Hunkly

41 if] *not in* Q

51 all] *not in* Q

V.2

46 mix] mixt

V.3

5 here a] here

6 and a] and

124 knighthood] Knight

V.5

15 SHALLOW] *Pist.*

24 FALSTAFF] *not in* Q

28 all] *not in* Q

99 *spero me*] *spero*

2

Readings adopted from Q, with the rejected F readings (many of which are accepted in other modern editions: see p.127). Q's readings (as given in this edition) are printed first, followed, to the right of the square bracket, by what appears in F. The list is selective: there are many further minor differences, and the profanities and colloquialisms omitted or amended in F are not included (unless the reading is listed for other reasons).

I.I

    44 armèd] able
    96 slain –] slaine, say so:
   103 tolling] knolling
   126 So] Too
   161 LORD BARDOLPH This . . . lord.] (*Vmfr.* This . . . lord. Q); *not in* F

I.2

    28 Dommelton] *Dombledon*
  36–7 smoothy-pates] smooth-pates
    43 Well] Well,
    48 in] into
   171 times] *not in* F
   185 your chin double,] *not in* F
 188–9 about . . . afternoon,] *not in* F
 216–22 but . . . motion] *not in* F

I.3

    26 cause] case
    28 and] on
    66 so,] a

II.I

    14 most beastly, in good faith] and that most beastly
    43 I] Sir *Iohn*, I
 46–7 in the channel] there
    54 or two] *not in* F
    66 thou upon] vpon
    71 all] all: all
    78 What] Fy, what a

88 liking his father] lik'ning him
112 You have, as it appears to me,] I know you ha'
114–15 and . . . person] *not in* F
120 with her] her
150 dost . . . me? Come,] *not in* F
165 better] bitter
166 lord] good Lord

II.2

16 once] ones
22–6 And God . . . strengthened.] *not in* F
30 at this time] *not in* F
71 virtuous] pernitious
78 petticoat] new Petticoat
88 blossom] good Blossome
93 lord] good Lord
128 POINS] *not in* F
168–9 descension] declension

II.4

1, 10 FRANCIS] 1. *Drawer.*
4 DRAWER] 2. *Draw.*
13–14 DRAWER . . . Dispatch! . . . straight.] *not in* F
53 DOLL Hang . . . yourself!] *not in* F
132–3 FALSTAFF No . . . Pistol.] *not in* F
144–6 word as . . . sorted] word Captaine odious
155 faitours] Fates
162 Troyant] Troian
176 *contento*] *contente*
279 Poins his] *Poines*, his
286 grace] good Grace
290 light – flesh] (light, flesh, Q); light Flesh,
296 now] euen now
310 chipper] chopper
315 thee] him
383–4 Come! . . . Doll?] *not in* F

III.1

24 deafing] deaff'ning
27 sea-son] (season Q); Sea-Boy
77 natures] nature
81 beginning] beginnings

III.2

19 Barnes] *Bare*

36 as the Psalmist saith] *not in* F

69 ever were] euery where

77–8 'a may be] he

130 much] not

172 prick] pricke me

192 Master Shallow] good Master *Shallow*: No more of that

253 Here's Wart;] Where's *Wart*?

264 Thas! Thas! Thas!] thus, thus, thus.

287 'Fore God, would you would.] I would you would, Master *Shallow*.

303–4 yet ... mandrake] *not in* F

305–8 and sung ... good-nights] *not in* F

314 thrust] truss'd

IV.2

24 Imply] Employ

28 His] Heauens

IV.3

2 place?] place, I pray?

82 lord] Lord, 'pray,

85 had the] had but the

120 human] *not in* F

IV.4

33 he is] hee's

39 time] Line

104 wet] write

terms] Letters

IV.5

50 majesty?] Maiestie? how fares your Grace?

55 He ... here.] *not in* F

72 pillèd] (pilld Q); pyl'd

76 tolling] culling

flower,] flower | The vertuous Sweetes, (*the lineation differs by approximately half a line in each line to* 80)

161 worse than] worst of

178 God] O my Sonne! | Heauen

220 You] My gracious Liege: | You

V.1
    8 Davy! Let me see, Davy] *not in* F
    9 yea, marry] *not in* F
    12 hade land] head-land
    21 lost] lost the other day
    24 tiny] tine
    29 backbitten] bitten
    43 little] but a very litle
    45 you] your Worship
    48 Come, come, come,] Come,
    60 him] of him
    74 without] with

V.2
    36 impartial] Imperiall

V.3
    25 Give Master Bardolph] Good M. *Bardolfe*:
    29 must] *not in* F
    56 tiny] tyne

V.4
    5 whipping-cheer] Whipping cheere enough
    6 two] two (lately)
    9 I go] I now go
    11 I] hee
    29 atomy] Anatomy

V.5
    4 Dispatch, dispatch!] *not in* F
    5 Shallow] *Robert Shallow*
    99 *tormenta, spero*] *tormento, spera*
        contenta] *contento*

Epilogue
    15–16 And ... Queen] *after* 32 *in* F, *and omitting* I
        23 seen] *seene before*

                                    3

Emendations incorporated in this edition (not including stage
directions and minor emendations, such as changes of punctuation that do not affect sense and the correction of obvious
misprints). Emendations that were first made (unauthoritatively)

in the second Folio (1632) are marked F2 (F1 in these cases refers to the first Folio). Most of the other emendations were first made by eighteenth-century editors such as Rowe, Pope, Theobald and Capell. Readings suggested by modern scholars are here attributed by name.

Induction

      35 hold] hole Q, F

I.1

      161 LORD BARDOLPH] *Vmfr.* Q; *not in* F

      162–3 MORTON Sweet ... honour; | The] *J. Dover Wilson, 1946; Bard.* Sweet ... honor, | *Mour.* The Q (F: ... honor. | ...)

      178 brought] F2; bring F1; *not in* Q

      192 My lord, your son] *this edition*; My Lord (your Sonne) F; *not in* Q

      201–2 religion; ... thoughts,] Religion, ... Thoughts: F; *not in* Q

II.2

      109 borrower's] borowed Q, F

      119 PRINCE HENRY] *not in* Q, F

II.4

      15 WILL] *this edition; Francis* Q; *2. Draw.* F

      19 FRANCIS] *this edition; Dra.* Q; *1. Draw.* F

      21 DRAWER] *Francis* Q; *2. Draw.* F

      47 Yea, Mary's joys] *this edition*; Yea ioy Q; I marry F

      82 swagger, 'a] *J. C. Maxwell, 1947*; swaggrer Q; Swaggerer F

      330 devil binds] *this edition*; diuel blinds Q; Deuill outbids F

IV.1

      36 appeared] appeare Q, F

      114 force perforce] forc'd, perforce F; *not in* Q

      137 indeed] and did F; *not in* Q

      183 not that.] not that, F2; not, that Q, F1

IV.2

      0 *New scene not marked in* Q, F

      19 imagined] imagine Q, F

IV.3

      o *New scene not marked in* Q, F
    41 Rome, three words] *A. R. Humphreys, 1966*; Rome,
        there cosin Q; Rome, F

IV.5

      o *New scene not marked in* Q, F
    82 have] *M. R. Ridley, 1934*; hands Q; hath F
  204 my] thy Q, F

V.3

    46 thee,] *J. Dover Wilson, 1946*; the Q, F

4

Stage directions (not including minor editorial adjustments such
as the provision of obvious exits and the addition of *aside* and
indications of the person addressed).

Induction

      o *painted full of tongues*] Q; *not in* F

I.1

      o *Enter ... door*] Q; *Enter Lord Bardolfe, and the Porter* F
      1 *Enter the Porter*] F (*in opening stage direction*); *not
        in* Q
      6 *Exit Porter*] *not in* Q, F

I.2

      o *Enter ... buckler*] *Enter sir Iohn alone, with his page
        bearing his sword and buckler* Q; *Enter Falstaffe, and
        Page* F
    52 *and his Servant*] *and Seruant* F; *not in* Q
  229 *Exeunt ... Servant*] *not in* Q, F

I.3

      o *Enter ... Bardolph*] *Enter th' Archbishop, Thomas
        Mowbray (Earle Marshall) the Lord Hastings, Faucon-
        bridge, and Bardolfe,* Q; *Enter Archbishop, Hastings,
        Mowbray, and Lord Bardolfe* F

II.1

      o *with ... Snare*] F; *and an Officer or two* Q
      7 *from behind them*] *not in* Q, F
    36 *and the Page*] *and the boy* Q; *not in* F

58 *and his men*] Q; *not in* F

131 *He takes her aside*] *not in* Q, F
   Gower] F; *a messenger* Q

134 *He gives him a letter*] *not in* Q, F

164 *Exeunt ... Page*] exit hostesse and sergeant Q; *not in* F

II.2

0 *Enter Prince Henry and Poins*] Enter the Prince, Poynes,
   sir Iohn Russel, with other Q; Enter Prince Henry,
   Pointz, Bardolfe, and Page F

65 *Enter ... Page*] Q; *Enter Bardolfe* F (*after* 68)

103 *reading the letter*] Letter F; *not in* Q

159 *Exeunt Bardolph and Page*] *not in* Q, F

II.4

0 *Enter ... Drawer*] Enter a Drawer or two Q; *Enter
   two Drawers* F

13 *preparing to leave*] *not in* Q, F

14 *Enter Will*] Q (*after* 18); *not in* F

21 *Exeunt Francis and Drawer*] Exit Q, F

31 *singing*] *not in* Q, F

33 *Exit Will*] *not in* Q, F

105 *Bardolph ... Page*] and Bardolfes boy Q; *and Bardolph
   and his Boy* F

155 *He brandishes his sword*] *not in* Q, F

178 *He lays down his sword*] *not in* Q, F

191 *He snatches up his sword*] *not in* Q, F

198 *drawing*] *not in* Q, F

200 *Falstaff thrusts at Pistol*] *not in* Q, F

202 *Exit Bardolph, driving Pistol out*] *not in* Q, F

206 *Enter Bardolph*] *not in* Q, F

222 *Music*] *not in* Q, F

228 *behind*] *not in* Q, F
   disguised as drawers] disguis'd F; *not in* Q

276 *coming forward*] *not in* Q, F

290–91 *laying his hand upon Doll*] *not in* Q, F

315 *turning to Prince Henry*] *not in* Q, F.

346 *Peto knocks at door*] Q; *not in* F

348 *Enter Peto*] F; *not in* Q

363 *Knocking within ... Exit Bardolph*] *not in* Q, F

364 *Enter Bardolph*] not in Q, F
376 *with Bardolph ... musicians*] not in Q, F
380 *at the door*] not in Q, F

II.1

0 *in his nightgown*] corrected Q; not in F
   followed by a page] with a Page F; alone corrected Q
3 *Exit page*] Exit F; not in Q
31 *Enter Warwick and Surrey*] F; Enter Warwike, Surry,
   and sir Iohn Blunt corrected Q

II.2

0 *Enter ... Silence*] Q; Enter Shallow and Silence: with
   Mouldie, Shadow, Wart, Feeble, Bull-calfe F
53 *Enter Bardolph ... him*] Q; Enter Bardolph and his
   Boy F (after 51)
100 *Enter Mouldy*] not in Q, F
121 *Enter Shadow*] not in Q, F
135 *Enter Wart*] not in Q, F
146 *Enter Feeble*] not in Q, F
169 *Enter Bullcalf*] not in Q, F
214 *Exeunt Falstaff ... Silence*] exeunt Q; not in F
234 *Enter Falstaff and the Justices*] Q; not in F
290 *Exeunt Bardolph and the recruits*] not in Q, F

IV.1

0 *Enter ... Forest of Gaultree*] Enter the Archbishop,
   Mowbray, Bardolfe, Hastings, within the forrest of
   Gaultree Q; Enter the Arch-bishop, Mowbray, Hastings,
   Westmerland, Coleuile F
24 *Enter Westmorland*] Q (after 25), F
180 *Exit Westmorland*] Q (after decide it.); not in F
226 *They go forward*] not in Q, F

IV.2

0 *Enter ... army*] Q (after IV.1.224); Enter Prince
   Iohn F
71 *Exit a captain*] Exit F; not in Q
86 *Shouts within*] shout Q; not in F
92 *Exit Westmorland*] Exit F; not in Q
96 *Exit Hastings*] Exit F; not in Q

IV.3

    0 *Alarum ... Colevile*] *Alarum Enter Falstaffe excursion.*
      Q; *Enter Falstaffe and Colleuile* F

   17 *He kneels*] not in Q, F

   23 *Retreat sounded*] *Retraite* Q; not in F
      Enter ... soldiers] *Enter Iohn Westmerland, and the*
      rest Q; *Enter Prince Iohn, and Westmerland* F

   74 *Exit Blunt with Colevile*] *Exit with Colleuile* F; *no.*
      in Q

   84 *Exeunt all but Falstaff*] *Exit* F; not in Q

IV.4

    0 *Enter ... lords*] *Enter the King, Warwike, Kent, Thoma:*
      duke of Clarence, Humphrey of Gloucester Q; *Enter*
      King, Warwicke, Clarence, Gloucester F

IV.5

    0 *They ... bed*] not in Q, F

   21 *Exeunt all but Prince Henry*] not in Q, F

   44 *He puts the crown on his head*] not in Q, F

   49 *and attendant lords*] not in Q, F

  139 *kneels*] not in Q, F

  223 *Enter ... lords*] *enter Lancaster* Q; *Enter Lord Iohr.*
      of Lancaster, and Warwicke F

V.1

    0 *Enter ... Page*] *Enter Shallow, Falstaffe, and Bardolfe*
      Q; *Enter Shallow, Silence, Falstaffe, Bardolfe, Page,*
      and Dauie F

    6 *Enter Davy*] not in Q, F

   47 *Exit Davy*] not in Q, F

   54 *Exit Shallow*] not in Q, F

   55 *Exeunt Bardolph and Page*] not in Q, F

   79 *within*] not in Q, F

V.2

    0 *Enter ... Chief Justice*] *Enter Warwike, duke Humphrey,*
      L. chiefe Iustice, Thomas Clarence, Prince Iohn, West-
      merland Q; *Enter the Earle of Warwicke, and the Lord*
      Chiefe Iustice F

   13 *, and attendant lords*] not in Q, F

   42 *Enter ... others*] *Enter the Prince and Blunt* Q; *Enter*
      Prince Henrie F

V.3

    0 *Enter ... Page*] Q; *Enter Falstaffe, Shallow, Silence, Bardolfe, Page, and Pistoll* F

  17 *sings*] not in Q, F

  29 *Exit*] not in Q, F

  32 *sings*] not in Q, F

  39 *Enter Davy*] Q; not in F

45, 52 *sings*] not in Q, F

  69 *One knocks at door*] Q; not in F

  70 *Exit Davy*] not in Q, F

  71 *to Silence, seeing him drink*] not in Q, F

  73 *sings*] not in Q, F

  79 *Enter Davy*] not in Q, F

103 *sings*] not in Q, F

V.4

    0 *Enter ... Doll Tearsheet*] *Enter Sincklo and three or foure officers* Q; *Enter Hostesse Quickly, Dol Tearesheete, and Beadles* F

V.5

    0 *Enter ... rushes*] *Enter strewers of rushes* Q; *Enter two Groomes* F

   4 *Exeunt*] F; not in Q

     Trumpets sound ... Page] *... and the Boy* Q; *Enter Falstaffe, Shallow, Pistoll, Bardolfe, and Page* F

  39 *The trumpets sound*] F after 40; not in Q

  40 *Enter ... among them*] *Enter the King and his traine* Q; *The Trumpets sound. Enter King Henrie the Fift, Brothers, Lord Chiefe Iustice* F

  75 *Exeunt King and his train*] not in Q; *Exit King* F

  93 *Enter ... officers*] *Enter Iustice and prince Iohn* Q; not in F

  99 *Exeunt ... Chief Justice*] *exeunt* Q (after 98); *Exit. Manet Lancaster and Chiefe Iustice* F

5

A list of some of the more interesting emendations suggested by other editors but not adopted in this edition.

I.1

 161 LORD BARDOLPH] TRAVERS
 183 ventured ... proposed,] ventured, ... proposed

I.3

 36–9 *see Commentary*
  47 least] last
  66 so,] so a

II.2

  71 POINS (*to Bardolph*] BARDOLPH (*to the Page*)
 102–3 writes ... every] writes – (*reads*) *John Falstaff, knight.* POINS Every

II.4

 330 devil binds] devil attends; devil bloats; devil's behind

III.1

  51 chance's mocks] chances mock

III.2

 148 SHALLOW] FALSTAFF
 302 invincible] invisible

IV.1

  34 rage] rags
  71 there] sphere; shore; flow
 178 At] And

IV.3

 60–61 Is ... lord] *as a verse line*
  62 A ... Colevile] *as a verse line*

IV.4

 10–17 *see Commentary*

V.2

 102 right justice] right, Justice

V.5

 17, 19 PISTOL] SHALLOW

6

Commentary on textual matters not included in the above lists will be found at the following places: I.2.121; II.2.75; III.2.43, 87, 314–15; IV.1.129; IV.5.33; V.3.17–22.

The Songs

1. 'When Arthur first in court' (II.4.32, 34)

Falstaff sings a garbled version of the ballad *Sir Launcelot du Lake*, which in Shakespeare's time was sung to the tune 'Chevy Chase' (also known as 'Flying Fame'). The best surviving version, given below, is found eight times in Thomas D'Urfey's *Pills to Purge Melancholy* (1719–20), and is close to a Scottish manuscript version of about 1650–75.

When Ar-thur first in court be-gan, And was ap-pro-ved king,___ By force of arms, great vict'-ries won, And con-quest home did bring.___

2. 'Do me right' (V.3.73–5; see also note to V.3.17–22)

This is from the drinking song 'Monsieur Mingo', which, with music by Orlando di Lasso, was published first in Paris in 1570 and in London in the same year by a Huguenot refugee, Thomas Vautrollier, with a partially expurgated text. The music reproduced here is based on the edition of M. Henri Expert, *Les Maitres musiciens de la renaissance française* (1894), pp. 72–5. English words (which are not a translation of the French) are

first found in a seventeenth-century manuscript in the Bodleian
Library (MS. Mus. f. 17–19). They are reproduced here from
the text appended to an article on the song in *Shakespeare
Quarterly* 9 (1958), pp. 105–16, by Dr F. W. Sternfeld, whose
further assistance is gratefully acknowledged.

Mon-sieur Min-go For quaff-ing doth pass In cup, cruse, can, or glass; In
cell-ar ne-ver was his fell-ow found To drink pro-found, By task and turn so
round To quaff, ca-rouse so sound, And yet bear so fresh a brain,
Fresh a brain, Sans taint or stain; Or foil, re-coil, or
quar-rel, But to the beer and bar-rel, Where he works to win his
name, Where he works to win his name; And stout doth stand, In Bac-chus' band, With pot in
hand, To pur-chase fame; For he calls with cup and can: Come try my
cour-age, man to man, And let him con-quer me that can, And
spare not, I care not, While hands can heave the pot, No fear falls to my lot; God
Bac-chus do me right, And dub me knight, Do-min-go.

Commentary

Q here refers to the Quarto edition of the play (1600), F to the first Folio (1623). Biblical quotations are modernized from the Bishops' Bible (1568, etc.), the official English translation of Elizabeth's reign.

The Characters in the Play: This arrangement is based on the grouping of the list headed *The Actors Names* at the end of the F version of the play (see pp. 121–2, 130), except that the names of the King's party have here been placed before those of the rebels. Some of the headings, descriptions, and names are added or modified from those in F's list, though the curious description *Irregular Humorists* and the order of those so described are as in F.

Act and scene divisions: F divides the play into acts and scenes, and names the Induction as such; Q makes no divisions at all. F's divisions are followed in this edition except in Act IV: see headnotes to IV.2, 3 and 5.

Locations: In only one stage direction in *Henry IV, Part II* does Shakespeare name the place where the scene is set: the Q opening direction to IV.1 locates it *within the forrest of Gaultree*. It has been common since the eighteenth century for editors to specify locations, but it is doubtful whether much is gained; when Shakespeare is concerned that we should be aware of the place of action he tells us by way of the dialogue (even in IV.1 he mentions Gaultree Forest in the first two lines of the scene). No other locations are provided in this edition. Too rigorous an insistence on place can imply for a present-day audience a realism – a relatively modern concept – that works against the understanding of Elizabethan drama.

INDUCTION

Many editors specify a location for Rumour based on the reference at 35–7 to the castle where Northumberland *Lies crafty-sick*. But Rumour is symbolic, not a particularized character like, say, Falstaff. No editor proposes a location for the speaker of the Epilogue, and it is just as inappropriate to do so for Rumour.

Dr Johnson regarded Rumour's speech as 'wholly useless, since we are told nothing which the first scene does not clearly and naturally discover' (though he conceded that it was 'not inelegant or unpoetical'). This implicitly emphasizes the recounting of facts with economy, and Johnson fails to allow for the atmosphere that Rumour evokes. There is, moreover, some virtue in laying a clear foundation for a situation, even if that means giving facts more than once. Rumour serves this function, telling us where we are in the well-known story of Henry IV and Henry V; he also warns the discerning that this will not be a play to make *smooth comforts false, worse than true wrongs* (40). There is an element in *Henry IV, Part II* that is distinctly uncomfortable.

0 *painted full of tongues*: This is part of a long-standing description of Rumour and the associated figure of Fame, common in the sixteenth century but going back to Virgil and Ovid. In 1553 the Revels Office paid for a coat and cap to be painted for Fame with eyes, tongues and ears.

3 *drooping*: Where the sun declines.

4 *post-horse*: Horse kept at an inn or staging point for use by those carrying post (or other travellers). The idea that rumours ride the wind has become a commonplace.

4, 19 *still*: Continually, always.

6 *slanders*: Rumour's speech is full of images of incert-
itude and deception; *false reports*, *the smile of safety*,
surmises, *jealousies*, *conjectures* and *Rumour* itself all
occur in nine lines. The sense of unease and doubt
is also suggested by such epithets as *covert*, *uncounted*
and *still-discordant wavering*, which are summed up
in the last sentence of the speech.

10 *safety*: This may mean here more than a sense of
physical security; *safety* could imply the salvation of
the soul. See note to I.2.43.

12 *Make*: Cause to be made.
fearful musters: Frightening enrolments of troops.
This line probably evoked for Shakespeare's audience
the preparations made towards the end of 1596 and
throughout much of 1597 against an expected Spanish
invasion. Such preparations were again being made in
1599, though that would be rather too late a date for
Part II. At a time when these preparations were
common, a dramatist could easily conjure up such
apprehensions, and specific dates may not be reliably
determined.

13 *big*: Pregnant, full (of events).

15 *And no such matter*: Though there is no substance in
such fears.

16 *jealousies*: Suspicious apprehensions of evil.

17 *so plain a stop*: So easily played upon. The stops
of a recorder (the *pipe* of 15) are the holes that are
covered or uncovered to produce different notes. A
similar image is used, though in a slightly different
way, in *Hamlet*, III.2.80–81.

18 *the blunt monster with uncounted heads*: The people,
seen as a mob, insensitive (*blunt*) and uncountable
because so numerous.

19 *wavering*: Vacillating.

21 *anatomize*: Analyse, dissect.

22 *my household*: Those I influence (and, by implication,
the audience).

23 *King Harry's victory*: The battle of Shrewsbury, which

Shakespeare dramatizes towards the end of *Henry IV, Part I*.

29 *Harry Monmouth*: Prince Hal, son of Henry IV, was born at Monmouth.

31–2 *the King ... death*: In *Part I*, V.4.37, the King is attacked by Douglas, and, when in danger, is rescued by Hal.

33 *peasant*: Country.

35 *hold*: Castle. Q and F both print *hole*, which makes a sort of sense. However, in Elizabethan ('secretary') handwriting 'd' is easily misread as 'e', and it is likely that Shakespeare wrote (or intended) 'hold'.

raggèd: There are two possibilities here. Combined with *worm-eaten*, *raggèd* suggests a broken-down castle, and those who support this interpretation argue that castles were falling into disarray in the later Tudor period. On the other hand *raggèd* could refer to the castellations and projecting stonework of Northumberland's *hold*, and *worm-eaten* might refer to the holes seemingly eaten into the walls to make arrow-slits. In *Richard II*, when Richard is brought to ruin at Flint Castle, Bolingbroke speaks of the castle's 'ruined ears' and later of its 'tattered battlements' (III.3.34 and 52). 'Tattered' can imply 'broken-down', but it too can suggest castellation (and indeed it has a particular architectural meaning, 'denticulated'). In both cases Shakespeare combines a description of a castle with a suggestion of ruin and disorder.

37 *crafty-sick*: In *Richard II* and in both parts of *Henry IV* Northumberland is made to seem the cunning politician. His absence from Shrewsbury, which contributed to the death of his son and the defeat of his cause, is ascribed to craft by Shakespeare, not by historians.

posts: Couriers.

tiring: Exhaustedly.

39–40 *From Rumour's tongues ... wrongs*: Rumour's final comment is applicable to more than the immediate situation – the arrival of news about the battle of

Shrewsbury. It is easy to find *smooth comforts false* in the play as a whole, and it is important for the audience to realize that upon the tongue of Rumour, the presenter of the story, *continual slanders ride*.

THE PLAY

1.1

The opening of this scene has attracted much attention, for it seems to provide evidence that three places of entry at stage level were available to the Elizabethan dramatist. In Q no entry is given for the Porter but the direction for Lord Bardolph specifies that he enters *at one door*, and his first line implies that the Porter is somewhere else. Some scholars have suggested that the Porter enters on the upper stage, but that involves a certain awkwardness unless Lord Bardolph can appear from a different direction and then Northumberland from a third.

A more interesting problem is the appearance in the play of two characters with the same name, though this is not unique in Shakespeare (there are, for example, two characters called Jaques in *As You Like It*). The duplication here is particularly strange in that Bardolph was probably originally called 'Harvey' in *Henry IV, Part I* (see An Account of the Text for *Part I*, p. 113–14), but, as with the original name for Falstaff, 'Oldcastle' (see note to I.2.121), it seems that pressure was brought to have the name changed. Shakespeare apparently then chose 'Bardolph' (a name which appears among a list of recusants that includes Shakespeare's father), not anticipating that in a second part to *Henry IV* this would present difficulties. It is possible that Lord Bardolph was originally called 'Umfrevile', since the abbreviation *Vmfr.* appears in Q as the speech-prefix at 161, and Sir John Umfrevile is referred to at 34. Lord *Robert* Umfrevile was present at Gaultree Forest but as a supporter of the King. The original Lord Bardolph was a rebel and died of wounds in 1408, after the battle of Bramham Moor. The cursory reference to his death at IV.4.97–9 makes it seem co-incident with the events at Gaultree Forest of 1405. Perhaps Shakespeare started by giving Lord Bardolph his proper name, toyed with changing the name, chose Umfrevile, then, realizing that it was the name of one of Bardolph's opponents, made do with the original and historically correct name. Something similar may be involved in the cases of Fauconbridge and Kent (see headnotes to I.3 and IV.4).

1 *keeps*: Guards.

3 *attend*: Await.

8 *stratagem*: Not 'plot' but 'violent and bloody act', a usage found elsewhere in Shakespeare's plays.

10 *high*: Too rich.

12 *certain*: Reliable.

13 *an*: If.

15 *in the fortune of*: As for what has befallen.

16 *the Blunts*: At the battle of Shrewsbury several knights were disguised as King Henry IV. One of these was Sir Walter Blunt, who was killed by Douglas (see beginning of V.3 in *Part I*). There was no second Blunt at Shrewsbury so far as historical records show; but Samuel Daniel (in his long poem *The First Four Books of the Civil Wars between the Two Houses of Lancaster and York* (1595), which Shakespeare knew) mentions the death of 'another Blunt' at Shrewsbury, and Holinshed tells of a Sir John Blunt who fought the French with distinction in 1412. *Henry IV, Part II* includes a non-speaking character called Blunt (see note to the stage direction at III.1.31); editors usually call him Sir John Blunt, Sir Walter's son.

18 *Stafford*: The Earl of Stafford was one of those disguised as Henry IV; Douglas killed him as well as Blunt (*Part I*, V.3.7–9).

19 *brawn*: Boar fattened for the table.

hulk: (Usually used of a ship) large, unwieldy person.

21 *So fought, so followed, and so fairly won*: This is reminiscent of the most famous of all rhetorical

figures, Julius Caesar's '*Veni, vidi, vici*', 'I came, I
saw, I overcame' (quoted by Falstaff at IV.3.41).
Caesar is, appropriately, referred to at 23.

23 *fortunes*: Good fortune, success.

27 *freely*: Openly.

   these news: In Elizabethan usage, *news* could be singular
   or plural.

   Travers: A character of Shakespeare's creation.

30 *over-rode*: Out-rode.

33 *comes*: Like *news*, *tidings* could be singular or plural.

34 *Umfrevile*: See headnote and note to 161.

37 *forspent*: Exhausted.

38 *breathe*: Rest, allow to breathe.

41 *ill*: This is F's reading. Q has *bad*, which makes good
   sense but could be a compositor's error unconsciously
   suggested by the previous word *had*. There is evidence
   that the compositor who set Q was particularly prone
   to changing words under the influence of similar
   shapes or sounds. Northumberland repeats *ill* at 51.

42 *spur ... cold*: Hotspur (Harry Percy) is now cold in
   death. His father plays on his name and this news at 50.

45 *jade*: Worn-out hack. (Cf. 'jaded'.)

46 *starting*: Leaping forward.

48 *Staying*: Waiting for.

52 *have not the day*: Has not won the battle.

53 *point*: Lace for tying a garment.

55 *by*: Past.

57 *hilding*: Contemptible.

59 *at a venture*: Recklessly.

   Morton: A character created by Shakespeare.

60 *like to a title-leaf*: Title pages of Elizabethan books
   served as an advertisement for the contents.

63 *a witnessed usurpation*: Evidence of encroachment
   (that is, the lines or wrinkles left in sand by the
   retreating tide).

72–3 *Drew Priam's curtain ... burnt*: No such instance is
   mentioned in the *Iliad*, but in the *Aeneid* Aeneas
   is warned of danger in a dream and wakes to find
   Troy ablaze.

74 *found . . . tongue*: Discovered the fire before the man could speak.

78 *Stopping*: Filling.

79 *stop my ear indeed*: Prevent my ever hearing again.

87 *is chanced*: Has happened.

88 *his divination lies*: His conjecture is false.

92 *spirit*: Here not the soul or character but the powers of perception.

94 *strange*: Reluctant.

95 *Thou shakest thy head*: This seems to imply a denial of Percy's death. Some commentators suggest that Morton's action is to incline his head in silent agreement; but it may be that he does shake his head slowly from side to side, not as a denial but in a gesture of sorrow.

96 *slain*: F reads *slaine, say so:*, which fills out the line to the correct number of syllables. But it may be an actor's or scribe's interpolation, for Q's shorter line allows for a dramatic pause.

102 *sullen*: Funeral.

108 *faint quittance*: Weak resistance.

109 *Harry Monmouth*: In this reference to Hal as the slayer of Hotspur, Shakespeare follows his own alteration of history in *Part I* (see Introduction, p. xxii). The dramatic value of a confrontation between them is obvious.

112 *In few*: In few words, in short.
    his death, whose: The death of him whose.

114 *Being bruited once*: As soon as it was noised abroad.

115 *best-tempered*: Of the finest temper (as metal).

116 *metal*: F spells the word *Mettle*, and Shakespeare is playing on the two meanings. The imagery of this passage (particularly 114–25) has often attracted the attention of critics. There are not only the obvious contrasts of well-tempered steel and dull and heavy lead, but, more subtly, the way in which the despondency of the troops is expressed in contrasting images which lead swiftly to their flight from the battlefield.

117 *abated*: Blunted.

123 *fled*: This unusual past form of 'fly' vividly suggests those fleeing from the battlefield as well as arrows.

128 *three times ... the King*: In *Part I* the death of Blunt in the guise of the King is dramatized and the death of Stafford is referred to (see notes to 16 and 18). Shakespeare may have had Shirley in mind as the third victim; Hal challenges Douglas with the words 'The spirits | Of valiant Shirley, Stafford, Blunt are in my arms' (*Part I*, V.4.39–40).

129–31 *Gan vail ... took*: Holinshed, describing how Henry's enemies were put to flight, says that Douglas, 'for haste', fell from a crag, was taken, but 'for his valiantness' was released. Shakespeare stresses Douglas's flight and fear rather than his valour. Twice in *Part I* he has Douglas flee, at V.4.42 in a stage direction and V.5.20, where it is said he 'fled with the rest' on seeing his men 'Upon the foot of fear'. Here he is said to stumble with fear; the *bloody* Douglas's flight is contrasted with his heroic pretensions, and might be compared with another doughty warrior's flight – Falstaff's from Gad's Hill.

129 *Gan*: Began to.
vail his stomach: Fail in courage.
grace: Excuse.

133 *power*: Armed force.

135 *at full*: In full.

137–9 *In poison ... well*: Paradoxically, poisonous drugs, used in appropriate quantities, may be curative; thus, what would have made Northumberland ill were he well may cure him now he is sick. Such bitter news might renew his strength so much that he can fight back and revenge his son's death. As Shakespeare dramatizes the events, this does not happen; Northumberland again lets his colleagues down by not arriving with his forces at Gaultree Forest, and his death at the battle of Bramham Moor is only glanced at (IV.4.97–9).

141 *under life*: Under the weight of the living man.

142 *fit seizure*: There is a slight (though effective) confu-

sion here between the weakness caused by fever and
the paroxysm of a fit.

143 *keeper*: Nurse.

144 *grief ... grief*: Bodily pain ... sorrow.

145 *nice*: There may be a pun here on the very specific
use of *nice* to mean 'slender' or 'thin' (as in *Othello*,
III.3.15, where policy is said to 'feed upon such nice
and waterish diet') and on the meaning 'unmanly'.
Wordplay on such an occasion as this is typically
Shakespearian. Cf. note to 42.

146 *scaly*: Made of overlapping plates of armour.

147 *coif*: Nightcap.

148 *wanton*: Effeminate.

149 *fleshed*: Initiated in bloodshed (as animals are for
hunting).

151 *raggèd'st*: Roughest.

154 *Let order die*: A serious, indeed a shocking, plea in
Elizabethan times, comparable with Falstaff's *woe to
my Lord Chief Justice!* (V.3.136). Northumberland's
passionate speech is reminiscent in style of his son's
outbursts in *Part I*, and it also recalls the moment
in *Richard II*, I.4.31–3, when Bolingbroke (as Henry
IV was then called) reverses order by doffing his
bonnet to an oyster-wench and bending his knee to
a brace of draymen. Here, Northumberland's cry is
reinforced by a plea that all natural restraints be
overturned and Cain's spirit reign in all men's hearts.
One cannot know the precise effect on an Elizabethan
audience, but this may be a good example of Shakespeare's skill in enabling his listeners to respond to
the speaker's emotion whilst remaining detached from
the plea itself.

156 *feed contention in a lingering act*: Foster dispute in a
long-drawn-out action.

157 *Cain*: Traditionally Cain committed the first murder
(Genesis 4).

158 *that*: So that.

159 *rude*: (1) Discordant (of the action dramatized);
(2) lacking polish (of the dramatist's art).

161 *LORD BARDOLPH*: Q's speech-prefix for this line is
     Vmfr. – presumably the Sir John Umfrevile of 34
     (see headnote). F's editor or compositor, perhaps
     puzzled, left the line out; if the conjecture that actors'
     parts underlie the F text is correct (see An Account
     of the Text, pp. 125–7), it could be that the line
     was not retained when a part for Umfrevile was
     abandoned. The line is sometimes given to Travers,
     but a comment on the Earl's behaviour comes more
     appropriately from a lord than from a servant.

162 *MORTON*: Both Q and F give this line to Lord
     Bardolph, beginning Morton's speech at 163. But this
     may be an error caused by the Q compositor's mis-
     reading a manuscript correction of the speech-prefix
     for 161; 162 seems to form a natural part of Morton's
     speech, and Q has a comma at the end of the line.

166 *cast th'event*: Calculated (cast up) the outcome.

168 *make head*: Raise an army.

169 *dole*: Distribution (perhaps with a pun on the meaning
     'sorrow').

170 *edge*: Perilous path along a narrow ridge.

171 *More likely to fall in than to get o'er*: In *Part I*,
     I.3.190–92, Worcester proposes a dangerous policy
     which he likens to walking over 'a current roaring
     loud | On the unsteadfast footing of a spear'. Hotspur
     replies, 'If he fall in, good night, or sink, or swim!'
     Shakespeare seems to be recalling that conversation
     here; the repetition of *fall in* is striking, since 'falling
     off' a narrow path would seem more logical. 'edge'
     could mean a cutting weapon (as in *Coriolanus*,
     V.6.113), so Shakespeare might well have associated
     an edge (path) with the spear which, as in medieval
     romances, was to provide the path across the 'current
     roaring loud'.

172 *advised*: Warned, apprised.

172–3 *capable | Of*: Susceptible to.

173 *forward*: Eager.

174 *trade*: Interchange.

177 *stiff-borne*: Obstinately pursued.

180 *engagèd to*: Concerned with, involved in.

182 *wrought out life*: Won through alive.

184 *respect*: Consideration.

185 *o'erset*: Overthrown.

186 *put forth*: (1) Put to sea; (2) stake.

189 *gentle*: Well-born (as 'gentleman').

Archbishop of York: Richard Scroop, who is variously described as the brother, cousin or godson of William Scrope, Earl of Wiltshire, who was executed at Bristol by order of Bolingbroke (*Richard II*, III.2.141–2). In *Part I*, I.3.264–5, Worcester tells Hotspur that the Archbishop 'bears hard | His brother's death'. There were many Scroops (or Scropes), and their relationships are complicated and easily misunderstood.

up: In arms.

191 *a double surety*: Bodily and spiritual allegiance.

192 *My lord, your son*: F's reading (Q omits 189–209) is *My Lord (your Sonne)*, indicating that Hotspur is *My lord* (as at 83). The brackets may be Shakespeare's, but they could have been introduced by a scribe (or the compositor), and it seems possible that *My lord* refers to Northumberland, continuing Morton's note of cautious deference in *my most noble lord* (187).

only but: Only.

the corpse: The bodies of men (whose souls (or hearts) were not in what they did); *corpse* could be either singular or plural.

193 *to fight*: As his soldiers.

197 *potions*: Medicine, poison.

201 *Turns insurrection to religion*: Makes rebellion a sacred duty. In the sixteenth and seventeenth centuries rebellion was not merely a civil offence; an attack on the sovereign was an attack on God's deputy on earth. It was, therefore, particularly serious if rebellion was supported by the religious, for it gave a seeming sanctity to what otherwise was regarded as sacrilegious. See second note to I.2.34.

202 *Supposed*: Believed to be. The word does not imply doubt of the Archbishop's sincerity.

204 *enlarge*: Enhance.

205 *Pomfret*: The castle where Richard II was murdered.

206 *Derives from heaven his quarrel and his cause*: Claims
   divine approval for the arguments for his course of
   action.

209 *more and less*: All classes of people.

210 *I knew of this before*: Typical example of a character
   being told what he already knows for the audience's
   benefit, though Northumberland's next line gives a
   sort of reason for his forgetfulness.

214 *posts*: Couriers.
   make: Collect.

I.2

0 *Enter Sir John ... buckler*: In Q Sir John is said to
   enter *alone, with his page bearing his sword and buckler*;
   F has *Enter Falstaffe, and Page*; *alone* probably implies
   that Falstaff enters in advance of the Page, who
   follows at a respectful distance; it is used in a similar
   way in Q's opening direction to III.1. The *sword and
   buckler*, carried as if in formal procession, represent
   Falstaff ironically as the hero of Shrewsbury, where
   he 'killed' the dead Hotspur (see *Henry IV, Part I*,
   V.4.126). J. Dover Wilson proposed that Falstaff
   should hobble in with a stick, because of his sore toe
   (see 247), so that his entry is a ludicrous imitation
   of Northumberland's with his *nice crutch* (I.1.45).
   buckler: Shield.

1 *giant*: Ironic – the Page is very small.

2 *water*: Urine.

4 *owed*: Owned.

6 *gird*: Gibe, jeer.

7 *foolish-compounded*: Compounded of folly.

8 *intends*: Inclines, tends.

14 *whoreson*: Abominable, but sometimes, as here, used
   with humorous familiarity.
   mandrake: The Page, being small, is likened to the
   plant with a tap-root subdivided so that it was said
   to look like a man.

14–15 *thou art fitter to be worn in my cap*: The Page is so

small he might more appropriately be worn as a
brooch in a man's cap than follow in his footsteps.

16 *manned with*: Attended by.

   agate: Small person, like the tiny figures that were
   carved on agates used as jewellery or for seals.

19 *juvenal*: Young man (perhaps intended as a play on
   the sound of *jewel*).

20 *fledge*: Covered with down.

22 *stick*: Hesitate.

   a face-royal: The meaning is simply 'a first-class
   face', but the implication may be that it cannot be
   touched (by a razor), as a stag-royal might not be
   hunted by any but the king. There is also a play
   on 'royal', a coin, and the 'face' of that coin. This
   meaning is taken up at 24–5

23 *a hair*: (1) A hair of the beard; (2) one iota.

26 *writ*: Called himself.

27 *grace*: (1) Title (as 'Your grace'); (2) favour.

28 *Dommelton*: F spells this *Dombledon*; the meaning of
   the word in its various forms in different dialects
   is 'blockhead'.

29 *short cloak*: Probably a garment fashionable in Tudor
   times rather than in Henry IV's reign.

   slops: Wide knee-length breeches.

33 *the glutton*: Falstaff refers to the parable of Dives
   and Lazarus (Luke 16), which clearly made a deep
   impression on him, for he refers to it twice in *Part
   I* (III.3.31, IV.2.24). His awareness of the Scriptures
   is strong. He refers to the Prodigal Son at II.1.143–4
   in this play and at IV.2.33 of *Part I*; and in *The
   Merry Wives of Windsor*, IV.5–7, his chamber is
   said to be painted 'fresh and new' with the story of
   the Prodigal. In view of his behaviour, his regard
   for these parables is ironic, but in view of his association with the morality tradition, the relationship
   is appropriate.

34 *his tongue be hotter*: Dives, when in hell, begged
   Lazarus to dip the tip of his finger in water and
   cool his tongue (Luke 16:24). Falstaff obviously

knows the details of the parable, not merely its
general outline.

Achitophel: Achitophel sided with Absalom in his
conspiracy against David, but his advice was rejected
in favour of Hushai's and he hanged himself (2
Samuel 16:20–17:22). The story was well known in
the sixteenth century. Achitophel is dramatized briefly
in George Peele's play *The Love of King David and
Fair Bethsabe* (printed in 1599), but he plays a large
part in the Latin drama *Absalom* written by Thomas
Watson some fifty or sixty years before Peele's play.
Watson's dramatization was probably unknown to
Shakespeare, but it well represents Tudor attitudes
as propounded by the preachers of the time, with
which he would have been familiar. Achitophel is
described as a perfidious adviser to David, but his
dilemma is well dramatized and much is made of
his anguish when rejected. There is not only dramatic
irony in Falstaff's mentioning Achitophel, whose
rejection and broken heart anticipate his own; the
biblical account indicates that the peculiar wickedness
of Achitophel's treachery was that 'the counsel of
Achitophel which he counselled in those days was
as a man had asked counsel at the oracle of God:
even so was all the counsel of Achitophel, both with
David and with Absalom' (16:23). Support for rebellion from men of God was as heinous in David's
time as in the Tudor period (see note to I.1.201).

35 *yea-forsooth knave*: A tradesman who could manage
no more than the mildest of oaths in making his
protestations.

bear ... in hand: Encourage with false expectations.

36 *stand upon*: Insist on.

36–7 *smoothy-pates*: Puritan tradesmen (the same who
were given to mild oaths) cropped their hair short
in a style later associated with the Roundheads.
Many editors choose the F reading *smooth-pates*, but
Q's version seems more appropriately to express
Falstaff's contempt.

37 *high shoes*: Built-up shoes (appropriate for upstarts).

37-8 *bunches of keys*: Symbols of (false) importance.

38 *is through*: Has agreed.

39 *taking up*: Agreement, bargain.

40 *had as lief*: Would as willingly.

   ratsbane: Poison.

41 *looked*: Expected.

   'a: He.

43 *security*: Security (of mind) usually meant 'false security', 'complacency', with an element of culpable negligence, especially in religious matters.

44 *horn of abundance*: (1) Cornucopia (in his trading); (2) cuckold's horn (citizens' wives were said to be particularly unfaithful).

45 *lightness*: Infidelity.

45-7 *yet cannot he see ... him*: The tradesman cannot see his wife's infidelity either by the light of his own cuckold's horn or by his wife's *lightness* – and his security is false.

46 *lanthorn*: The old form of 'lantern', preserved here for the sake of the pun.

48 *in Smithfield*: 'In' was commonly used for 'into' in the sixteenth century (and later). F and many editors print *into*. Live animals were sold at Smithfield (originally a 'smooth field') from well before the Tudor period until 1855. The horses sold there had a poor reputation.

50 *Paul's*: The nave of St Paul's Cathedral was used as a place where servants might find new masters.

51 *An*: If.

51-2 *a wife in the stews*: Reference to a wife now completes a trio found in a popular saying of the time that a man must not choose a wife in Westminster, a horse in Smithfield or a servant in Paul's, 'lest he choose a quean, a jade or a knave'. A 'quean' is a prostitute; hence Falstaff's reference to the *stews* (brothels).

52 *Lord Chief Justice*: Sir William Gascoigne, appointed Lord Chief Justice in 1401, was a man of independence. He refused to sentence the Archbishop of

York to death, and, traditionally at least, he was
responsible for committing Prince Hal to the King's
Bench prison, though this distinction has been claimed
for two other judges (one being Gascoigne's successor,
Sir William Hankford). Gascoigne's reappointment
by Hal (V.2) is contrary to fact. He was summoned
to the first parliament of Henry V's reign but he either
was dismissed, resigned or died before that parliament met on 15 May 1413; Hankford was appointed
from 29 March of that year, according to the patent
of his office, though 1414 is given by one authority.
Three dates have been put forward for Gascoigne's
death, 1412, 1413 and 1419. There was nothing remarkable in a Lord Chief Justice's being concerned with
such a relatively trivial matter as that dramatized
here. Alongside Gascoigne, Shakespeare (and some
members of his first audience) may also have thought
of the then current Lord Chief Justice, Sir John
Popham, who was reputed to have enjoyed a riotous
youth – like Prince Hal – before settling down to
the studies which led in due course to high office.

52 *Servant*: Tipstaff.

54 *for striking him*: The first known reference to this
incident is no earlier than Sir Thomas Elyot's *The
Book Named the Governor* (1531). It is also dramatized
in *The Famous Victories of Henry V*, which was
performed a few years before *Henry IV, Part II*. In
Elyot's account Hal only threatens the Lord Chief
Justice, but in the anonymous play there is a stage
direction, '*He giveth him a box on the ear*'.

55 *close*: Concealed.

58 *in question*: Examined judicially.

72–100 *What! A young knave ... of your health*: Shakespeare
employs here the comic device (still in use) where
a comedian bullies a weak character and then is
obsequious to a stronger one.

72–3 *Is ... wars*: The singular form of the verb with a
plural subject was acceptable in Elizabethan grammar.

80 *Setting my knighthood and my soldiership aside*: Knight-

hood was, properly, too honourable an estate to admit
of lying, and the soldier was supposed to be too
brave to descend to deceitfulness. Thus theoretically
Falstaff is doubly protected against accusations of
lying, but for the sake of the point he will doff both
these honours.

81 *in my throat*: Outrageously.

87 *grows to*: Is integral to.

89 *hunt counter*: Follow the wrong scent, are completely
mistaken. There is a pun on 'Counter' as the name
of a debtors' prison, or, more generally, a petty
legal officer who arrested people for debt and
served writs.

97 *age*: This is F's reading; Q has *an ague*, which is
possible, since it relates to the Lord Chief Justice's
sickness (95), but it may be a compositor's error.
To say an old man had 'yet some smack of youth'
would suggest that, despite his years, he had retained
a spirit of youthfulness, and could be a compliment.
Falstaff's suggestion that the Lord Chief Justice has
some smack of age implies that he is prematurely
old; and this is reiterated in the following phrase –
that the Lord Chief Justice has *some relish ... of
time*. Falstaff is superficially solicitous for the health
of the Lord Chief Justice, but simultaneously continues to insult him by harping on the degree to
which he has aged. It is just possible that a particularly weak pun is intended on *age*/'ague'; cf.
gravity/*gravy* (163–4).

98 *saltness*: This could mean youthfulness or maturity
and is appropriately ambiguous, Falstaff meaning one
thing but being able, if challenged, to claim he intends
the opposite.

108 *apoplexy*: Paralysis. Falstaff's account of the symp-
toms in the lines that follow is correct. Henry IV
did suffer from *apoplexy* but not as early as this; see
headnote to IV.4.

114 *What*: For what, why.

116, 118 *it ... his*: Its ... its. These forms of neuter possessive pronoun were being replaced by 'its' in Shakespeare's lifetime. In F 'its' appears ten times, on eight occasions in very late plays.

116 *original*: Origins.

   grief: Anxiety.

118 *Galen*: Greek physician of the second century AD, still highly regarded in the seventeenth century. Falstaff may be showing off, but, as with the Bible (see note to 33), his knowledge is more than merely superficial.

121 *FALSTAFF*: Q's speech-prefix here is *Old.*, which abbreviates Falstaff's original name, Oldcastle. See An Account of the Text, p. 120.

124 *punish you by the heels*: Put you in the stocks (or in prison).

129 *in respect of poverty*: Because he is too poor to pay a fine.

131 *make some dram of a scruple*: Feel a particle of doubt. *dram* and *scruple* are quantities for measuring potions (128).

134 *for your life*: Of a capital nature (that is, in which his life might be forfeit).

135–6 *advised ... land-service*: This is a cunning quibble; *land-service* was military service, and whilst engaged in the campaign culminating at Shrewsbury Falstaff was immune from arrest. But *land-service* might well refer to the service he had attempted at Gad's Hill – robbery – and he was *advised* not to risk facing a charge on that account.

138 *infamy*: Deliberately misunderstood by Falstaff, who treats it as if it were a fabric.

147 *misled*: This may be simply a repetition of *misled* at 145, but (esp. with the puzzling sentence that follows – see next note) it could be the dialect form 'mizzled', meaning 'confused' or 'mystified'. This word was in use in Shakespeare's day and could be spelt 'misled'.

147–8 *I am ... my dog*: Dr Johnson, in his edition of Shakespeare, bluntly commented, 'I do not understand this joke', and no one since has offered a satisfactory interpretation. It is possible that a topical

character is referred to. The Prince returns the
compliment at II.2.100–101: *I do allow this wen to be
as familiar with me as my dog.*

151 *exploit on Gad's Hill*: See *Henry IV, Part I*, II.2.

152 *th'unquiet time*: A phrase used by the historians Hall
and Holinshed in the titles of their accounts of the
reign of Henry IV.

152–3 *your quiet o'erposting that action*: Having your offence
quietly passed over.

157–9 *To wake ... burnt out*: Falstaff responds to the Lord
Chief Justice's proverb (a version of 'let sleeping
dogs lie') by comparing it with a tag meaning 'to
have one's suspicions aroused'. The comparison
seems a little forced, but Falstaff may be extending
the expression to mean 'to sense trouble': to arouse
a sleeping dog, as to have one's suspicions aroused,
promises trouble. The Lord Chief Justice's response
seems both a rebuke and a warning: the candle of
Falstaff's life is more than half over, and what has
been used up (which would hardly have the Lord
Chief Justice's approval) was the *better part*; what
is to come can surely only bring Falstaff more trouble.
The relationship of these expressions is difficult to
pin down precisely, but the general sense seems clear.

160 *wassail candle*: Large candle used at feasts and
designed to last the whole night.
tallow: Made from animal fat, which Falstaff presumably considers more appropriate for him than
wax, which is secreted by bees.

161 *wax, my growth*: Punning on *wax* meaning 'to grow'.
approve: Prove.

163, 164 *gravity ... gravy*: If the two first syllables are
pronounced alike (as there is some evidence they were
in Shakespeare's time) a kind of pun is obtained.
The humour is not original to Shakespeare; John
Lyly, in his play *Eudymion* (published 1591), puns
on 'grave' and 'gravity'.

164 *of gravy*: Loosely, of being bathed in sweat.

166 *ill angel*: Each man and woman was said to be

attended by a good and an evil angel, and these
were dramatized in earlier drama, one warning and
one tempting. Shakespeare burlesques their advice
in Launcelot's monologue in *The Merchant of Venice*,
II.2.1–28. Here Falstaff's association with the Morali-
ties is lightly touched on. See also II.4.330.

167 *your ill angel is light*: An angel was a coin worth
a third of £1; when clipped it was said to be *light*
(of some of its metal). There may be an allusion
to Satan's power to transform himself into 'an angel
of light' (2 Corinthians 11:14); if so Shakespeare
may have expected his audience to remember the
adjacent verses, which speak of false apostles and
deceitful workers (13) and of those 'whose end shall
be according to their works' (15), the fate in store
for Falstaff.

168 *take*: Accept.

170 *go*: (1) Walk; (2) pass as good money.
cannot tell: (1) Don't know; (2) cannot count (as
good money).

170–71 *these costermongers' times*: A costermonger was originally a man who sold apples ('costards') from a
barrow. The costermonger lived by his wits (so
Falstaff's contempt may rebound on him), but the
implication of the phrase is that life is reduced to
the lowest kind of buying and selling.

171–2 *bearherd*: The man who looked after bears used for
bear-dancing or bear-baiting was poorly regarded.
The spelling in Q, *Berod*, probably indicates the
pronunciation.

172 *pregnancy*: Quick-wittedness.

172–3 *tapster ... reckonings*: The intellectual ability of a
tapster is to be found only in his capacity to deliver
a bill for what has been drunk.

173–4 *appertinent*: Belonging.

177 *livers*: The liver was thought to be the seat of violent
passions.
galls: Bile.

178 *in the vaward of our youth*: Falstaff repeats his claim

to be young, but presumably those in the forefront or vanguard (*vaward*) of youth are the most advanced in years and so approaching middle age.

179 *wags too*: (1) Waggish as well as youthful; (2) waggish just as are young people.

182 *characters*: (1) Characteristics; (2) letters.

moist: Watery.

182–3 *a dry hand*: Said to be a sign of old age.

183 *a decreasing leg*: Shakespeare may be using *decreasing* to mean 'weakening' or 'shrinking' (in the hams), but he may be suggesting that, as Falstaff's girth increases, so his legs seem to diminish in length and to be less fitted to support his weight.

185 *single*: Feeble.

188–9 *I was born ... afternoon*: Falstaff probably means he was born mature, but as a nineteenth-century editor (R. G. White) suggested, it might also be implied that Falstaff, as a dramatic creation, was born at the time of the theatre performance (which, in the public theatres of Shakespeare's day, was in the afternoon).

189 *something a*: A somewhat.

190 *hallooing*: Shouting (when following hounds or on the battlefield).

191 *singing of anthems*: In *Part I*, II.4.128–9, Falstaff wishes he were a weaver so that he might sing at his work, as weavers (many of whom were puritans) were noted for doing: 'I could sing psalms – or anything.' See also note to 33.

193 *caper with me*: Challenge me to a dancing contest.

193–4 *a thousand marks*: £666. The mark was the value of two-thirds of £1.

194–5 *have at him*: I'll be at him.

197 *sensible*: (1) Reasonable; (2) capable of feeling the pain of the blow.

checked: Rebuked.

198 *marry*: A corruption of 'Mary' (the Virgin), commonly used as a mild oath.

198–9 *ashes ... sack*: This modification of the biblical

mourning to that of much less deep regret (based on the proverbial 'to mourn in sack and claret') is an example of the turn of wit that seemed second nature to Falstaff in *Part I* but is much less apparent in this play.

old sack: The precise nature of the wine Falstaff drank is not known; *sack* may have been a general term for sweet white wine of the sherry and Canary varieties. Old sack was preferred to new.

209 *look you*: Take care to.

212–3 *I brandish anything but a bottle*: In *Part I*, V.3.55, Hal, much to his annoyance, finds sack instead of a pistol in Falstaff's holster.

213 *spit white*: It is not clear what is meant here. Editors since the eighteenth century have attempted to pin the meaning down by reference to a variety of Tudor sources. The most likely meaning is probably 'to spit clean', that is, healthily. As one Tudor authority put it, 'white spittle, not knotty, signifieth health'.

221–2 *perpetual motion*: The idea of perpetual motion, although not new, attracted some attention in Elizabeth's reign.

228 *crosses*: Yet another money pun: (1) coins with a cross on one side; (2) afflictions.

230 *fillip*: Strike smartly.

three-man beetle: Ram or sledgehammer so large that three men are needed to use it.

233 *pinches*: Torments.

233–4 *both the degrees prevent my curses*: Both age and youth have their own curses which anticipate mine.

236 *What ... purse*: Pages carried the master's purse and made payments on his behalf (as at II.4.368).

237 *groats*: Fourpenny pieces.

241 *this to the Prince*: The letter that Bardolph delivers at II.2.94.

242–3 *Ursula, whom I have weekly sworn to marry*: At II.1.84–90 Mistress Quickly asserts that Falstaff once swore to marry her. Whether she is Ursula or whether

Falstaff has been swearing to marry another is not
clear. In *Henry V* Mistress Quickly is given the first
name Nell.

248 *halt*: Limp.

colour: Pretext.

250–51 *commodity*: Self-interest.

I.3

Q here includes an entry for Fauconbridge, but there
is no part for him to play and he does not appear
in F. Holinshed mentions him as one of the rebels,
and it is presumably from that source that Shakespeare
took the name. See also headnote to IV.4 and An
Account of the Text, p. 120. The other rebels mentioned by Holinshed all enter here.

0 *Mowbray*: Son of the Mowbray banished for life in
Richard II.

Hastings: Historically not a lord but a knight, Sir
Ralph Hastings.

1 *Thus have you heard* . . . : The Archbishop's first line,
like Falstaff's in I.2 and the Hostess's in II.1, refers
to an action or conversation already completed. This
simple dramatic device enables the new scenes to
move with pace from the beginning and it helps to
avoid any slackening of momentum as the various
actions of the play are introduced. It is now necessary, of course, for Shakespeare to indicate what
is proposed, and so the Archbishop asks for his
colleagues' reactions to the plan.

cause: Matter in dispute.

4 *Lord Marshal*: Only a courtesy title; the Mowbrays
claimed to be Earl Marshals of England, but the
office had been given to Westmorland.

5 *allow*: Grant.

7 *in*: Within.

9, 77 *puissance*: Strength.

10 *file*: Roll.

11 *men of choice*: Picked men.

12 *supplies*: Reinforcements.

largely: Abundantly.

26 *cause*: Matter of concern. This is the reading in Q;
   F prints *case*. 'Cause' with this meaning occurs elsewhere in Shakespeare's works.

27 *who*: Hotspur.
   lined: Fortified.

28 *air and promise*: F has *on* for *and*, which makes easy
   sense. But Q's reading has been described as a 'particularly forceful hendiadys' (a complex idea expressed
   by two words joined by 'and'). It is possible that F's
   reading represents a weakening by someone copying
   Shakespeare's text without fully understanding it.
   The *air* on which Hotspur had to live was, of course,
   his father's *promise* to send reinforcements (in *Henry
   IV, Part I*).

29 *project*: Anticipation.

33 *winking*: Shutting his eyes (to the facts).

36–55 *Yes ... or else*: Omitted from Q, perhaps because
   of the complexity of the opening lines (36–9) and
   because the lengthy version of the parable is covered
   adequately, so far as the play's action is concerned,
   by 58–62.

36–9 *Yes ... th'appearing buds*: This difficult passage has
   often been emended. This edition follows F except
   that a comma has been added after *Indeed*; a comma
   is used instead of a colon after *action*; a dash is used
   in place of a colon after *hope*; and a comma is
   omitted after *spring*. The passage can be interpreted:
   'Yes, *if* the present occasion for war, the action now
   imminent – the cause already afoot – *does* live so
   in hope (just as do the buds which appear in an
   early spring).'

41–62 *When ... tyranny*: A lengthy version of the parable
   of the builder, Luke 14:28–30: 'For which of you,
   disposed to build a tower, sitteth not down before
   and counteth the cost, whether he have sufficient to
   perform it? Lest at any time after he hath laid the
   foundation and is not able to perform it, all that
   behold it begin to mock him, saying, "This man began
   to build, and was not able to make an end."'

42 *model*: Architectural plan.

43 *figure*: Design.

44 *rate*: Calculate.

45 *ability*: To pay.

47 *offices*: Rooms.

52 *Consent*: Agree.

55 *his opposite*: Its contrary, that is, all that stands against the success of our building plan, and, by implication, our political plot.

60 *his part-created cost*: The half-built object of his expenditure.

62 *waste*: Wasteland (with the implication of the wasteful use of effort and resources).

65 *The utmost man of expectation*: Every man that we could possibly expect.

70 *as the times do brawl*: In these discordant times.

74 *sound*: Ring (as does an empty metal vessel).

76 *several*: Various.

81 *is it like should*: Is likely to. At I.1.134–5 it was stated in Lord Bardolph's presence that the forces were led by Lancaster and Westmorland.

82 *Duke of Lancaster*: This title actually belonged to Prince Henry. Prince John was born at Lancaster and is called John of Lancaster by Holinshed. See also note to IV.1.129.

84 *substituted*: Delegated.

85 *notice*: Information.

89–90 *An habitation ... heart*: An echo of Luke 6:49: 'But he that heareth and doeth it not is like a man that without foundation built an house upon the earth; against which the flood did beat vehemently, and it fell immediately.'

91 *fond*: Foolish.
   many: Multitude.

94 *trimmed*: Dressed, tricked out.

99 *now thou wouldst eat thy dead vomit up*: The dog that returns to its vomit was proverbial in Shakespeare's day and is found in the Old and New Testaments (Proverbs 26:11 and 2 Peter 2:22, the latter refer-

ring to the expression as 'a true proverb').

100 *What trust is in these times*: Shakespeare has just
had Falstaff inveigh against *these costermongers' times*
(I.2.170–71). Northumberland, by supporting Bolingbroke against Richard, played a large part in creating
these times. The rebels, like Falstaff, must stand partly
self-convicted by their condemnation of others.

103–5 *Thou . . . Bolingbroke*: Recalling York's description of
the entry into London of Richard and Bolingbroke,
one disgraced, one triumphant (*Richard II*, V.2.1–40;
the throwing of dust occurs at 6).

108 *seems*: The singular form for the plural; see note to
I.2.72–3.

109 *draw our numbers*: Assemble our army.

II.1

0 *the Hostess*: Mistress Quickly.

1, 6 *Master*: Fang and Snare would not be entitled to be
called *Master* (they are, respectively, a sergeant and
his yeoman), but the Hostess often elevates the rank
of those she addresses. At 67–8 the Lord Chief Justice
is called *your grace*, the form of address reserved
for royalty, dukes and archbishops, and Pistol is to
her a *Captain* (II.4.134).

1 *entered the action*: Begun the lawsuit (on the Hostess's
behalf).

5 *Sirrah*: It has been suggested that Fang should be
attended by a boy to whom *Sirrah* is addressed, but
it is at least as likely that, as sirrah could be used
for either sex, he is speaking to the Hostess, or else
that he is addressing Snare (and then notices his
seeming absence); as this line follows the Hostess's
questions about Snare, Fang might be calling him
up to display his lustiness to her.

7 *from behind them*: This is an editorial addition based
on the assumption that Snare follows so closely on
his master's heels that Fang does not see him – an
obvious opportunity for comic business. It has been
suggested that, since the company had an exceptionally thin actor for the part of the First Beadle

(see note to the opening stage direction of V.4), he
may also have played Snare. The seeming absence
of a thin Snare could easily be made visually comic.

13 *he stabbed me*: The Hostess, like so many characters
of this kind in the plays of the period (for example,
the vintner's wife, Mistress Mulligrub, in John Marston's *The Dutch Courtesan*, published 1605), speaks
a double language. Her simple protestations are full
of words that need no stretch of imagination to take
on sexual meanings: *stabbed*, *weapon*, *foin*, *thrust*,
undone, and so on.

16 *foin*: Technically, to thrust with a pointed weapon;
but see previous note.

21 *vice*: Q reads *view*, but that may be a misreading of
the manuscript caused by the printer's inclining
unwittingly to an easier meaning. F's *vice* means
'grip', appropriate for Fang.

23 *infinitive*: Infinite. The Hostess has a love of fine
words (for all her imprecision about their meanings
and forms); perhaps she picks them up from her
customers – that is the source of Mistress Mulligrub's
elevated vocabulary (*The Dutch Courtesan*, III.4.8–10).

23 *upon my score*: In my accounts ('on the slate').

25 *continuantly*: Immediately (for 'incontinently'). Q
prints *continually*: but, as A. R. Humphreys puts it,
'F's fine word is surely Shakespeare's.' Q's reading
is probably a mistaken attempt to 'correct' the
Hostess's grandiose error; scribes and compositors,
because they are trained to produce a correct text,
are naturally reluctant to copy a word they assume
to be accidentally wrong.

25–6 *Pie Corner – saving your manhoods*: Pie Corner, the
south-western corner of Smithfield, where it is joined
by Giltspur Street, was noted for its cook-shops, at
which pigs were dressed during Bartholomew fair. It
has been suggested that the Hostess's apology (*saving
your manhoods*) is for mentioning a place redolent of
killing and cooking pigs. But would Fang and Snare be
so sensitive? It may be that Pie Corner sold other flesh

than that of the pig. In Ben Jonson's play *Bartholomew
Fair* (1614), which shows respectable women being
corrupted in the fair and becoming 'mistresses o' the
game', a distinction is drawn between eating pig 'I'the
heart o'the fair; not at Pie Corner' (I.5.152). This may
simply refer to the greater attractions of the fair itself,
but there might also be an allusion to other noted attributes of Pie Corner. *Wit's Recreations* (1640) uses the
phrase 'cornered π' in a sense that seems clearly sexual,
with the Greek letter ('pi') as a visual symbol. See also
notes to 26 and 68.

26 *buy a saddle*: There were many saddlers near
Smithfield. But as the Hostess is inclined to sexual
innuendo *saddle* may also imply that which is
mounted – a prostitute.
indited: For 'invited'.

27 *Lubber's*: For 'Libbard's', that is, 'Leopard's'.
Lumbert: Lombard.

28 *exion*: For 'action'.

29 *case*: Again there is a sexual meaning (the female
genitals), illustrated by the discussion of the 'geni-
tive' case in *The Merry Wives of Windsor*, IV.1.53–65;
the example given, '*horum, harum, horum*', is taken
to refer to 'whore' by Mistress Quickly, who cries
'Vengeance of Jenny's case'.

31 *one*: Reckoning.

36 *Bardolph*: A Bardolph appears in a list of recusants
which also includes Shakespeare's father; and the
names Bardolph and Pistol appear in muster-rolls of
artillerymen of 1435. See also headnote to I.1.

37 *malmsey-nose*: Malmsey was a sweet red wine, and
the colour has spread to Bardolph's nose.

39–40 *do me . . . your offices*: The *me* is an 'ethic dative',
implying 'for me', as in *Cut me* (44). Here there is
also a sexual pun in *do me*.

41 *whose mare's dead*: What's the fuss? (cf. Prince Henry
at IV.5.10–11).

45 *quean*: Prostitute.
channel: Gutter.

48, 50 *honeysuckle . . . honeyseed*: For 'homicidal' and 'homicide'.

49 *God's officers and the King's*: The officers execute the law on behalf of the King's courts, and, as the King is God's deputy, the officers are, indirectly, *God's officers*.

50 *queller*: Destroyer.

53 *A rescue*: This is, curiously, an ambiguous expression, its meaning depending upon who shouts it. Here it means that a rescue is being attempted and help is needed by the officers of the law; but it was also the cry of those who sought to rescue someone being arrested.

54 *bring a rescue*: A recognized idiom, not the Hostess's mistake.

wot: Wilt (dialectal).

55 *ta*: Thou (dialectal).

56 *hempseed*: The Hostess continues her variations on 'homicide', but this one is appropriate, since *hemp*, used to make rope, was already associated with hanging (for instance in the word 'hempstring' for someone who deserved hanging).

57 *rampallian*: Ruffian.

57–8 *fustilarian*: A nonce word (the Page seems to have caught the Hostess's word disease). It may be derived from 'fusty', or 'fustian' (that is, someone wearing such fabric); it is associated tentatively in the *OED* with 'fustilugs', a fat, frowzy woman.

58 *I'll tickle your catastrophe*: A catchphrase of the period.

62 *stand to*: Stand by.

63 *What*: Why.

67–8 *your grace*: See note to 1, 6 above.

68 *Eastcheap*: Like Pie Corner (see note to 25–6), Eastcheap was a centre for cookshops and butchers, and it is described by Stow in his *Survey of London* (1598) as 'a flesh market'. This has been taken as an appropriate setting for the gluttonous Falstaff, but as a market of flesh in the sexual sense (see

note to II.4.339) it would be appropriate for the Hostess.

74–5 *ride thee a nights like the mare*: Haunt your sleep with nightmares.

76 *ride the mare*: Sexual, of course, but it links with Falstaff's greeting at 41 (*whose mare's dead?*) and the Hostess's complaint at 31–2 that she has *borne, and borne, and borne*.

77 *vantage of ground to get up*: Superior position to get astride the mare (a military expression (cf. II.3.53), with a sexual innuendo here).

79 *temper*: Disposition.

84–5 *parcel-gilt*: Partially gilded (usually on the inner surface).

85 *Dolphin chamber*: Rooms in public houses were each given names to distinguish them.

86 *sea-coal*: Mineral coal, brought by sea from Newcastle to London, as distinct from charcoal.

87 *Wheeson*: Whitsun (dialectal).

88 *liking his father*: This is Q's reading; F has *lik'ning him*. The Q compositor might have misread 'lik'ning' in his copy as 'liking', but as 'like' was an accepted form of 'liken' it might simply represent his 'preferred spelling' (what he took to be the proper form of the word). On the other hand the scribe who prepared the manuscript for F might have written 'lik'ning' as *his* preferred spelling. There is no sure explanation for the change from *his father* to 'him'. Possibly whoever prepared the F manuscript thought it was the Prince who was being compared to the *singing-man*; that might suggest that any allusion to a pretender (see next note) was lost on him.

singing-man of Windsor: Singing-men were professional musicians of cathedrals and royal and university chapels; in general they were well regarded, though about this time they were subject to some criticism, by puritans and others, as fulfilling no useful role and being given to drink. But that would not be ground for the Prince's objection to Falstaff's

comparison. It may be that a particular singing-man
was or had been a pretender to the throne, and in
view of the way Henry IV *came by the crown* this
would be a serious and very dangerous allusion. A
tenuous link has been suggested with John Magdalen,
a priest who was involved in the plot against Henry
IV by 'The grand conspirator Abbot of Westminster',
which Shakespeare touches on at the end of *Richard
II* (V.6.21–3).

91   *Keech*: Rolled-up animal fat.

92   *gossip*: Neighbour (as a familiar term of address).

93   *mess*: Small amount.

95   *green*: Unhealed.

97   *familiarity*: For 'familiar'.

98   *madam*: A knight's wife was entitled to be called
'madam'.

99–100   *didst ... thirty shillings*: There is a touching sim-
plicity as well as something comic in the Hostess's
running on from the avowal of love to the request
for money.

100   *book oath*: Oath taken on the Bible.

103   *her eldest son is like you*: This is a skilful piece of
impertinence, implying not only that the Hostess is
unreliable but that the Lord Chief Justice may have
erred in times past (see note to I.2.52). But Falstaff's
attempt to direct attention away from his own villainy
fails.

104   *in good case*: Well off (but see note to 29).

105   *distracted her*: Driven her mad.
       for: As for.

120   *current*: Genuine (as 'current coin', reflecting *sterling
money*).

121   *sneap*: Rebuke.

123   *curtsy*: Bow (used for either sex).

128–9   *You speak ... wrong*: See note to V.3.134–6.

128   *having power*: Being empowered.

129   *in the effect of your reputation*: In accord with that
reputation which you claim is yours.

139   *By this heavenly ground*: The Hostess confuses the

expressions 'by heaven' and 'by this ground', producing an effective paradox.

140 *fain*: Content.

142 *Glasses*: Glasses were replacing metal drinking cups
at this time; by pawning her *plate* the Hostess can
become fashionable.

the only: The best, the only acceptable.

drinking: The action is made to represent the vessel
itself – a usage of this word not recorded in *OED*.
It is possible that Shakespeare had in mind the Tudor
meaning of a 'drinking' as a convivial revel; but the
precise meaning is strained.

143 *drollery*: Comic picture, caricature.

143–4 *the story ... waterwork*: That is, paintings on cloth
of two of the most popular subjects of the time, in
watercolour or distemper, imitative of tapestry. There
were complaints throughout the sixteenth century of
such work from Germany and the Netherlands (hence
the reference to a *German hunting* scene), depriving
Englishmen of work.

145 *worth ... bed-hangers*: Falstaff implies that such
tapestries as the Hostess owns are fit only for bed-
hangings (of a four-poster).

147 *humours*: Moods.

148 *wash thy face*: Presumably the Hostess has been
crying.

draw: Withdraw.

152 *nobles*: Gold coins.

160 *Will I live*: As sure as I live!

161 *Hook on*: Follow, stick close.

162 *Doll Tearsheet*: *Doll* was commonly used as a name
for a prostitute. Coleridge suggested that the surname
should be 'Tearstreet', which would fit not only her
occupation but the line *This Doll Tearsheet should be
some road* (11.2.160). But *Tearsheet* is not inappropriate; in John Fletcher's *Valentinian* (c. 1614), III.1,
a whore is defined as 'a kind of kicker out of sheets'.

168 *Basingstoke*: There is no reference in Holinshed or
Hall to Henry's staying at Basingstoke at this time.

Q reads *Billingsgate*, presumably the compositor's mistake.

177 *presently*: Immediately.

181–2 *shall I ... dinner*: Falstaff's invitation is singularly inappropriate. It is as if he were, rather feebly, trying to gain the others' attention by any means in order to become the centre of the action.

186 *take ... up*: Recruit.

192 *grace*: The meaning seems to be between 'propriety' and 'ornament' (usages common by Shakespeare's time); the word may here have the specific sense 'procedure' (which Falstaff goes on to illustrate: *tap for tap ...*), though the *OED*'s earliest example of this is from 1607.

193 *lighten*: Enlighten.

II.2

Prince Henry as dramatized at his first appearance in *Henry IV, Part II* is in sharp contrast to the devil-may-care Hal of the tavern scenes of *Part I* and the bold and successful soldier to which he had matured at the end of the earlier play. There is a strong feeling of ennui and self-disgust. It is with some force that he denies that he is *as far in the devil's book* as Poins and Falstaff (42–3). In the jape on Falstaff that he devises with Poins (163–70) Shakespeare dramatizes the Prince's growing weariness with his tavern life. The trick planned here is no more imaginative than his joke on Francis in *Part I* (II.4), and when it is carried out (II.4) he shows little of the enthusiasm with which he played the earlier game.

In Q an entry is also given here for Sir John Russell (and an unnamed '*other*'). This was the name originally used for Peto in *Part I* (see An Account of the Text of that play, pp. 113–14, and headnote to I.1 above). Only Prince Henry and Poins are required, and the two extra characters, given in F as Bardolph and the Page, are not needed until line 65. Presumably Shakespeare had the character Bardolph in mind, though he used one of the three

names originally intended for *Part I* (Oldcastle for
Falstaff, Harvey for Bardolph and Russell for Peto).

0 *Prince Henry*: In accord with the rather different role
he performs in this play, he is referred to here as
Prince Henry instead of Prince Hal, which was used
in *Part I*.

Poins: There is no historic source for Poins, though
there was a Poyntz family in Gloucestershire, the
county where Falstaff's recruiting scene is set. F
frequently uses the spelling *Pointz*, but no connection
with the family has been proved.

3 *attached*: Laid hold of.

4–5 *discolours the complexion of my greatness*: (1) Makes
me pale (with *weariness*); (2) tarnishes my princely
reputation.

6 *show*: Look, appear.
small beer: Beer thinned with water (served to
children). Prince Henry's point is not that it is
undignified for him to drink such beer but that what
he enjoys is inferior in quality. His tone could
be mildly ironic, but the dominant mood is one of
self-disgust.

7 *loosely studied*: Negligent in what should concern
him.

11 *creature*: Food (after 1 Timothy 4:4: 'every creature
of God is good, and nothing to be refused if it be
received with thanksgiving').

12–13 *What ... thy name*: That the new-made man soon
forgets the names of his former associates was a
common theme in the drama of the day. The Prince
says it is shameful in him to remember Poins's name,
but later in the play he will be ready to banish the
memory of the friends of his youth.

15, 16 *viz ... once*: Q reads *with* for viz., F has *ones*
for *once*. Both readings may have been caused by
mistaking the letters of the hand in which the copy
was written, but the reading of 'once' as 'ones' may
have been due to the word's being heard wrongly
by the compositor as he said the words he was setting

(aloud, or to himself), or it may be that the spellings were not automatically associated with the separate meanings now given to the two words. In this edition it has been assumed in both cases that the word of 'easier' meaning is erroneous.

16 *bear*: Bear in mind.

17 *for superfluity*: As a change of wear.

19–20 *it is ... racket there*: If Poins has a shirt to his back he will be found playing tennis, *racket* meaning (1) the tennis-racket; (2) an uproar.

21–2 *low countries ... holland*: As elsewhere in Shakespeare, *low countries* means the sexual parts of the body, and, by extension, brothels. *shift* means (1) scheme; (2) shirt; (3) change of clothing. *holland* means the country of that name in the Low Countries and a fine linen. Poins has been so busy begetting bastards (23–4) that his linen has been spoiled (by dirt or disease?), pawned (to pay for his low pleasures) or used for baby clothes (23–4), so that he lacks a superfluity of shirts and cannot now play tennis. However, so many puns and combinations of meaning are possible in these and the following lines that the permutations are almost endless.

22–6 *And God ... strengthened*: This passage was omitted from F, perhaps, it has been suggested, on the grounds of taste or because it was thought profane; but it might have been excised because it was too complex to make its point clearly enough.

22–3 *those that ... linen*: Those babies that cry from out of the remnants of your shirts (in which they are swaddled).

23–4 *inherit His kingdom*: Echoing Matthew 25:34, 'go to heaven'.

24–5 *not in the fault*: Not to be blamed (for being illegitimate).

25–6 *Whereupon ... strengthened*: The air of disillusionment about the conclusion of Prince Henry's description of the way the peoples of the earth are replenished accords with the mood of 5–6.

28 *idly*: Carelessly.

35 *stand the push*: Can stand up to.

44 *Let the end try the man*: Proverbial. This recalls Prince
   Henry's speech in *Part I*, I.2.193–215, describing how
   he will surprise men by his reformation.

47 *ostentation*: Show (with no suggestion of boastfulness).

54 *keeps the roadway*: Holds to the common way (of
   thinking).

56 *accites*: Induces (and possibly 'summons' – a legal
   usage; hence *your most worshipful*).

58 *lewd*: Debased (rather than 'licentious').

59 *engraffed*: Attached.

63 *second brother*: Younger brother (who, having no
   inheritance, must make his own way in the world).

63–4 *a proper fellow of my hands*: Good with my fists, a
   fine, bold fellow.

68 *transformed him ape*: The Page may be cheekily
   'aping' Bardolph by imitating his walk or gestures,
   but it would be in accord with the play (and particularly with the Prince's disgust for vanity and the
   emptiness of life) if the Page had been tricked out
   in a ridiculous livery. That which was Christian has
   been transformed to beastliness and, specifically, a
   devil (see second note to II.4.330).

71 *virtuous*: F reads *pernitious*, which at first sight
   seems more appropriate; but the unusualness of Q's
   virtuous provides a phrase that has individuality
   (which is to be expected of Shakespeare). It is also
   a subtle joke: virtue's colour was proverbially that
   of blushing – red – and red is the colour of Bardolph's
   drunken face.

74 *get a pottle-pot's maidenhead*: Knock off a two-quart
   pot of ale.

75 *e'en now*: Just now, a moment ago. For Q's idiomatic
   calls F has *call'd*.
   red lattice: Alehouses had red lattice windows.

82 *Althaea's dream*: Dr Johnson pointed out that
   Shakespeare was mistaken in his mythology, for he
   confounded Althaea's firebrand with Hecuba's. 'The

firebrand of Althaea was real: but Hecuba, when she was big with Paris, dreamed that she was delivered of a firebrand and that consumed the kingdom.' However, there are references in *Henry VI, Part II*, I.1.232, and *Troilus and Cressida*, II.2.110, which show that Shakespeare – if he wrote the line in the former, and by the time he wrote the latter – knew both dreams; so it may be the Page, not Shakespeare, who is mistaken.

88 *cankers*: This image appears many times in the literature of the period and especially in Shakespeare. A canker-worm was a caterpillar, or any insect larva which infected and destroyed from within the buds and fruit of plants. It was most frequently associated with the rose.

89 *sixpence to preserve thee*: The Elizabethan sixpenny piece was decorated with a cross, and that (not the coin itself) is to *preserve* the Page as a *Christian* (67).

94 *a letter*: See I.2.240.

96 *martlemas*: A corruption of 'Martin-mas', the Feast of St Martin (11 November), which was associated with plenty, especially of meat, since cattle that could not be fed through the winter were slaughtered about this time and their meat preserved. In *Part I*, I.2.156–7, Hal likens Falstaff to 'the latter spring' and 'All-hallown summer' (fine weather associated with All Saints' Day, 1 November). The implication of all three descriptions is the fullness of Falstaff's body, vigour and years. For his age he is in fine fettle (and a St Martin's summer, like an All-hallown summer, is fine weather late in the year), but this spell of 'late spring' immediately precedes winter and the death of nature.

100–101 *I do allow ... dog*: At I.2.148 Falstaff spoke of the Prince as his *dog*; here the roles are reversed.

100 *wen*: Tumour, swelling (hence, in Dr Johnson's words, 'a swollen excrescence of a man').

103 *John Falstaff, knight*: Q and F both give these words to Poins, but some editors, logically enough, transfer

them to the Prince. However, if actors' parts underlie F (see An Account of the Text, pp. 125–7), its reading would strongly support Q in giving the words to Poins; and if we suppose that he looks at the letter (as suggested in the stage direction supplied in this edition), the arrangement of Q and F can be maintained quite naturally.

108 *takes upon him not to conceive*: Pretends not to understand.

109 *borrower's*: Q and F both read *borowed*, and some sort of strained sense can be taken from this. But a misreading of manuscript, which would probably have lacked the apostrophe in *borrower's*, would easily explain the error. A man bent on borrowing is only too willing to ingratiate himself, doffing his cap, which 'Plays in the right hand, thus' (*Timon of Athens*, II.1.19).

112 *fetch it from Japhet*: Prove it by tracing their ancestry back to Japheth (Noah's third son, who was said to be the ancestor of all Europeans, Genesis 10).

112–14 *Sir John ... Prince of Wales*: Falstaff has inverted the correct order by naming the sender first instead of last. The whole letter is pompous and presumptuous.

115 *certificate*: Formal document, patent.

119–20 *I commend me ... leave thee*: This, presumably, is Falstaff's idea of Roman *brevity*.

122 *at idle times*: When you have nothing better to do.

124 *by yea and no*: A mild puritan oath; see also I.2.35.

139 *old boar*: At I.1.19 Falstaff is called *brawn*.

140 *frank*: Pigsty.

141 *the old place*: There was a Boar's Head tavern in Eastcheap in the early Tudor period. It is never named by Shakespeare, but the inference that it is the tavern at which Falstaff sups is drawn from 139–41.

143 *Ephesians*: Good drinking companions. The relevance of the name is pointed out here by the phrase *of the old church*; St Paul's Epistle to the Ephesians (5:18) warned them against excess, particularly of wine.

147 *pagan*: Prostitute.

151 *town bull*: Made available to all farmers of the district

160 *should be*: Is likely to be.

some road: As much frequented as a highway (from a proverbial saying).

161–2 *the way between Saint Albans and London*: A much used thoroughfare.

163–4 *bestow himself*: Behave.

167 *drawers*: Drawers of beer, tavern waiters.

168 *From a god to a bull*: Jupiter (*Jove*) transformed himself into a bull for love of Europa.

168–9 *heavy descension*: Great fall.

171 *weigh with*: Counterbalance.

II.3

1 *daughter*: Daughter-in-law.

2 *Give even way unto my rough affairs*: Protest no more about my harsh course of action.

3 *Put not you on the visage of the times*: Do not look as bleak as are the times.

11 *endeared*: Bound by affection.

18 *stuck*: A particular use of the word to express the fixity and lustre of a heavenly body in its sphere.

19 *the grey vault of heaven*: This may mean lowering grey skies (against which the sun stands out the more brightly); but *grey* was used for 'blue' (as in *Titus Andronicus*, II.2.1, 'The hunt is up, the morn is bright and grey').

21, 31 *glass*: Mirror, ideal example.

23 *He . . . his gait*: Any man who did not emulate Hotspur's style of walking might as well have had no legs.

24 *speaking thick*: The precise nature of Hotspur's defect (or peculiarity) of speech is not clear; *thick* could mean 'huskily' or 'rapidly' when applied to speech, and the second meaning may be implied if those who normally spoke *tardily* (26) affected Hotspur's manner. Rapid speech would be appropriate for an impetuous character such as Hotspur. The characteristic seems to be Shakespeare's invention.

29 *affections of delight*: Tastes for pleasure.

30 *humours of blood*: Moods.

31 *mark*: Guiding object.

34 *unseconded*: Unsupported.

36 *abide a field*: Face a battle.

38 *defensible*: Able to provide means of defence.

40 *precise and nice*: Precisely and meticulously. The words are almost synonymous here, and their rhyme suggests a caustic note in Lady Percy's voice.

45 *Monmouth*: Prince Henry.
Beshrew your heart: A mild expression of reproach.

52 *taste*: Trial.

53 *get ground*: Gain mastery.

57 *suffered*: Allowed.

59 *rain upon remembrance with mine eyes*: Water the plant of remembrance (rosemary) with the water of my tears.

61 *recordation*: Remembrance.

64 *still-stand*: Stand-still, point of balance.

67 *I will resolve for Scotland*: As usual, Shakespeare chooses to blacken Northumberland's character. Historically, although the outcome was no different, North-umberland left for Scotland only when he saw that the Archbishop had moved too hastily. He makes no further appearance in the play, but his death (at the battle of Bramham Moor in 1408, three years after Gaultree Forest) is indirectly mentioned at IV.4.94–101.

II.4

This scene makes an illuminating comparison with II.4 of *Henry IV, Part I*. Apart from the rejection, it is the only time that Prince Henry and Falstaff meet in this play, and the scene lacks the panache and exuberance that spill over in II.4 of *Part I*. The style of this scene is set by the mood of II.2 (see headnote), and, most graphically, by Falstaff's instruction (33) to empty the chamber-pot, given between two lines of a drinking song. John Masefield described this as the 'finest tavern scene ever written'; but it could be argued that II.1 and II.4 of *Part I* are even more effective, the first for its realism, the second as an epitome of good fellowship.

1–21 The distribution of speech-prefixes at the opening
of the scene differs in Q and F, and neither is
adequate. The first seven speeches are allocated in
Q to Francis, Drawer, Francis, Drawer, Francis (then
an entry is given after 18 for Will), Drawer, Francis,
then an exit is marked. This edition brings Will on
earlier, allocates to him lines 15–18 (in Q he has
nothing to say), and, since he is the last of the drawers
to enter, retains him until 33 to carry away the
jordan, a task given to Francis by many editors
(there is no direction at that point in Q or F). F's
opening stage direction is *Enter two Drawers*, and
Francis is not named; the speeches are allocated
alternately between First and Second Drawer; lines
13–14 are omitted; and there is no entry for Will.
See An Account of the Text, pp. 123–4.

1–2 *apple-johns*: Long-keeping apples, at their best when
shrivelled.

6 *putting off his hat*: Standing bare-headed in mock
respect.

10 *cover*: Lay the cloth (playing on *putting off* at 6).

11 *noise*: Band of musicians. In Marston's *The Dutch
Courtesan*, II.3.112–13, the tavern has available 'Mr
Creake's noise', referred to as fiddlers.

14 *straight*: Very soon.

19 *old utis*: High old time; *utis* may be a Warwickshire
or Worcestershire dialect word for 'noise', 'confusion', and it may also mean a period of festivity
– strictly, the 'octave', that is the eighth day, or
period of eight days, of a festival.

23 *temperality*: The Hostess's own compound of 'temper'
(temperament, physical condition) and 'quality'.
pulsidge: Not simply one pulse beating well, but all
the pulses of the body; again a word of the Hostess's
own.

26 *canaries*: A light, sweet wine from the Canary Islands.

27 *searching*: Discovering the weak spots of the body
(with the implication – exemplified by Doll's being

sick of a calm – that it disturbs the bowels).

perfumes: For 'perfuses'.

29 *hem*: A hiccough.

32, 34 *When Arthur ... king*: This is a garbled version of
the ballad *Sir Launcelot du Lake*, which was sung in
Shakespeare's time to the tune 'Chevy Chase' (see
The Songs).

33 *jordan*: Chamber-pot.

Exit Will: See note to 1–21.

36 *calm*: For 'qualm'.

37 *sect*: This stands for 'sex' and for Doll's profession.
The *sect* referred to is the Family of Love, a genuine
religious sect, whose name was much used by Elizabethan dramatists (such as Marston and Middleton)
for prostitutes.

39 *muddy rascal*: A *rascal* was a young deer, said to be
muddy when out of season and sluggish.

47 *Yes, Mary's joys*: Q reads *Yea ioy*. Shakespeare uses
'joy' elsewhere as a term of endearment; in *Antony
and Cleopatra*, I.5.57–8, it is used by Cleopatra of
herself, but with a slight suggestion that 'mistress'
is implied (Antony's 'remembrance lay | In Egypt
with his joy'). But as a term of affection, it makes
poor sense in the context of what is being said here
and in the tone of this exchange between Falstaff
and Doll. F's reading is *I marry* ('I' commonly represents 'Ay' in texts of this time), which makes sense
but does not explain how the Q reading came to be
as it is. The expression 'a maiden of joy' (equivalent to the French *'fille de joie'*) was used in 1585,
and that sense might be implied in some way in the
'joy' of the text, though not in the form in which
we have it. Editors have suspected that *Yea joy* may
misrepresent some profanity which F modified (as
it did systematically throughout the play; see An
Account of the Text, pp. 122–4); 'Iesu' has been
suggested for *joy*, though even then the sense runs
on awkwardly from Falstaff's preceding speech.

There is one possible clue. In this line Doll

mentions two gifts, implying that prostitutes do no
more than give men the diseases they receive from
them, and Falstaff picks on this and adds three more
jewels. From the eighteenth century editors have
marked Falstaff's additions in inverted commas as if
they came from a song. This is an imaginative suggestion, but the song has not been identified. But the
five precious jewels, connected with the word 'joy',
are intriguing. In the Middle Ages Mary, mother of
Jesus, was said to have five Joys, her son's
Annunciation, Nativity, Epiphany and Resurrection,
and her Assumption. There was, of course, another
Mary, Mary Magdalen, and it is possible that Doll
suggests that what is granted the prostitute is a
perversion of the Joys of Mary, mother of Jesus,
as those appropriate to a pre-penitent Mary Magdalen.
The *jewels* might all stand for venereal sores, as
ouches certainly could. The F reading could easily have
been produced by a scribe or compositor of the period
without any prompting, but it could equally have
been suggested by the appearance of 'Mary' in the
manuscript underlying F. This would certainly have
been modified in the process of reducing profanity,
and *I marry* would be a likely substitute.

Any emendation can only be a guess, but the
Q text as it stands is distinctly awkward in tone
and in the progression of speeches; and an accidental
omission of 'Mary's' seems possible, since the compositor who set Q was one of the two who omitted
words in some twenty-seven places in setting the
second Quarto of *Richard II*. The reading *Yea, Mary's
joys* offers one way of overcoming the problem posed
by Q and explaining the change made in F.

48 *ouches*: (1) Gems, brooches; (2) carbuncles, sores.
   See previous note.

48–51 *to serve ... chambers*: Military phrases, all used with
   sexual innuendo.

53 *DOLL Hang ... yourself*: F omits this line, probably
   in error.

conger: A term of abuse. The *conger* is the sea-eel; a sexual innuendo is implied.

54 *the old fashion*: Like the old days.

56 *as rheumatic as two dry toasts*: The temperament was thought to be controlled by the balance (or imbalance) of the four humours. By *rheumatic* the Hostess presumably means 'choleric'. Like *toast* Falstaff and Doll are hot and dry, and, as Dr Johnson put it, they 'cannot meet but they grate one another'.

57 *confirmities*: For 'infirmities'; the *con*- prefix suggests the coming together, the grating, of Doll and Falstaff.

57–8 *What the goodyear*: The derivation of this exclamation is far from clear. It is possibly a dialect form of 'What the devil!'; it may be derived from a Dutch expression meaning 'As I hope for a good year'; or, with much less certainty though some plausibility, it might (as Sir Thomas Hanmer, one of the earliest editors of Shakespeare, suggested) be derived from a French word, '*gouje*', a prostitute.

58 *bear*: (1) Put up with afflictions; (2) support a man's weight (as at 61); (3) give birth to children.

59 *the weaker vessel*: That woman is the weaker of the sexes is an ancient fallacy, and the expression *the weaker vessel* is biblical (1 Peter 3:7). It is given a sexual turn at 61–2.

62 *hogshead*: Large cask.

venture: Cargo.

63 *Bordeaux stuff*: Wine of Bordeaux (*stuff* and the echo of 'boarding' may be sexual innuendoes).

67 *Ancient Pistol*: An ancient was an ensign or standard bearer. Falstaff is the captain, Peto the lieutenant, Pistol the ensign and Bardolph the corporal. The name *Pistol* is particularly suggestive. A Pistol and a Bardolph appear in muster-rolls of artillerymen of 1435. Shakespeare may have known the Italian word '*pistolfo*', which John Florio (whom it is thought Shakespeare knew) translated in 1611 as 'a roguing beggar, a cantler, an upright man that liveth by cozenage'. There is also in the ancient's name a

suggestion of 'pizzle' (see notes to 112, 124 and 156); and the Tudor pistol was a fearsome, erratic weapon, likely to go off with a roar at half-cock, very much as is the character Pistol.

69 *swaggering*: (Then a new word) hectoring, blustering.

72 *I'll*: I'll have.

78 *pacify yourself*: Keep yourself quiet (or, if *pacify* is a mistake for 'satisfy', 'be you assured').

   comes: The singular form for the plural.

81 *Tilly-fally*: Fiddlesticks.

83 *Tisick*: For 'phthisic', a consumptive cough.

   debuty: A corrupted form of 'deputy', used by others besides the Hostess, for a deputy alderman, or the citizen charged with keeping order in a ward or district.

85 *Master Dumb*: Clergy who merely read out others' sermons instead of preaching their own were called 'dumb dogs', not being able to bark (from Isaiah 56:10).

86 *by*: Nearby.

87 *civil*: Well-behaved.

87–8 *are in an ill name*: Have gained a bad reputation.

88 *I can tell whereupon*: I now understand why (for admitting such as Pistol).

94 *tame cheater*: This seems to be a particular usage of these words created by Shakespeare, and it is one which later authors (including Sir Walter Scott) took up. 'Cheater' originally meant one who looked after the royal escheats (that is, land which reverted to the king), but in Shakespeare's day it was coming to mean such a person who operated dishonestly. It is the *honest* escheator that the Hostess has in mind at 100. 'Cheater' was applied to gamesters, presumably alluding to those who resorted to sharp practice, and the *tame cheater* is thought to have been the decoy who lured the innocent card-player into a game in which he could be fleeced. Thus in *The Fair Maid of the Inn* (1625) by John Fletcher (and probably others) a tame cheater is described as a 'decoy duck'. The implication is that Pistol is the

last man to frighten anyone; after all, as Thomas
Dekker explained in *The Bellman of London* (1608),
cheaters seldom swear or swagger, for fear of frightening off their prey.

96 *Barbary hen*: Guinea fowl (used to mean 'slut' or
'prostitute').

108 *charge ... discharge*: Drink a toast (with a sexual
innuendo and playing on the military meanings –
loading and firing a pistol).

111 *bullets*: Testes.

112 *She is pistol-proof*: (1) She will not succumb to you;
(2) she is past child-bearing (taking up the meaning
of *pistol* as a discharging weapon, and punning on
'pizzle').

112 *not hardly*: Scarcely (a colloquialism; the *not* is
redundant).

114 *proofs ... bullets*: The Hostess sees no hidden meanings – she is simply confused – in contrast to Doll,
who immediately realizes what *charge* means (119–22).

120 *mate*: Companion, fellow.

121–2 *I am meat for your master*: A proverbial expression,
here with a sexual innuendo. (There may be wordplay on *meat* and *mate*.)

124 *bung*: (1) Pickpocket ('bung' was a cant word for purse);
(2) pizzle (the other meaning of *bung* – something
that fills a hole).

125 *chaps*: Cheeks.

126 *play the saucy cuttle*: The precise meaning of this
delightfully evocative expression is not clear, but its
implication is obvious. A cuttle was the knife used
for cutting purses, and it seems that Doll is warning
Pistol not to try any tricks with her.

127 *basket-hilts*: An expression of contempt for a swords-
man; literally, a sword hilt with steel basketwork to
protect the hand.
Since when: Since when were you a true soldier?

128 *points*: Laces, here those used for securing armour.
Doll implies that Pistol is dressed more impressively
than he behaves.

129 *Much*: An expression of scornful disbelief.

130 *murder*: Destroy.

132–3 FALSTAFF *No more* ... *Pistol*: F omits these lines. Some editors attribute this to their indecency, but on that basis most of the scene up to this point might also have been excised. It is more likely that the compositor's eye accidentally slipped from Falstaff's *No* to the Hostess's (134).

134 *Captain*: The Hostess's rapid promotion of Pistol may indicate her desire to pacify him.

142 *stewed prunes*: Pistol lives on what others leave, not only in the sense of food, but also as a pimp. Prunes were thought to be a cure for venereal disease, and 'stews' were brothels. Pistol lives off the takings of mouldy prostitutes.

144–6 *word* ... *ill-sorted*: For these lines F has only *word Captaine odious*, a weak modification which avoids the *odious* meaning of *occupy*: 'fornicate'. Here (in contrast to 132–3) the change seems deliberate, because of the new sense that is produced; but in comparison with what has gone before these lines are hardly odious enough to be censored (and the word is so used elsewhere in the period). It is just possible that the alteration was made to avoid the implication of some topical allusion, now irrecoverable.

145–6 *ill-sorted*: In bad company.

152–5 *To Pluto's* ... *here*: As in his development of Falstaff (and Shylock) from characteristics inherited from the earlier drama, with Pistol Shakespeare goes far beyond the braggart soldier, the *miles gloriosus*, from whom he stems. Falstaff and Shylock transcend the stock dramatic elements of their origin because Shakespeare creates a kind of humanity for them. Pistol's development is different. Shakespeare takes a dramatic stereotype and gives him a passion, a passion for a kind of literary rant that might appeal to such a braggart soldier were he a real person. Shakespeare's peculiar genius appears in his skilful control over this creation. Shylock and more especially Falstaff are inclined to take over their plays. This problem does not arise with Pistol, yet he is invested with a colour and an imagination that make him seem, like Falstaff and Shylock, a world away from the ordinariness of his origins.

Much of what Pistol says is drawn from, or imitative of, the rant of drama, and, as J. W. Lever showed in *Shakespeare Survey 6* (1953), pp. 79–90, his classical learning seems to be derived from a passage in John Eliot's *Ortho-epia Gallica* (1593) where a braggart is portrayed. In this speech Pistol seems to be indebted to Eliot and to the dramatists Peele, Greene and Kyd.

152–3 *Pluto's damnèd lake*: Probably a confusion for the River Lethe or Styx of Hades, which Pluto ruled.

153 *Erebus*: The son of Chaos and Night; also a name for the underworld itself.

155 *faitours*: The word is akin to 'factor', but in Shakespeare's time it meant an impostor or cheat. It seems to have puzzled those involved in producing F, because they replaced it with *Fates*.
Hiren: Probably a confusion of 'iron' (that is, Pistol's sword) and 'Irene' from a lost play by George Peele, *The Turkish Mahomet and Hyrin the Fair Greek*, written some five years before *Henry IV, Part II*.

156 *Peesel*: The spelling indicates the pun implicit in *Pistol*/'pizzle'. See notes to 67 and 114.

157 *beseek*: Beseech (either a blunder or a dialect form).
aggravate: Another malapropism.

158 *good humours*: Fine goings-on.

158–62 *Shall pack-horses ... Greeks*: Pistol borrows from Marlowe for 158–60 (*Tamburlaine, Part Two*, IV.3.1–2: 'Holla, ye pampered jades of Asia! | What, can ye draw but twenty miles a day') and from Eliot's *Ortho-epia Gallica* for the next two lines.

161 *Cannibals*: This is not an error for 'Hannibals' (as might be expected were the Hostess speaking); it is drawn from Pistol's source, Eliot: 'I fear not to fight

with a whole army if it be not of these miscreant Tartarians, Cannibals, Indians, and Muscovites.'

162 *Troyant*: Trojan.

163 *Cerberus*: The three-headed dog that guarded the underworld, here made a king.

164 *fall foul for toys*: Fall out over trifles.

169 *Give crowns like pins*: Tamburlaine gave his followers kingdoms.

174 *feed and be fat, my fair Calipolis*: A paraphrase of lines from Peele's play *The Battle of Alcazar*, where Muly Mahamet offers his starving mother lion's flesh saying, 'Feed then and faint not, my fair Calipolis ... Feed and be fat that we may meet the foe.' This, like Pistol's other allusions to plays, would have been familiar to Elizabethan audiences.

175 *give's*: Give us.

176 *Si fortune me tormente sperato me contento*: Which language Pistol thinks he is speaking is uncertain. It is closest to Italian, though, if Pistol's sword is Spanish and the motto is inscribed on it (as was common), Spanish would be expected. He means, 'If fortune torments me, hope contents me.' Later he offers a slightly different version of his tag (V.5.99).

177 *give fire*: Shoot.

178 *sweetheart*: Pistol's sword.

179 *full points*: Full stops.

etceteras nothings: Both words carry the same innuendo – the vagina.

181 *neaf*: Hand. Pistol's substitution of a dialect word (meaning 'fist') for 'hand' makes a ridiculous end for his high-flown phrase.

182 *seen the seven stars*: Enjoyed companionship at night. The *seven stars* have been identified as the Pleiades and as Ursa Major, the latter being the more arithmetically precise. Falstaff has a similar phrase at III.2.209.

184 *fustian*: Ranting.

185 *Know*: (1) Recognize; (2) have intercourse with.

185–6 *Galloway nags*: Prostitutes (lively as Galloway nags but which any man might ride).

187 *Quoit him*: Chuck him (like a quoit).

187–8 *shove-groat shilling*: In the game of shove-groat (the ancestor of shove-ha'penny), Edward VI shillings were popular as the coins to be pushed up the board. The implication is that Pistol should be given the push in the same way as the coins were.

191 *Shall we have incision? Shall we imbrue*: Both questions mean 'Shall I let blood?' The terms are from surgery.

We: The royal plural.

192 *death rock me asleep*: Either Anne Boleyn or her brother George wrote a lyric beginning 'O Death, rock me on sleep' as they both awaited execution in 1536.

194 *Untwind*: Untwine.

Sisters Three: The three Fates. Clotho held the spindle of life's thread; it was drawn by Lachesis and cut by Atropos.

195 *toward*: Forthcoming.

200 *tirrits*: A word of the Hostess's own, combining 'terror' and 'fits'. It may have been suggested to Shakespeare by the spelling 'tirets' (for 'terrets', a harness ring) in Holinshed's account of Henry IV's reign.

204 *whoreson . . . villain*: Doll uses these as terms of endearment. Falstaff's gratified response to the attentions he receives and his repeated recall of his ability in standing up to a mere swaggerer such as Pistol illustrate his decline.

206 *shrewd*: Vicious.

211 *ape*: Fool (used affectionately).

214 *Hector*: Leader of the Trojan forces during the siege of Troy.

215 *Agamemnon*: Leader of the Greek forces besieging Troy.

215–16 *the Nine Worthies*: These were three pagans, Hector, Alexander and Julius Caesar; three Jews, Joshua,

David and Judas Maccabeus; and three Christians, King Arthur, Charlemagne and Godfrey of Bouillon (who led the First Crusade).

220 *canvass*: An expression from hawking, meaning 'catch in a net'; here with a sexual innuendo, of course.

225 *thou followed'st him like a church*: As churches are immobile (*the* Church, indeed, being founded on a rock), this presumably implies that Falstaff did not move an inch.

226 *tidy*: Tender and fat.

Bartholomew boar-pig: See the note to II.1.25–6.

227 *foining*: Sword-thrusting (with an innuendo, as at II.1.16).

229–30 *death's-head*: Skull, used as a memento mori. A real skull might serve as a constant reminder of death as it stood on a man's desk, and the design of a skull was used on jewellery. Prostitutes wore rings so engraved; in *The Dutch Courtesan*, I.2.48–9, they are said to have 'their wickedness ... always before their eyes, and a death's-head most commonly on their middle finger'.

231 *what humour's*: What mood is.

233 *pantler*: Pantryman.

chipped bread: Cut off the crusts of loaves.

235–6 *His wit's as thick as Tewkesbury mustard*: Falstaff's analogy does not work as he intends. Tewkesbury's famous mustard was noted for its sharpness, not its thickness, so the reference to it would compliment Poins rather than disparage him. It seems unlikely that the confusion is on Shakespeare's part, and it must be that Falstaff's wit is solidifying, not Poins's.

236–7 *conceit*: Wit, imagination.

237 *mallet*: Wooden hammer (proverbial for dullness).

239 *of a bigness*: Of equal size. A well-formed leg was important for a man of fashion.

240 *conger*: The conger-eel was considered a heavy food and likely to dull the wits.

fennel: A herb used to flavour fish; it is supposedly good for the digestion, hence its association with eel.

241 *flap-dragons*: In the game of flap-dragons – an exercise in foolish bravado – small objects (the *flap-dragons*: sometimes raisins, or, as here, candles) were floated in liquor. Then either the liquor had to be drunk with the objects alight, or the objects were to be snatched into the mouth from the burning liquor.

241–2 *rides the wild mare*: This probably refers to a schoolboy game, still played, which has many different names. The *mare* is formed by some eight boys bending down one behind the other, the first propped against a wall; other boys then run up one after another and jump astride the mare with the object of seeing how many boys it takes to make the mare collapse.

242 *joint-stools*: Stools with well-joinered legs; jumping over them was another high-spirited game.

244 *sign of the leg*: Elizabethan shops indicated what they sold by displaying an object representing it. Falstaff means that Poins wears boots as well fitting as those of the bootmaker's advertisement.

244–5 *breeds no bate with telling of discreet stories*: This means either that Poins causes no strife (*bate*) with his stories, because they are discreet; or (more likely) that he does not commit the offence of restricting himself to stories that are discreet (that is, he amuses the Prince with indiscreet gossip).

245 *gambol*: Playful.

250 *nave*: Hub (with a pun on 'knave', Falstaff being as round as a wheel).

250–51 *have his ears cut off*: The penalty for defaming royalty.

253 *elder*: (1) Elder-tree; (2) old man.

254 *his poll clawed like a parrot*: The precise meaning is not clear. Falstaff's hair seems to have been ruffled so that he looks like a parrot – presumably because Doll has been running her hand through his hair. But parrots do not normally look particularly ruffled, though in excitement their feathers can be disturbed. Some verbal link may be intended between *poll* (parrot) and 'Doll'.

259–60 *Saturn and Venus . . . conjunction*: Saturn, representing
old age, and Venus, representing love, were thought
to be unlikely partners, and astrologers believed
(erroneously) that the two planets were never *in
conjunction* (in apparent proximity).

260 *fiery trigon*: The twelve signs of the zodiac were
grouped into four trigons (triangles), one of which
contained the three fiery signs, Aries, Leo and
Sagittarius.

his man: Bardolph, with the *fiery* countenance.

261 *lisping*: Speaking lovingly.

tables: Literally, a notebook for assignations; here
used to mean 'whore' – the Hostess.

263 *busses*: Kisses.

268 *kirtle*: Dress.

274 *hearken a'th'end*: See what time will show (proverbial).

276–7 *Anon, anon, sir*: This is the response that drawers
customarily made as they rushed about serving drinks.
In *Henry IV, Part I*, II.4.20–100, the Prince and
Poins have a game with the drawer Francis, making
him repeat the cry interminably. Here, as soon as
they speak these words Falstaff recognizes them, as
if he recalled the episode. In fact he had not arrived
on the scene then, but doubtless an audience would
not remember this so exactly; possibly Shakespeare
also did not.

279 *Poins his*: The Q reading reproduced here is a posses-
sive construction which would now be rendered by
'Poins's'. F has a comma after *Poins*, which implies that
Poins is the brother of this *bastard son of the King's*.

280 *sinful continents*: With a pun on the meanings 'con-
tainers of sin' and 'sinful contents'.

289 *compound*: Lump.

290 *by this light*: A common oath, which Falstaff then
extends to refer to Doll – *this light flesh and corrupt
blood*.

294 *if you take not the heat*: If you do not (as an iron
does) take up the *heat* of the moment so that you
may give it out again (that is, join in).

295 *candle-mine*: Falstaff is so gross that candles could be mined from him.

296 *honest*: Chaste.

301–2 *as ... Gad's Hill*: This recalls Falstaff's claim that he ran away at Gad's Hill because he knew his opponent was the Prince, and 'The lion will not touch the true prince' (*Part I*, II.4.265).

314 *the wicked*: The unregenerate, a puritan idiom, Falstaff taking the guise of a puritan preacher.

322 *close with*: Side with.

324 *zeal*: Another word with puritan associations, immortalized in the name Zeal-of-the-Land-Busy in Jonson's *Bartholomew Fair*.

326 *dead elm*: Falstaff is no longer a *withered elder* (253) but a *dead elm*. The elm is noted for its size and notorious for the ease with which it rots from the centre and collapses. Traditionally it was the support of the vine, as Falstaff is for the products of the vine.

327 *pricked*: Marked (as in a list).

328 *privy-kitchen*: Personal kitchen (presumably, as kitchens tend to be the hottest part of a house, the hottest part of hell).

329 *malt-worms*: Drunkards (those who love the *malt*). *For*: As for.

330 *good angel*: See note to I.2.166.

binds: Q has *blinds*, F *outbids*; editors have offered a variety of interpretations of these words. But, as the editor of the New Variorum edition puts it, 'It may be ... that Shakespeare wrote something different from both [*blinds* and *outbids*] and that both are guessed.' The emendation suggested here, *binds*, is close to the Q reading, and 'blinds' is a very possible error for it; Q's compositor was prone to mistakes of this kind (see note to I.1.41; in the second Quarto of *Richard II*, on which he worked, 'sparkes' is printed as 'sparkles'). *binds* is appropriate to the context and also to Falstaff, who is well versed in biblical matters and religious language (see 314 and 324, and notes to I.2.33, 34 and 191). Besides its common meaning of 'make fast', 'bind' has a specific religious meaning: when Christ says to Peter that he is the rock upon which the Church will be founded He tells him: 'whatsoever thou shalt bind in earth shall be bound in heaven, and whatsoever thou shalt loose in earth shall be loosed in heaven' (Matthew 16:19, repeated at 18:18). Falstaff is suggesting that the boy is bound (1) in this spiritual and ecclesiastical way to the Devil, and (2) as an apprentice to 'a devil', Bardolph. As the Prince says at II.2.66–8, Falstaff was given the boy Christian and he is now transformed into an ape – probably equivalent to a devil, for in the Middle Ages the 'old ape' was the Devil (in the devotional manual *The Ancrene Riwle*, *c.* 1230), and in Elizabethan times Antichrist was said to be 'the Ape of our Lord Christ'.

334 *burns*: Infects (with venereal disease).

335 *damned*: Usury was forbidden by Church and state.

337 *quit*: (1) Forgiven (in a religious sense); (2) repaid.

339 *suffering flesh to be eaten in thy house*: (1) Allowing meat to be eaten in your house (on fast days); (2) using your house as a brothel; *flesh* could mean sexual intercourse (as, for example, in the phrase 'exchange flesh', *The Winter's Tale*, IV.4.278) or, in 'a piece of flesh', a woman, especially a prostitute.

340 *howl*: This probably picks up the religious implications of what has gone before and suggests howling in hell.

341 *mutton*: (1) Sheep meat; (2) prostitute.

345–6 *says that which his flesh rebels against*: Utters a word – *gentlewoman* – which serves to gloss over that which his sexual appetite now finds repugnant.

351 *posts*: Messengers travelling post-haste.

354 *Bare-headed*: Indicative of the urgency of the captains' search (to go bare-headed was very unusual).

356 *I feel me much to blame*: The Prince, who has not entered very wholeheartedly into the action of this scene (in contrast to his behaviour in the equivalent scene in *Part I*), begins now to feel positive guilt.

358 *the south*: The south wind (supposed to bring stormy
      weather).

363 *unpicked*: Unenjoyed.

366 *presently*: Immediately.

367 *stay*: Wait.

368 *Pay the musicians*: Unless Falstaff's purse has been
      replenished since I.2.237 the musicians will fare badly.

372 *post*: Post-haste.

378 *peascod-time*: The time when peas firm in their pods. 'In
      Peascod-time' was a very popular tune in the sixteenth
      century. One of the ballads most frequently sung to it
      was 'The Lamentable Ballad of the Lady's Fall', and
      that would be quite likely to occur to an Elizabethan
      audience, if not to the Hostess. The first verse begins:

> Mark well my heavy doleful tale,
>   You loyal lovers all;
> And heedfully bear in your breast
>   A gallant lady's fall.

      The tune is given by Chappell in *Popular Music of
      the Olden Time*, I (1859), p. 198. The other song most
      sung to the tune was 'The Ballad of Chevy Chase'.

378–9 *an honester and truer-hearted man*: Falstaff is, of course,
      anything but honest and true-hearted. What is more,
      as this scene has shown, the Hostess knows that only
      too well. Her words (as two nineteenth-century
      editors, Charles and Mary Clarke, put it very well)
      'serve better than pages of commentary' to indicate
      Sir John's powers of fascination.

384 *blubbered*: With face tear-stained.

III.1

      This scene was omitted in some copies of Q. See
      An Account of the Text, p.121. The King's speech
      is curiously different in the Q and F versions; see
      Collations 1 and 2 in An Account of the Text.

0 *nightgown*: Dressing-gown.
      followed by a page: On Q's reading *alone*, see note
      to I.20. F has *with a Page*.

5 *O sleep, O gentle sleep*: On many occasions Shakespeare comments on the difficulty with which sleep comes to the troubled mind. This half-line seems to echo the opening of a sonnet by Sir Philip Sidney, 'Come, sleep, O sleep, the certain knot of peace' (*Astrophil and Stella*, 39), but with Shakespeare there is a very strong association between inability to sleep and those troubled by doubts as to the course of action they should adopt, whether they are rightly in authority – as is Henry V (*Henry V*, IV.1.250–77) – or are usurpers (*Macbeth*, II.2.35–40). Even in this respect the association is not peculiar to Shakespeare (see first note to 31).

9 *cribs*: Hovels.

10 *uneasy pallets*: Uncomfortable beds.

13 *state*: Grandeur.

15 *vile*: Lowly.

17 *watch-case*: The meaning is not known. Some editors suggest that a sentry-box is meant; and the expression has also been interpreted as equating the King in his bed with the restless mechanism of a watch-case. The former meaning, if grounded in fact, would be simple and straightforward, but there is no firm evidence for it. The second suggestion is strained; but it would lead on naturally to the *common 'larum-bell*, especially as in Shakespeare's time there were already watches which could sound an alarm.

21 *visitation*: Violent buffeting.

24 *slippery*: Swiftly passing.

25 *hurly*: Uproar.

27 *sea-son*: Q has *season*, F *Sea-Boy*. A sort of sense can be wrung from *season*, but it is more probably the *ship-boy* (19) who is referred to. *sea-son* is a trifle awkward; it sounds rather like elegant variation on Shakespeare's part, and he may have had second thoughts and changed 'son' to 'boy'. On the other hand, that is exactly the kind of change, from the unusual to the obvious, that is made by copyists;

sea-son seems idiosyncratic enough to be Shake-speare's; *sea-boy* could be his or anyone's.

29 *to boot*: Into the bargain.

30 *happy low, lie down*: In Q the word *happy* is enclosed in parentheses, a device that was sometimes punctu-ational and sometimes indicated an aside. Neither usage seems appropriate here, and it has been suggested that *happy* was meant to be deleted, especially as there are twelve syllables in the line. The meaning may simply be 'you who are happy in being low-born, lie sleeping'; but it is just possible that the King addresses *lie down* to himself.

31 *Uneasy lies the head that wears a crown*: Erasmus had expressed this idea in his *Institutio Principis* (1516) and it was already proverbial in Shakespeare's time; but his phrasing has made it seem his own creation. *Enter Warwick and Surrey*: Q gives an entry here (and at V.2.42) for Blunt, but he has no lines in the play. However, a mute called Blunt is required to lead Colevile away at IV.3.74, and there would be no harm if a stage extra who played that part also appeared here, especially as at 35 the King bids *good morrow to you all, my lords* (though *all* could mean only two). Like Blunt, Surrey has no lines to speak, but the King calls for him by name in line 1. See the note to I.1.16 and An Account of the Text, p. 120.

42 *his*: Its.

43 *little*: A little.

46 *the revolution of the times*: Although the King is concerned with rebellion, he means simply 'the changes wrought by the passage of the times', just as changes are seen with the progress of the seasons.

47 *continent*: Dry land.

51 *chance's mocks*: The absence of the apostrophe in Q and F has led some editors to read *chances* as a plural noun, either followed by a comma or with *mock* as a verb. But 'the mockeries (or "tricks") of chance' seems likely, especially with *changes* at 52.

53 Q has three and a half lines here which do not
appear in F. It has been suggested that they were
censored from F because they are so pessimistic as
to be offensive to Christians; but this is not wholly
convincing. The complete passage (modernized) reads:

> With divers liquors! O, if this were seen,
> The happiest youth, viewing his progress through,
> What perils past, what crosses to ensue,
> Would shut the book and sit him down and die.
> 'Tis not ten years gone,
> Since Richard and Northumberland, great friends . . .

It will be noted that the fifth of these lines not only
is a half-line but also runs on exactly in metre and
in sense from *With divers liquors!* Half- or part-lines
are not an impossibility (see V.2.67 and V.5.75); but
the passage omitted from F seems an awkward interpolation. A. R. Humphreys suggested that it was an
addition made at some stage, perhaps marginally, to
an early draft, since, if it were Shakespeare's final
intention to retain it, he would surely have given more
weight to the half-line, for instance by writing *'Tis*
in full. On these grounds the passage is omitted
here. See An Account of the Text, pp. 127–8, and
the notes to IV.5.76–7 and 178.

53, 55, 56 *not ten years . . . two years . . . eight years*: The events
which culminated in the affair at Gaultree Forest
took place in 1405. A full decade would take one
back well before the break between Richard and
Northumberland; Richard was deposed in 1399 and
the battle of Shrewsbury took place in 1403.

61, 66–7, 71–3 *Gave . . . into corruption*: Shakespeare may here
have in mind more than one scene of *Richard
II*. When Richard is at Flint Castle, Northumberland
obeys Bolingbroke's order to 'send the breath of
parley | Into his ruined ears' (*Richard II*, III.3.33–4).
Northumberland's face-to-face defiance of Richard
comes in the deposition scene (IV.1.221–74). The

words echoed here at 66–7 and 71–3 are part of
Richard's speech to Northumberland at V.1.55–68.

62 *cousin*: Often used imprecisely for any blood relation
or (as here) as a mark of friendliness between people
not related to each other.

Nevil: The Earl of Warwick at this time was a
Beauchamp, not a Neville; and he does not appear
at all in *Richard II*.

64 *rated*: Berated.

69 *necessity*: When Bolingbroke returns to England,
breaking his banishment, he maintains, indeed swears,
that he comes only for what is rightfully his, invoking
the specious plea, 'As I was banished, I was banished
Hereford; | But as I come, I come for Lancaster'
(*Richard II*, II.3.112–13). Even in the course of
claiming what is his, before the confrontation with
Richard, he orders the execution of Bushy and Green
(III.1), an act which only the King (or a judge with
the King's authority) might command. There is no
question that he is a usurper, a fact which still trou-
bles his son when, as Henry V, he prays before
Agincourt: 'Not today, O Lord, | O not today, think
not upon the fault | My father made in compassing
the crown!' (*Henry V*, IV.1.285–7). Henry IV blames
Exton for Richard's murder but admits (*Richard II*,
V.6.39) that he 'did wish him dead' (and in this play
(IV.5.93) he accuses his son of wishing for his death
with the words *Thy wish was father, Harry, to that
thought*). It is unlikely that Shakespeare intended Henry
to seem guiltless in encompassing the crown; his
part in Richard's deposition and murder, his remorse,
his son's sense of inherited guilt, run through the
sequence of plays too insistently for him to escape
blame (see also note to IV.5.185). On the other hand
he undoubtedly returned to an England despoiled,
and this also Shakespeare graphically shows, particularly in the scene with the Gardeners in *Richard II*
(III.4). To that extent, *necessity*, the needs of England,
was something that Henry IV as Bolingbroke was

forced to respond to. The meaning of necessity is well illustrated in one of Oliver Cromwell's speeches to Parliament (1654): 'Necessity hath no law. Feigned necessities, imaginary necessities . . . are the greatest cozenage that men can put upon the Providence of God, and make pretences to break known rules by.' The balance between self-seeking and selfless concerns is nicely held here. See also note to 88, 89.

77 *Figuring the natures of the times deceased*: Reproducing the forms of the past.

79 *chance*: Outcome.

80 *who*: Which.

81 *intreasurèd*: Safely stored.

83 *necessary form*: Inevitable pattern.

88, 89 *necessities*: Henry, perhaps a trifle ironically, repeats the word from 69 to summarize Warwick's philosophical explanation of the inevitability of certain causes and the effects that follow.

99 *A certain instance*: Unquestionable evidence.
Glendower is dead: Glendower supported the rebels in *Part I*. The historical Glendower did not die for another decade – after Henry IV, in fact, though Holinshed reports his death in 1409, four years after the events here dramatized. In 1405, however, Glendower's son was captured in a scuffle at Usk, and it may be this that Shakespeare had in mind.

101 *unseasoned*: Late.

102 *take*: Accept.

103 *inward*: Internal (civil).
out of hand: Off our hands.

104 *Holy Land*: At the very end of *Richard II* Henry IV, full of remorse for Richard's murder, says, 'I'll make a voyage to the Holy Land | To wash this blood off from my guilty hand.' At the beginning of *Henry IV, Part I* (I.1.19–21 and 100–101) he recalls his intention but is forced by rebellion at home to postpone his crusade. This levying of a force to fight for Jerusalem anticipates historical events by about a decade. The historical Henry IV planned an

expedition 'to recover the city of Jerusalem from the infidels' (as Holinshed puts it) in 1412, and ships, men and materials were collected to this end. The King here refers to his proposed expedition, and at IV.4.1–10 he will report *Our navy is addressed, our power collected* in order to fight on *higher fields*. However, Henry was taken ill before he could leave, and the nearest he got to Jerusalem as King (for he had made a pilgrimage there as Duke of Lancaster in 1392–3) was the Jerusalem Chamber at Westminster, where he died (see note to IV.5.234–9).

III.2

This is undoubtedly one of the great comic scenes in English drama. Its success depends at least as much on the two Justices as on Falstaff, and it is possible that Shakespeare, conscious of the decline in the fortunes of Falstaff, deliberately provided an alternative source of comedy, one lacking the sourness which characterizes much of Falstaff's part in this play. The scene is set in Gloucestershire, though we are not told that until IV.3.81. Shakespeare may seem to be mocking country life if the scene is taken out of context; but if it is considered as part of the play as a whole, its kindly humour and warm humanity show a marked contrast with the comic scenes set in London and the events at Gaultree Forest.

Q's opening stage direction brings on the two Justices alone, presumably indicating that the prospective recruits should enter one by one as their names are called. F, however, brings them all on at once with the Justices. This has been thought to reflect Elizabethan stage practice, and it has been followed in a number of modern productions. But the dialogue seems to suggest that the recruits appear individually: at 95 Falstaff asks to see them, and at 98–100 Shallow says *Let them appear as I call* and then asks for the first man – *where is Mouldy?* Moreover, there is no certainty that F represents stage practice here, since it several times gives entries long before the

characters are required on stage. This *may* reflect
the use of actors' parts (see An Account of the
Text, pp. 125–7), for although the parts could provide
the words said (and added) they might prove inadequate as a guide for allocating entries. If all the
recruits enter at the beginning of the scene, the business associated (quite properly) with them takes away
from the comedy of the two Justices, part visual,
part verbal; and it produces one guffaw from the
audience instead of the sequence of laughs that can
begin with the Justices' entry and continue as each
recruit appears.

  3 *rood*: Cross.

    cousin: See the first note to III.1.62.

  7 *black woosel*: Black ousel (blackbird). Ellen, alas, is
not a blonde, and at the time dark-haired girls were
out of fashion.

 13 *Clement's Inn*: Situated in the Strand; one of the Inns
of Chancery, which prepared law students for the
Inns of Court and were considered inferior to them.

 15 *lusty*: (1) Lively; (2) lascivious.

 17 *roundly*: Thoroughly, without ceremony.

 20 *Cotsole*: For 'Cotswold'.

20–21 *swing-bucklers*: Swash-bucklers.

 22 *bona-robas*: Smarter prostitutes ('good stuff', as Florio
put it in 1598).

 29 *Scoggin*: A Henry Scogan was court poet to Henry
IV (and a friend of Chaucer); a John Scoggin served
Edward IV as a jester, and his surname became
synonymous with 'buffoon'.

 30 *crack*: (Cheeky) lad.

 31 *Samson Stockfish*: *Samson* gives a fine impression of
Shallow's boldness; but 'stockfish' is dried cod. For
an Elizabethan audience a slight pause between the
two names would give the right comic effect; but
this must largely be lost on an audience today.

31–2 *behind Gray's Inn*: In Gray's Inn Fields.

 36 *Death, as the Psalmist saith* . . .: Psalm 89:48: 'What
man is he that liveth and shall not see death?'

37 *How*: What price is.
   Stamford fair: Stamford, in Lincolnshire, was famous
   for its great horse and cattle fairs, held in February,
   Lent and August.

43 *John o'Gaunt*: Henry IV's father. Here and later in the
   scene F spells out *of*; Q uses the colloquial form *a*.

45 *clapped i'th'clout at twelve score*: We cannot now tell
   whether hitting the centre of a target (marked by a
   small piece of cloth, a *clout*) at 240 yards was, by the
   standards of the time, easy, exceptional or impossible. The evidence we have is contradictory. It seems
   unlikely that a countryman would not know what
   a good shot was, and though Shallow might be
   exaggerating the range (see next note) he probably
   knows what he is talking about here.

46 *a forehand shaft a fourteen and fourteen and a half*:
   These distances are 280 and 290 yards, not impossible if an arrow is shot high into the air; but Shallow's
   point is that when Double fired he aimed at his target
   by keeping it in sight above his bow hand (shooting
   a forehand shaft), and this seems very improbable. The
   comedy is probably no deeper than a gentle mockery
   of the old story-teller given to exaggeration.

49 *Thereafter as they be*: According to their quality. The
   phrase has a country ring about it; if it sounded
   strange to a London audience it would have helped
   to reinforce the sense of a different locality.

54 *SHALLOW*: In Q, as first printed, this speech (as well
   as the next) was given to Bardolph. In the course of
   printing, his name was removed, and when this portion
   of the play was later reset (because of the insertion
   of III.1) it was again omitted. F seems to clear up
   the problem satisfactorily by giving the speech to
   Shallow, who, as the host, would be likely to greet
   the new arrivals. If actors' parts underlie F (see An
   Account of the Text, pp. 125–7) one would expect
   them to have given the correct allocation of speeches.

56 *esquire*: A rank between gentleman and knight.

60 *tall*: Valiant.

63 *backsword man*: One who fenced, for practice, with a stick with a basketwork hilt.

65 *accommodated*: Seemingly a word coming into favour at the time, and Shallow immediately pounces on it. This points to the interest Shakespeare's audience could be expected to have in new words.

69 *phrases*: 'Phrase' could be used to mean a single word.

75 *word of exceeding good command*: Very good military term.

80 *It is very just*: That is very true.

83 *like*: Thrive.

86 *Surecard*: Q gives the name as *Soccard*, but that text is very unreliable with names (for example it has *Billingsgate* for 'Basingstoke' at II.1.168, and *Weminster* for 'Westminster' at II.4.350). *Surecard* offers some sort of meaning (as do the names of other characters in this scene). It can mean a certainty (a trump card); and the great eighteenth-century editor Edmond Malone maintained that it was a word for 'boon companion' in the seventeenth century, though no evidence for that statement has survived.

87 *Silence*: Here and in a number of other places this name is spelt *Scilens* in Q. This very unusual spelling also occurs in a short section of the manuscript additions to the play *Sir Thomas More*, and many scholars adduce this similarity as part of the evidence for Shakespeare's having had a hand in the revision of that play. The unusual spelling (which is not known to occur elsewhere in the work of the man who set Q – and indeed in resetting part of this passage he altered the spelling to *Silens*) suggests that the copy used in printing Q may have been Shakespeare's own manuscript. See also An Account of the Text, p. 127.

87–8 *in commission*: As Justice of the Peace.

92–282 Falstaff also recruits men in *Part I*, where he freely admits to having 'misused the King's press damnably' (IV.2.12–13). His behaviour can look comic enough to us, but corrupt recruiting practices (which dated back at least to the time of the historic Henry IV's youth) were a matter of particular social concern at the end of the sixteenth century. The Vice element in Falstaff's character may well have struck an Elizabethan audience in this respect, especially when he admits to having led his men where they were so 'peppered' that not three of them are left alive (*Part I*, V.3.35–7). This recruiting scene is in the main comic; but the comedy springs chiefly from the Justices, who are well-intentioned, and the recruits, who are not all as mean as they may be made to appear (see 228–32), and it is to some extent counterbalanced by the corrupt practices of Falstaff and Bardolph. In *Part I*, IV.2.13–34, Falstaff describes how he recruits only those able to buy themselves out of service, pocketing what they pay him and replacing them with 'tattered prodigals'. It is the tattered prodigals we see here; the best physical specimen, Bullcalf, is allowed, together with Mouldy, to bribe his way out of service.

 93 *sufficient*: Able.

103 *friends*: Family.

110 *Prick him*: Mark him down on the list.

111 *pricked*: Mouldy plays on *Prick* at 110, using *pricked* with the meanings (1) grieved; (2) soured (mouldy), and with obvious sexual wordplay.

112 *dame*: Probably 'wife', not 'mother', in view of the sexual innuendoes in *undone* and *husbandry*.

117 *spent*: Used up (again with sexual innuendo – hence Mouldy's query in the next line).

120 *other*: Others.

121 *Shadow*: The name refers to Shadow's thinness (he is wasted away to nothing) and also suggests the practice of recruiting 'shadows' (see the note to 134). Shadow might well have been played by Sincklo (see note to V.4.0).

123 *cold*: (1) Cool; (2) cowardly.

128–31 *Thy mother's son ... substance*: This speech lacks the sprightliness of wit typical of the Falstaff of *Part I*.

This is a laboured invention dependent on the uncertainty of fatherhood and a play on Shadow's name. It is demonstrable that he is his mother's son, but his father may be a shadowy unreality; and the son cannot be more than an image (that is, the shadow) cast by the father, and images and shadows are without substance; there is little of Shadow's putative father to be found in him.

133 *serve*: (1) Serve as a soldier; (2) suffice, do well enough.

134 *a number of shadows fill up the muster-book*: The *muster-book* includes the names of some non-existent men (commonly called *shadows*) to enable Falstaff to claim more money than he is really entitled to. Cf. Morton's comment on Percy and his army, I.1.192–3. *fill up*: To fill up.

135 *Thomas Wart*: A list of men from Gloucestershire fit to serve the King in 1608 includes a Thomas Warter, who was a carpenter (see note to 142–3), and, being of 'lower stature', was 'fit to serve with a caliver' (at 264 Wart begins caliver drill). This might all be coincidence (and the date of the muster-roll is a decade after the play was written); but as Shakespeare seems to have known the area well (see note to V.1.33–4), it is possible that he knew Warter, who could have been bearing his caliver for some years before the date of the surviving roll.

140 *ragged*: As well as describing Wart's clothes, this could mean 'with projecting lumps' (as warts have).

142–3 *his apparel . . . pins*: Wart is so tattered that he cannot bear any further (physical) pricking. His clothes are like a loose timber *frame* held together on his back by *pins* (pegs or pieces of dowelling for joining timbers).

148 *SHALLOW*: Many editors give this speech to Falstaff, but Q and F both indicate that it is spoken by Shallow. The question is properly Falstaff's, but Shakespeare's allocation is perfectly natural: when several people are present at an interview it is not

uncommon for one person to ask another's questions. If actors' parts underlie F (see An Account of the Text, pp. 125–7) a faulty allocation of speeches in Q should have been revealed and corrected in F.

149, 151 *A woman's ... tailor*: Tailors were traditionally cowardly (hence the surprise of the tailor in the nursery story who kills nine, and the expression 'Nine tailors make a man'); but see 228–32. *tailor* also implied the sexual organs, male or female.

152 *pricked*: Clothed (with a sexual innuendo; see previous note).

153 *battle*: Army.

158 *magnanimous*: Courageous.

163–4 *put him to*: Enlist him as.

165 *thousands*: Evidently Feeble is lice-ridden.

179–80 *ringing ... coronation day*: Bell-ringing to celebrate the anniversary of the King's coronation.

181 *gown*: Dressing-gown.

184–5 *two ... four*: Commentators have remarked that these numbers do not tally, and that this is because Shakespeare was careless in such little matters. But there is nothing careless here. At 93 Falstaff mentions *half a dozen* men (a general number, from which he can select those he wants); he sees five; at 242–3 it is apparent that the precise number to be taken from those available is four, but, because he can make a little money by releasing two men and substituting for one of them, he takes only three.

187–8 *I cannot tarry dinner*: I cannot waste time taking dinner (but he makes an effort; and dramatic if not real time is allowed for the delay).

191 *the Windmill in Saint George's Field*: The Windmill may have been an inn; but St George's Field lay close by Southwark, which was noted for its brothels.

192 *Master Shallow*: F has *good* before *Master*, and then repeats *No more of that*. This may be what Shakespeare wrote; but it is the sort of change that actors tend to introduce and might stem from actors' parts (see An Account of the Text, p. 127).

196 *away with*: Endure, bear (probably with a sexual innuendo).

200 *Doth she hold her own well*: Shallow asks whether she withstands the ravages of time (to which he and Falstaff are succumbing) and, presumably, disease. It is a little surprising that Falstaff should still know of her after so many years.

209 *We have heard the chimes at midnight*: This most evocative phrase is reminiscent of (and similar in meaning to) Pistol's *We have seen the seven stars* (II.4.182).

212–13 *Hem, boys*: A drinking cry.

215 *Corporate*: For 'Corporal'; Bullcalf mistakes the word in the manner of the Hostess.

stand: Act as.

216–17 *four Harry ten shillings in French crowns*: Ten-shilling pieces and French crowns became current only in Tudor times (*Harry* is Henry VIII), and early in the reign of Elizabeth they were devalued. We should presumably compute Bullcalf's sum at the devalued rate, as that is the value an Elizabethan audience would understand. He is offering £1, which he would pay as five French crowns, formerly worth six shillings each but later only four shillings.

223 *Corporal Captain*: A neat mixture of precision – *Corporal* – and promotion – *Captain*.

226 *forty*: Mouldy offers forty shillings (£2), making with Bullcalf's £1 the £3 that Bardolph offers Falstaff at 238.

228–32 *a man . . . next*: Having been mocked for cowardice, Feeble now shows commendable spirit (and a fluent knowledge of popular proverbs).

229 *bear*: Have.

245 *past service*: Falstaff is referring primarily not to the service of the King but to Mouldy's sexual service of his wife (a duty he has alluded to at 113).

246 *come unto it*: Are matured enough for service; when Bullcalf is no longer a calf he will be capable of the same service as the *town bull* (see note to II.2.151).

251–3 *Care I . . . spirit*: Should a soldier be chosen for his
       outward appearance or his spirit? Falstaff juxtaposes
       two contemporary approaches to recruiting, manip-
       ulating them dishonestly to suit his own purpose.
       See also note to IV.1.155.

       thews: Muscles.

       assemblance: The precise meaning is unsure. The
       word was used by Caxton a century before *Part II*
       was written, and it seems to combine 'appearance'
       and 'bodily frame'.

255 *with the motion of a pewterer's hammer*: Very rapidly.

256 *come off and on*: This is uncertain in meaning; it
     may be a military metaphor, meaning 'retire and
     advance' but with the sense of having a name *off*
     the list and *on* (properly, on the list, then off – just
     as advance should take place before retiring).

256–7 *he that gibbets on the brewer's bucket*: This is even
       more obscure than the phrase before. To *gibbet* is
       to hang or be hung from a gibbet; *bucket* may mean
       a beam (from an old French word, '*buquet*'), hence,
       it has been suggested, a pig hung by the heels after
       being slaughtered 'kicks the bucket' (though equally
       convincing alternative explanations are offered for
       that phrase). It is conceivable that the expression is
       an antecedent to 'kicking the bucket' for 'dying',
       and as such implies 'a quick release from earthly
       misery' – a meaning that is at least in accord
       with Falstaff's images of swiftness. It has also been
       suggested that a *brewer's bucket* is a brewer's yoke
       for carrying pails of liquor. See also the use of
       bucket (probably for 'pail') at V.1.19.

257 *half-faced*: Thin-faced, like a profile (half-face) on
     a coin.

259 *as great aim*: As likely a target.

261–2 *give . . . great ones*: Again this is a parody of
       military writing of the time, but it is also Falstaff's
       own philosophy: he would have as his men those
       who will not be missed, so that he may more easily
       make money out of them, and he must stand clear

of the great (such as the Lord Chief Justice).

262 *caliver*: A light firearm.

264 *traverse. Thas! . . .*: *traverse* can refer to bodily movement from side to side, and some editors and producers
have Wart engage in a little rapid marching; but
traverse also means to move the rifle or gun to a
different position, and although the first recorded
use of the word in that sense in the *OED* is of 1628,
it may well be the meaning here. *Thas!* probably
represents the unintelligible sound barked out by
those who drill troops and could indicate Wart's
taking aim at first one group of the audience, then
a second and a third. Both instructions would fit
arms drill better than foot drill.

267 *chopped*: Dried up.

shot: A secondary meaning may be intended: a *shot*
was an animal left after the best of the flock or herd
had been selected.

Well said: This could mean 'Well done' (as at V.3.9).
But Falstaff may be addressing it to himself; there
are other instances of characters being intrigued with
the language they use: cf. *accommodated* (65–79) and
occupy (II.4.144–6).

268 *scab*: Referring to Wart's name, rascal.

tester: Sixpence.

270 *Mile End Green*: Used as a drilling ground for citizens of London in Elizabethan times.

lay: Lodged.

271 *Sir Dagonet*: King Arthur's fool.

271–2 *Arthur's show*: An archery display held on Mile End
Green by a society of archers which named itself after
King Arthur and the Knights of the Round Table.

272 *quiver*: Nimble.

273–4 *manage . . . you in*: Elizabethan firearms took so long
to reload that, in order to keep up a fairly continuous
sequence of fire, the front rank of men, after firing,
ran round to the back to reload whilst the second rank
fired, and so on, until the first rank was ready again.

273 *piece*: Firearm.

275 *Bounce*: This imitates the sound of a gun firing, and
    was also a catchword of the time. Robert Armin, in
    A Nest of Ninnies (1608), writes, 'Bounce is the world's
    motto'; this line does not appear in the earlier version
    of the book published in 1600 (called *Fool upon Fool*),
    so presumably the word came into fashion about,
    or shortly after, the time of *Henry IV, Part I*.

288 *have spoke at a word*: Mean what I have said.

291 *fetch off*: Delude, cozen.

295–6 *Turnbull Street*: A haunt of thieves and prostitutes.

296 *duer*: More punctiliously.

297 *Turk's tribute*: The tribute due to the Sultan of Turkey
    was said to be exacted with the utmost rigour. Cf.
    V.2.47–8.

298–301 *like a man ... knife*: Falstaff illustrates the insignif-
    icance of Shallow by likening him to a man shaped
    in a moment's idleness from a scrap of cheese rind.
    He goes on to liken him to a radish (and radishes
    might accompany cheese, so the progression is logical
    enough) with a split root so that it looked like a
    man's legs; above these a head is carved, but there
    will be little room for a body. So Shallow is mere
    waste (like the rind of cheese) and a 'no-body'
    (like the carved radish). Falstaff's disparagement of
    Shallow is comic enough, but, unfortunately for
    Falstaff, Shallow engages our sympathy in spite of
    his silliness. Seeing his hospitality so abused goes a
    little way to prepare an audience for the rejection
    of Falstaff.

301 *forlorn*: Meagre.

302 *thick*: Dull, not acute.

    invincible: The reading of both Q and F, but editors
    have suggested that it is an error for 'invisible' (the
    two words could look alike in Elizabethan hand-
    writing). If so, the misreading has produced a more
    difficult word instead of an obvious one – not the
    direction of change one expects. If it were certain
    that F's reading was produced independently of Q's,
    that would be very strong evidence that *invincible*

is correct. It is at least noteworthy that the scribe who prepared the manuscript for F did not make the very plausible substitution of 'invisible'. *invincible* suggests that only acute sight could overcome the limitations imposed by Shallow's puny dimensions.

304 *mandrake*: The point of the insult is that the mandrake (see the second note to I.2.14) was thought to be a sexual stimulant, which, as represented by Shallow, even whores found excessive.

306 *overscutched housewives*: *overscutched* means 'overbeaten'; *housewives* was pronounced 'hussives', hence 'hussies'. Falstaff's implication is that a whore who has often been punished by beating (see V.4.5 and note) has been long at the game and is of the lowest grade of prostitute. There may be a play on 'scut', technically the tail of the hare but also a term of abuse and meaning the female sexual organs.

306–7 *the carmen whistle*: Carters were famous for whistling and singing. The *Fitzwilliam Virginal Book* includes a piece by William Byrd called 'The Carman's Whistle'.

307 *fancies*: Fantasias.

307–8 *good-nights*: Serenades.

308 *Vice's dagger*: The Vice in the morality plays traditionally brandished a thin wooden dagger.

311 *tilt-yard*: Tournament ground.

311–12 *burst his head*: Had his head broken. Presumably Shallow, far from being a close friend of John of Gaunt, was so insignificant that he had to struggle among the crowd in order to see, and, getting among the officials (*marshal's men*), was roughly pushed into place.

314–15 *eel-skin*: This (in slightly differing spellings) is the reading of the corrected Q and of F. However, the uncorrected Q reading, *eele-shin*, may be correct, for 'elsin' is a northern dialect word for a shoemaker's awl. Confusion of 'eel-skin' and 'elf-skin' occurs in *Part I* (see Commentary, note to II.4.240), also with the implication of slightness.

315 *treble hautboy*: The smallest and narrowest of the hautboys, an early relation of the oboe.

316 *beefs*: Fat cattle.

318 *a philosopher's two stones*: One of these stones, so the alchemists believed, would give eternal life, and the other would allow base metals to be turned into gold. Falstaff means to make Shallow his 'golden goose'.

319 *dace*: A small fish used as bait to catch pike.

320 *the law of nature*: The strong destroying the weak.

IV.1

Q provides an entry here for *Bardolfe* (Lord Bardolph) but he has nothing to say; Shakespeare probably realized as he worked from the histories that Bardolph was in Scotland and took no part in the affair at Gaultree Forest. F provides an entry for *Colevile* (see note to IV.3.0), and anticipates Westmorland's entry, though it also has a direction that he should enter at 24.

0 *within the Forest of Gaultree*: This is Q's only mention of location. F's stage direction does not include it, and it is not necessary, as the first lines establish the locale. The forest is that referred to in the modern place-name Sutton-on-the-Forest (known as Sutton sub Galtris in 1242), about eight miles to the north of York, where the novelist Laurence Sterne lived.

3 *discoverers*: Scouts.

8 *New-dated*: Of recent date.

11 *hold sortance*: Be in accord.
   quality: Rank.

15 *overlive*: Survive.

16 *opposite*: Adversary.

17 *touch ground*: Strike bottom (as a ship against a rocky shore, hence line 18).

23 *just proportion*: Exact number.
   gave ... out: Estimated.

24 *sway on*: Advance.

34 *guarded*: Ornamented.
   rage: The reading of both Q and F. Most editors now emend to 'rags', although they admit that Q

and F are not necessarily wrong. 'Guarded with rags' is a splendid paradox; but *rage* is obviously in tune with the general import of the passage. It could easily be a misreading of 'rags'; but the fact that Q and F agree lends support to *rage*, even though we cannot be certain that F has it from an independent source.

35 *countenanced*: Approved.

44 *good letters*: Erudition, scholarship.

45 *figure*: Symbolize. For the heinousness of ecclesiastical support for rebellion, see note to I.1.201 and second note to I.2.34.

47 *translate*: With the additional meanings of 'transform' and, in a technical usage for the movement of bishops from one see to another, 'transfer'.

52 *point of war*: Short bugle or trumpet call given as a signal in the field.

54–7 *we are ... for it*: It is commonplace in Elizabethan literature for disturbance in the state to be reflected in or explained as disturbance in some other sphere. Thus at IV.3.107 Falstaff speaks of *this little kingdom, man*, and strange births and disorder in the seasons are mentioned at IV.4.122–4. In *Richard II* England is a garden, full of possibilities for order and beauty (as seen by Gaunt) but rank and overgrown (as seen by the Gardener). Here the Archbishop explains himself by reference to bodily disorders, their cause and cure.

57 *bleed*: In war and also as patients were bled in the treatment of fever. King Richard, 'though no physician', argues that it 'is no month to bleed' when he is trying to avert conflict (*Richard II*, I.1.153–7); and at 60 here the Archbishop also disclaims the role of physician (but see 64–5). Richard's speech is mocking in tone (as the precise triple rhymes imply – 'incision' with 'physician'), but the Archbishop's dilemma is in theory more genuine, though whether he feels it very deeply is open to question. As a leader of the Church he is bound to advocate peace, but, as he sees it, there is a *rough torrent of occasion* (72)

which oppresses the peace and against which only
force can prevail.

64 *rank*: Bloated.

67 *justly*: Precisely.

71 *our most quiet there*: This is F's reading (55–79 are
not in Q); the sense is awkward but not impossible,
there referring back to *the stream of time* at 70, and
most used adjectivally, as elsewhere in Shakespeare.
Various emendations for *there* have been suggested,
of which the best are 'shore' and 'sphere'.

72 *occasion*: Events.

73 *griefs*: Grievances.

74 *articles*: Items listed in a deposition. (See IV.2.36.)

78 *access*: Accented on the second syllable.

83 *instance*: Entreaty.

84 *Hath*: The singular form for the plural.

90 *suborned*: Traitorously induced.

   grate on: Harass.

92–4 After 92 an uncorrected version of Q has this line:
And consecrate commotions bitter edge. After 93, it has:
To brother borne an household cruelty, – both lines
are omitted from the corrected Q and from F. Some
editors think these lines were excised by mistake
during the proof-correction of Q, it being argued
that the cut in Q which begins at 101 should have
begun at 99. It will be noted that 99 and 100 begin
with the same words as the lines quoted above (*And*
and *To*). The reason for omitting 101–37 would
doubtless be that they refer in too close detail to
the deposition of Richard, a matter upon which
Elizabeth was particularly sensitive. It has been
suggested that 99 and 100 were to be omitted because
they are similarly objectionable; but they are so
general, and so little different from what the
Archbishop says in his immediately preceding speech,
that this argument is difficult to accept. Certainly
the passage is awkward. The Archbishop's declaration that it is the well-being of all – *the commonwealth* – that he seeks to defend seems peculiarly

unctuous, but of course that may be what Shakespeare
intended. The first line omitted reads well, but the
second has been thought by other editors to be
corrupt. In the manipulation of type, it was much
harder to remove two lines from either side of an
intervening line than two adjacent lines, so it is
unlikely that a compositor would have removed the
lines on either side of 93 if his instruction was to
remove two adjacent lines; but nothing is beyond
the bounds of possibility. Certainly two lines were
marked to be removed; certainly F, though elsewhere
it restores many passages missing from Q, does not
include these lines. Since a separate manuscript source
must have been available to produce F, if only to
supply the lines that it adds, and since there is no
other firm evidence or convincing conjecture, these
cuts made in the course of printing Q are observed
in this edition.

93 *brother general . . . commonwealth*: This reads awkwardly, and, coupled with the excision of the adjacent
lines, seems to have caused some puzzlement to those
who prepared Q and F. Q has no comma after *commonwealth*, suggesting that the Archbishop is addressing
Westmorland as a brother army commander. F has a
comma (as in this edition), indicating that *commonwealth*
and *brother general* are in apposition. We cannot be
certain that the comma is Shakespeare's; but it seems
more likely that the Archbishop is claiming to be
fighting on behalf of the general brotherhood of man,
his fellow subjects.

94 *quarrel*: Reason for complaint.

95–6 *There . . . to you*: With superb arrogance Westmorland
asserts that he, as authority's representative, can
determine that no wrongs exist, and that if they did
it would be for authority to decide if they needed
redress. This is said by the man who, to seek redress
of his own wrongs, was one of the first to join
Bolingbroke against Richard, and it is wholly in accord
with his duplicity here (however justifiable that may

technically be; see note to IV.2.121). In Holinshed
it is Westmorland, not Lancaster, who tricks the
rebels.

100 *unequal*: Unjust.

101–37 *O . . . the King*: Omitted in Q; see note to 92–4.

102 *Construe the times to their necessities*: Interpret the
present time according to the dictates of expediency.

109 *signories*: Estates. In *Richard II* Mowbray, Duke of
Norfolk, is banished (I.3), and his death abroad is
reported by Carlisle (IV.1.91–102); immediately
before this Bolingbroke restores Norfolk's 'lands and
signories' (87–9).

114 *force perforce*: The same expression appears at IV.4.46
and *Perforce must move* at IV.5.35. F has *forc'd*, for
force, but in Elizabethan handwriting 'e' is easily
confused with 'd'.

116 *rousèd*: Raised (and excited).

117 *daring of the spur*: This probably means that the
horses were so keen to be off that they dared the
riders' spurs to prick them into action.

118 *armèd staves in charge*: Lances at the ready.
beavers: Visors (of their helmets).

123 *warder*: Mace. (Richard's dramatic act, preventing
the combat between Mowbray and Bolingbroke,
occurs at I.3.118 of *Richard II*.)

129 *Hereford*: F spells the word here in three syllables
(though a disyllable is more appropriate for the
metre) but at 136 as *Herford* (as is commonly done
in *Richard II*). Henry IV was known as Henry
Bolingbroke, Duke of Hereford, before he assumed
John of Gaunt's title, Duke of Lancaster (see also
note to I.3.82).

133 *ne'er had borne it out of*: Would never have carried
the victory away from.

143 *set off*: Set aside.

146 *it proceeds from policy*: Events will show that Mowbray
speaks prophetically here and at 181–2. *policy* could
mean 'dissimulation'.

149 *a ken*: Sight.

152 *battle*: Army.

    names: This may simply mean 'men', but it could mean 'men of distinction' (cf. *Henry V*, IV.8.104).

155 *reason will*: It stands to reason that. Falstaff has contrasted the physical and spiritual qualities of the soldier (see note to III.2.251–3). Westmorland argues that in both respects his men are stronger than those of the rebels.

160 *commission*: Pronounced '-i-on', as are *question* (165) and *action* (170, 190).

161 *In very ample virtue*: With the full authority.

163 *stand*: Insist.

164 *intended in*: Signified by.

165 *muse you make*: Am surprised you ask.

166 *schedule*: Statement.

167 *general*: Joint, common.

168 *several*: Individual.

170 *ensinewed to*: Joined together in.

171–2 *Acquitted ... our wills*: Provided we are pardoned for this present action, and our demands being met, then ...

174 *awful*: Q's spelling, *aweful*, points to the meaning.

178 *At either end*: *At*, the reading of both Q and F, is usually emended to 'And', giving the simple sense 'And either conclude' instead of the less obvious, but surely acceptable 'At either extremity'. Q's meaning cannot have puzzled those who prepared the copy for F.

    frame: Bring to pass.

179 *difference*: Battle.

184 *large*: Generous, all-encompassing.

185 *consist*: Insist.

187 *our valuation*: The way we are esteemed.

189 *nice*: Trifling.

    wanton: Frivolous.

191 *That, were our royal faiths martyrs in love*: So that, even if our faithfulness to the King was put to the test of dying for love of him.

192–4 *We shall ... partition*: For winnowing corn a gentle breeze was required to blow off the lighter chaff,

leaving the ears of corn for milling. The wind that
will blow on the former rebels will be so rough that
their virtues will be dismissed with their faults: even
death in the King's cause would not suffice to prove
their loyalty. Shakespeare may be making a contrast
with one of the earliest rebels of Henry's reign,
Aumerle, who is pardoned at the end of *Richard II*,
and as Duke of York leads the van at Agincourt
and is killed (*Henry V*, IV.6).

195–6 *weary ... grievances*: Tired of finding fault at every
opportunity, however trivial.

197 *doubt*: Suspicion.

198 *the heirs of life*: Those who survive the person executed.

199 *tables*: Notebooks, records.

201 *history*: Recount.

203–4 *so precisely ... occasion*: Eradicate from this land
everything which his fears draw to his attention.

208–12 *an offensive wife ... execution*: Those who seek
Shakespeare's biography in his writing suggest that
there is personal experience here; but he evidently
observed much, and there are no grounds for drawing
this conclusion.

211 *hangs*: Suspends.

213 *wasted*: Used up.

217 *offer*: Threaten.

219 *atonement*: Reconciliation.

224 *just distance*: Halfway. (See headnote to IV.2.)

226 *Before*: Be forward, lead on (a usage not found in
the *OED*).

IV.2

Most editions mark a partial exit at IV.1.226 and
begin a new scene. The traditional scene divisions
are preserved here for readers' convenience; but F,
which carefully divides the play into acts and scenes,
marks no division here and none is required since
the action is continuous. Shakespeare's source, Holinshed, is uncertain as to what happened and gives
two versions; the second refers to a meeting between
the disputants 'just in the midway betwixt both the

armies' (cf. *just distance 'tween our armies*, IV.1.224).
The rebels and Prince John confront one another
immediately in the play, and the audience has to
imagine that the location has shifted to halfway
between the armies.

8 *iron*: (1) Armoured; (2) merciless.

   man: Q reads *man talking*. It could be that the compositor was half-anticipating the next word, *Cheering*,
but it seems more likely that Shakespeare first wrote
'talking', then substituted 'cheering', but failed to
cancel 'talking'.

10 *the word to sword*: The word of God to war. In
Shakespeare's time *word* and *sword* sounded similar.

13 *countenance*: Support, approval.

14 *set abroach*: Open up.

17 *the books of God*: (1) Works of divinity; (2) God's
grace.

18 *speaker*: The Speaker in Parliament acts as interme-
diary between the members and the sovereign, a part
of his role that was of much greater significance in
Tudor and Stuart times than today.

20 *opener and intelligencer*: Interpreter and messenger.

21 *sanctities*: Holiness (or saints).

22 *workings*: Perceptions.

24 *Imply*: Insinuate. (F has the easier reading *Employ*.)

26 *taken up*: Enlisted.

28 *substitute*: Deputy. The sovereign was God's deputy
on earth.

30 *up-swarmed them*: Raised them up in swarms.

33 *misordered*: Disordered, confused.

   in common sense: As everyone can see.

34 *monstrous form*: This can be glossed as 'distorted
shape' or 'abnormal course', but the word *monstrous*
suggests one of the terrible creatures which rise first
from the sea and then from the earth in Revelation
13. This is the beast that stands for Antichrist, a
role in which, as a rebel against God's deputy, the
Archbishop finds himself, whether he likes it or not.

35 *hold . . . up*: Maintain.

36 *parcels*: Details.
   grief: Grievances.

38 *Hydra*: Many-headed. Hydra was the many-headed
   snake of Lerna which grew two heads for each one
   cut off.

39 *Whose dangerous . . . asleep*: Shakespeare has conflated
   Hydra, with its many heads (and doubtless eyes to
   go with them), and Argus, Juno's watchman, who
   had a hundred eyes and was charmed asleep by the
   music of Mercury.

44 *though*: Even if.

46 *theirs shall second them*: This continues the many-
   headed Hydra idea, made specific at 48, which also
   recalls the King's reported fear that one rebel killed
   Revives two greater in the heirs of life (IV.1.197–8).

47 *success of mischief*: A succession of disturbances.

49 *generation*: Offspring.

51 *sound the bottom*: Plumb the depths.

54–65 *I like . . . amity*: Holinshed remarks that when
   Westmorland saw the rebels' strength 'he subtly
   devised how to quail their purpose'. Shakespeare
   transfers the 'subtle device' to Prince John (though
   Westmorland is still party to the plan), in order, it
   has been suggested, to associate the duplicity with
   the royal household. Divorced from the horrors and
   exigencies of war, we may deplore Prince John's
   stratagem, but the fear of civil war was doubtless
   strong enough to allow an Elizabethan audience to
   accept any means of putting down rebellion. The
   Council of Constance (1410–15, contemporaneous
   with the reign of Henry IV) had decreed that faith
   need not be kept in dealings with heretics; and in
   Elizabethan eyes rebels were in much the same cat-
   egory. Prince John could claim (as indeed he does at
   112–14) that in undertaking to redress the grievances
   he does not promise to do so in any particular manner.
   He simply redresses them as he thinks fit, not as the
   rebels expect and desire. See also note to 121.

57 *lavishly*: Freely.

61 *several*: Respective.

79 *happy*: Appropriate.

80 *something*: Somewhat.

81 *Against*: In the face of.

83 *coz*: Cousin (as at III.1.62).

85 *passing*: Exceptionally.

88 *had been*: Would have been. It is ironic that the contest in which Mowbray's father took part, and which opens this four-part dramatization of the dispute between the houses of York and Lancaster, was also 'resolved' without a blow being struck (*Richard II*, I.3).

93 *trains*: Followers, armies.

95 *coped*: Encountered, fought.

107 *high treason*: This was defined in 1350–51, during the reign of Edward III, as an act 'compassing or imagining' the death of the king or his immediate family, killing his judges (who represented him in the administration of justice), levying war in the king's dominions or aiding the king's enemies.

109 *capital treason*: This is not a specific charge: treason was a capital offence and the adjective is simply a reminder of the penalty.

attach: Arrest.

115 *with a most Christian care*: We may take this ironically, but Prince John is doubtless sincere according to his interpretation of the Christian duty to rebels.

116 *look*: Expect.

117 *and such ... yours*: See second note to 122.

118 *shallowly*: Without adequate consideration.

119 *Fondly*: Ill-advisedly.

120 *stray*: Strays, fleeing stragglers.

121 *God ... today*: This is a traditional expression of indebtedness to God for victory. Henry V is even more forthright after Agincourt:

> ... be it death proclaimèd through our host
> To boast of this, or take that praise from God
> Which is His only. (*Henry V*, IV.8.113–15)

But Henry's men fought against odds; Prince John has won by a trick, so it is not the military virtues of courage and resolution that he attributes to God, but the subtle device that quailed the rebels' purpose (see note to 54–65). There is a similar, and certainly ironic, offer of praise to heaven at the end of Marlowe's play *The Jew of Malta*, in which victory is also gained by deceit. Prince John's stratagem is coldly efficient. There is nothing noble here, but nor has he risked the lives of his troops. His condemnation of the rebels is expressed in rhymed couplets, which, together with some alliteration, suggest a degree of self-satisfaction that prevents his winning our admiration. It is not long since he could swear, by the honour of his blood, that his father's purposes had been mistook (55–6); and we have now seen *his* purposes 'honourably' mistook.

122 *Some guard*: Some (of you) escort.

these traitors: This is F's reading. Q has *this traitour* (and it omits F's *and such acts as yours* in 117), but F is correct in suggesting that the Archbishop was not the only one of the rebels to be executed.

IV.3

F has no indication of a new scene here, despite the care with which it divides up the play; but *Exeunt* is marked at the end of IV.2 (F's IV.1), and that clearing of the stage technically ends the scene.

Like so much of *Henry IV, Part II*, this scene has a parallel in *Part I*, in this case Falstaff's supposed killing of Hotspur (V.4).

0 *Alarum*: A call to arms.

Excursions: Military attacks, sorties.

Sir John Colevile: In F Colevile is also brought on at the beginning of IV.1 (see note to 65); no exit is provided for him, so that he would leave at the end of IV.2 (F's IV.1) and would then have to re-enter immediately. That there is a time lapse between the two scenes is apparent from 24. Sir John Colevile of the Dale was a real person, but he is not mentioned

in the histories as being involved in the affair at
Gaultree Forest. With Hastings and others he was
executed at Durham when the King, after settling
matters in Yorkshire, moved north to attack the Earl
of Northumberland. But it has been suggested that
Colevile was pardoned, for a man of the same name
fought with Henry V in the campaign in France which
led to Agincourt; but names and descriptive adjuncts
could be passed on like noble titles. No certain reason
can be given for Shakespeare's choice of Colevile.
He might with historical accuracy have chosen Sir
John Lampley or Sir Robert Plumpton. It may be
that he was simply attracted by the name (which
might mean that he wished to engage the audience's
sympathies for Colevile, especially in view of his
resolute character); or he may have chosen it because
it was also the name of a contemporary Scottish spy
of ill repute (which would make his defeat by Falstaff
redound more obviously to the latter's credit). The
first explanation seems more probable.

Since the eighteenth century editors have expanded
this stage direction to indicate that Falstaff and
Colevile enter 'meeting'. The entry need not be so
arranged; for example, they might well enter at
sword-point, one facing the other, Falstaff backing
on to the stage first, asking his questions as Colevile
appears. Such an entry, with Falstaff backing away
but triumphing verbally and on the strength of his
reputation, would be appropriate to his character.

1 *condition*: Rank.

7–9 *dungeon . . . Dale*: The dale, like the dungeon, is *deep*.

13–14 *they are . . . death*: Sweat-drops become tears.

13 *lovers*: Friends.

18–19 *I have . . . of mine*: Falstaff's fatness speaks for itself
in all languages.

20–21 *indifferency*: Ordinary kind.

22 *womb*: Belly.

30 *but it should be*: If it were not.

31 *check*: Reproof.

34 *expedition*: Speed.

35–6 *foundered nine score and odd posts*: Lamed 180 and more
      post-horses.

40–41 *the hook-nosed fellow of Rome*: Julius Caesar.

41 *three words*: Q reads *there cosin*; F omits both words.
    This emendation, proposed by A. R. Humphreys,
    seems to provide what is required, since the Latin
    of Caesar's famous saying is precisely three words:
    '*Veni, vidi, vici*'. As Humphreys points out, Falstaff
    would be unlikely to be quite so impertinent as to
    address Prince John as cousin, and in any case he
    has little liking for him.

44 *Here ... yield him*: Falstaff's gesture makes an
    intriguing contrast with Hotspur's behaviour which
    was the source of Henry's complaint at the begin-
    ning of *Henry IV, Part I* (I.1 and 3); Hotspur refused
    to surrender his prisoners to the King (and indeed
    he was duty-bound to surrender only Mordake, who
    was of blood royal), but Falstaff yields Colevile,
    whom he was entitled to keep, without being asked.

46–7 *a particular ballad*: A ballad all about me. In *Part I*,
      II.2.43–5, Falstaff threatens to have ballads made on
      his companions and 'sung to filthy tunes'.

49–50 *show like gilt twopences to me*: Look like counterfeit
       coins in comparison with me. Twopenny pieces were
       often gilded so that they could be passed as half-
       crowns.

51–2 *the cinders of the element*: The stars of heaven.

55 *heavy*: Troublesome (also punning on Falstaff's weight).

57 *thick*: (1) Dim (as of a light); (2) thick (of Falstaff's
    body).

60 *Colevile*: This was pronounced as three syllables (see
    72), so some editors arrange this and the next two
    lines as two verse lines.

65 *Had they been ruled by me*: If they had taken my
    advice. Presumably Colevile had more sense than to
    trust Prince John. Some editors take this line as
    evidence that he should be present from the begin-
    ning of IV.1 (see note to IV.1.0), but he is given

no lines which would prove that the rebel lords had
the benefit of his advice. His remark must refer to
an incident not dramatized, or it is simply the general
observation of a soldier who feels he knows better
than his commanders.

71 *Retreat is made*: The signal for retreat has been
sounded.

stayed: Stopped.

73 *present*: Instant.

74 *Blunt*: See note to the stage direction at III.1.31.

78 *cousin*: Westmorland.

82 *stand*: Act as.

83 *in my condition*: Some editors gloss *condition* as 'natural
disposition', but Prince John's natural disposition,
from what we have seen, is hardly to speak better
of anyone than he deserves. He may mean 'in my
capacity' (as victorious commander and therefore
expected to speak well of his troops).

87–8 *a man cannot make him laugh*: Dr Johnson commented,
'He who cannot be softened into gaiety cannot easily
be melted into sadness.'

90 *proof*: Fulfilment.

92 *male green-sickness*: Green-sickness (chlorosis) was
a form of anaemia in young girls.

93 *get wenches*: Falstaff, an advocate of meat and
strong drink (to him indicative of virility), argues
that fish-eating and thin drink make a man anaemic
and so capable of begetting only girls. If there is a
sexual innuendo in *skill in the weapon is nothing without
sack* (111–12), that would tally with his assertion
here. But there was a proverb that 'Who goes drunk
to bed begets a girl', and this Falstaff seems to belie.

94 *inflammation*: Passions inflamed with drink.

95 *sherris-sack*: The white wine from Jerez, Spain –
sherry; but see note to I.2.199.

97 *Curdy*: Curd-like, thick.

98 *apprehensive*: Quick to apprehend or respond.

forgetive: Inventive (pronounced with the 'g' soft,
as in 'forge').

100 *becomes*: It is possible that the subject of *becomes* is
     shapes (see note to I.2.72–3), but probably Falstaff is
     loosely harking back to *good sherris-sack* (95), which
     becomes excellent wit by the process he has described.

102–3 *the liver*: See first note to I.2.177.

105 *parts' extremes*: Bodily extremities.

107 *this little kingdom, man*: See note to IV.1.54–5.

108 *vital commoners ... inland petty spirits*: Spirits of
     three kinds, natural, animal, and vital, were believed
     to permeate the blood and be carried by it to the
     various parts of the body, determining spiritual as
     well as physical characteristics.

111–14 *skill ... use*: Falstaff argues that sack gives the soldier
     courage to use his *weapon* and enables the scholar
     to use his *hoard* of *learning*. There may also be a
     sexual innuendo, despite the proverbial belief that
     drink prompts desire but inhibits performance; see
     note to 93.

113 *hoard ... devil*: Treasure was said to be guarded by
     devils or evil spirits.

114 *commences ... act*: Punning on the use of these words
     at Cambridge and Oxford Universities respectively
     for the conferring of degrees – enabling students to
     put to use their *hoard* of *learning*.

117 *husbanded*: Cultivated.

120 *human*: Secular.

127 *tempering*: Referring to the warming of soft wax
     between the fingers before using it to make a seal.

128 *seal with him*: (1) Come to an agreement with him;
     (2) mould him, like wax, to my purpose.

IV.4

We know from IV.5.233 that the Jerusalem Chamber
in Westminster Abbey is the location of IV. 4 and
IV.5 (which form a single continuous scene: see headnote to IV.5). Events are compounded; historically
the affair at Gaultree Forest dates from 1405, and
the victory at Bramham Moor (97–9) from 1408.
Henry was with the forces that marched north from
York (when the historical Colevile was executed; see

note to IV.3.). By 1408 the last armed rebellion of the reign had been put down, but Henry was already suffering from what was described as leprosy, visited on him, according to 'foolish friars' (as Holinshed puts it), for his having executed the Archbishop of York; but the disease was probably congenital syphilis. He became much more seriously ill in 1412 and by the end of that year was incapacitated. He died on 20 March 1413.

Q's stage direction gives the Earl of Kent an entry here, but he has no lines to speak. In 1413 he had been dead for five years, and the title was then vacant until 1461. Perhaps Shakespeare at first thought Kent would be 'available' for this scene because he was working from events of 1405, 1408 and 1413 simultaneously, but then realized that Kent was dead at the time of the King's illness and dropped him. Alternatively he may have confused the Lord Fauconbridge whose name appears in the Q entry to I.3 with William Neville, also a Lord Fauconbridge, who was granted the title of Earl of Kent in 1461.

  0 *carried in a chair*: This is not in Q or F, but it makes the King's illness apparent and his fainting more practicable without over-dramatization.

    Clarence: Historically he was in France at this time.

  2 *debate*: Struggle.

  3 *to higher fields*: On a crusade; see note to III.1.104.

  5 *addressed*: Made ready.

  6 *substitutes in absence*: Deputies.

    invested: Empowered with authority.

  7 *level*: Accessible.

20–48 *How chance ... gunpowder*: This plea for brotherly accord is probably inspired by a passage in Stow's *The Annals of England* (1592), though in Stow the King gives his advice to Prince Henry, not Clarence. He says he fears that after his death 'some discord shall grow and arise between thee and thy brother, Thomas Duke of Clarence, whereby the realm may be brought to destruction and misery, for I know

you both to be of great stomach and courage'. Prince
Henry promises he will honour and love his brothers
above all men 'as long as they be to me true'.

27 *omit*: Neglect.

30 *observed*: Humoured.

34 *humorous*: There is probably some wordplay here.
The word means 'capricious', which accords with
sudden, but there may be a suggestion of another
meaning of 'humorous': 'moist'. This is appropriate
to *winter*, and also suggests one of the four bodily
humours controlling the mental disposition.

35 *flaws congealèd*: Icy squalls.
spring of day: Daybreak.

41 *Confound*: Destroy.
working: Exertion.

45 *suggestion*: Suspicion.

48 *aconitum*: Aconite or wolf's-bane, to the Elizabethans
a poison; its medicinal qualities were not discovered
till much later.
rash: Violent.

52 *Canst thou tell that*: These words appear only in F.
Like those at 120 and 132 they could have been added
merely to fill out a line and may not be Shakespeare's.

54 *fattest*: Most fertile.

58 *blood weeps from my heart*: It was thought that every
sigh caused a drop of blood to drain from the heart.

64 *lavish*: Unrestrained.

65 *affections*: Inclinations.

66 *fronting*: Confronting.
opposed: Hostile.

67 *look beyond him*: Warwick protests that the King
exaggerates the Prince's current misdemeanours –
goes too far.

75 *Cast off his followers*: This suggests that the cold-
ness of blood which Falstaff finds in the Lancasters
(IV.3.114–20) will play its part in determining Prince
Henry's behaviour, despite all the sack that Falstaff
has induced him to drink. It anticipates the rejection
of Falstaff, and it looks back to the plan of action

Prince Henry outlined for himself in *Henry IV, Part I*, I.2.193–215. See also IV.5.155 and V.2.125–9.

77   *mete*: Appraise.

      other: Others.

79–80 *'Tis seldom ... carrion*: This may recall Judges 14:8, where Samson, turning aside from his path, saw a swarm of bees which had made honey in the carcase of a lion. The meaning of the King's words is that Prince Henry is unlikely to renounce his pleasure, however corrupt; but an Elizabethan audience might well remember that the circumstances of the honey and the lion led to Samson's famous riddle: 'Out of the eater came meat, and out of the strong came sweetness' (Judges 14:14), 'the strong' being the dead lion, the carrion; and the association of corruption with sweetness could readily be linked with the myth of the regenerate Hal.

90   *every course in his particular*: The general sense is clear enough – 'each incident in every detail' – but the word *course* is not easily glossed precisely. It has been explained as 'proceeding' and as 'phase', but what might be implied is the meaning used in bear-baiting, where a course was one of a succession of attacks. This meaning is used by Shakespeare (in *Macbeth*, V.6.11–12, and *King Lear*, III.7.53), and it would be appropriate here, since the insurrection put down at Gaultree was one of a series of attacks 'baiting' Henry IV.

      his: Its.

92   *haunch*: Hind part, latter end (an expression one would expect to be comic, like 'the buttock of the night', *Coriolanus*, II.1.48–9).

93   *Harcourt*: Shakespeare's creation.

97–9 *The Earl ... overthrown*: This refers to the battle of Bramham Moor (1408), in which the historic Northumberland at last behaved with distinction – and was killed. Shakespeare allows him no glory. See also headnote to I.1.

99   *shrieve*: Sheriff.

101 *at large*: In full.

104 *wet her fair words still in foulest terms*: F has *write* for
wet and *Letters* for *terms*. As A. R. Humphreys puts
it, the F reading 'seems a little glib and may indicate botching', but to explain the Q reading 'requires
three specialized interpretations in nine words', that
is, *wet* as a variant of 'wit', meaning 'bequeath'; *words*
as 'that which is granted'; *terms* as 'conditions' (though
that is not very 'specialized'). These interpretations
were proposed by Hilda M. Hulme in *Explorations
in Shakespeare's Language* (1962).
still: Always.

105 *stomach*: Appetite.

113 *look up*: Cheer up.

119 *wrought the mure*: Made the wall.

120 *and will break out*: Omitted from Q; see note to 52.

121 *fear*: Alarm.

122–5 *Unfathered heirs ... between*: Disturbance in the state
is reflected in unusual events in nature (see note to
IV.1.54–7). Prince Henry makes a point of the return
to normality in terms of *ebb* and *flood* at V.2.129–33.

122 *Unfathered heirs*: Children unnaturally conceived,
specifically by parthenogenesis. Such 'virgin births'
could be miraculous, but the offspring could be (like
the *loathly births of nature*) monstrous, ill-formed
creatures and were sometimes said to result from
the intercourse of a witch and an incubus (evil spirit).

125–8 *The river ... died*: Holinshed states that the Thames
flowed three times 'and no ebbing between' on 12
October 1412. But there is no record of any such
events in conjunction with the death of Edward III.

132 *Softly, pray*: Omitted from Q; see note to 52.

IV.5

As at IV.2 and IV.3, F does not mark a new scene
here. The action is continuous and the move to *some
other chamber* could easily be represented by movement across the stage. Otherwise, a formal change
of scene would have to be made in the middle of
the King's speech, which is absurd. However, as most

editors mark a new scene at this point, the tradition
is again followed here for readers' convenience.

Except perhaps at 107 Shakespeare makes nothing
of Holinshed's detailed account of an event of 1412,
when the Prince, seeking to remove Henry IV's
suspicions that he wished to usurp the throne, knelt
before him, gave him a dagger and invited him to
kill him, saying 'that his life was not so dear to him
that he wished to live one day with his [the King's]
displeasure'. *The Famous Victories of Henry V* bases
a scene on this.

The incident of the Prince's removal of the
crown is briefly described in Holinshed, where those
attending the King believe him dead and so inform
the Prince, who then takes away the crown. In *The
Famous Victories* the pattern of the incident is closer
to Shakespeare's version and, although the speeches
are much briefer, there is some similarity of tone,
with especially close parallels in the Prince's answer
to the King (139–77). In Samuel Daniel's poem
*The First Four Books of the Civil Wars between the
Two Houses of Lancaster and York* Henry (not the
Prince, as at 24–9 here) addresses the crown, and the
interchange between father and son after the King
has awoken includes the advice closely paralleled
at 204–15.

2 *dull*: This hardly goes with *hand*. It may be a transferred epithet, describing the music and meaning
  'inducing drowsiness'.

6 *changes*: Turns pale.

9 *heaviness*: Sadness.

10–17 Editions, including Q and F, vary in the treatment
  of these lines as prose or verse. The arrangement
  here allows for a movement from the prosaic to the
  poetic; Prince Henry's comment at 15–16 deliberately jars in content and tone with the verse immediately before and after.

14 *altered*: Good news might be expected to bring an
  alteration for the better, not for the worse, as is here

implied. But at IV.4.102 the King has said *wherefore should these good news make me sick?*, and although the Prince was not then present, his response here continues that train of thought.

25 *ports*: Gates.

28 *biggen*: Nightcap.

32 *gates of breath*: Mouth and nose.

33 *downy*: Q spells this *dowlny*, and F has *dowlney*; both spell *down* at 34 *dowlne*. Like the Q spelling *Scilens*, this has been taken to be of Shakespearian origin (see An Account of the Text, p. 127).

34 *suspire*: Breathe.

37 *rigol*: Circle.

43 *as immediate from*: As I am next in line to.

44 *Derives itself*: Descends.

50 *your majesty*: F adds *how fares your Grace?* This could be authorial, but it could well be an actor's interpolation, especially if actors' parts underlie F (see An Account of the Text, p. 127).

65 *part*: Action.

70 *thoughts*: Worries.

72 *engrossed*: Collected.

   pillèd: Pillaged. F has *pyl'd* (that is 'piled'), which makes easier sense; but Q's reading, followed here, has an appropriate forcefulness.

75 *arts and martial exercises*: Arts and arms were the two branches of a gentleman's education.

76 *tolling*: Levying (a toll – that is, the pollen).

76–7 *flower . . . wax*: F reads *flower* | *The vertuous Sweetes*, the line being completed with *our Thighes packt with Wax*. This disturbs the lineation as far as 80, and if 'The virtuous sweets' is included in a modern edition it has to be made a half-line on its own; the lineation can then follow that of Q. The source of 'The virtuous sweets' is not easily determined. It seems unlikely that Shakespeare, or even the most insensitive of writers, would deliberately add it and allow it to dislocate the following lines, especially as the addition also disrupts the sense; and it does not sound like an actor's interpolation. It is conceivable that Shakespeare started a modification, did not complete it and failed to score out this phrase, so that it was mistakenly included in F.

79   *Are murdered*: It is not the worker bees but the drones that are murdered, as Shakespeare knew, since he refers to the killing of the 'lazy yawning drone' in *Henry V*, I.2.204.

79–80   *This ... engrossments*: Proverbially the bee produces sweetness from even the bitterest flowers. Shakespeare reverses the normal course of nature (cf. IV.4.121–5), and he also inverts the syntax: *engrossments* ('accumulations') is the subject of the sentence and *taste* is the object. *Yields* is either the singular form for the plural (see note to I.2.72–3) or an error, induced by *taste*.

80   *ending*: Dying.

82   *determined*: Put an end to.

84   *kindly*: Natural (filial).

86–8   *tyranny ... eye-drops*: The Prince's sorrow would move even those who normally drink nothing but blood.

86   *tyranny*: Cruelty (and the tyrant himself).
       quaffed: Drank.

93   *Thy wish ... thought*: An idea already proverbial in Shakespeare's time.

95   *chair*: Throne.

99   *dignity*: High estate; cloud suggests both its height and its insubstantial nature.

100   *so weak a wind*: The wind was said to hold up the clouds; the King's breath sustains his life and thus his kingship.

101   *dim*: (1) Weak; (2) darkening to its close.

104   *sealed up*: Confirmed.

107   *a thousand daggers*: This is a common enough expression, but it may reflect the story of Prince Henry and the dagger (see headnote).

116   *compound*: Mix.

118   *Pluck down my officers*: Perhaps a suggestion that Prince Henry will dismiss the Lord Chief Justice.

119 *form*: Decorum, law and order.

120 *vanity*: Worthlessness, futility.

124 *confines*: Territories.

125 *dance*: Dancing was often associated with such vices as drinking and swearing, and it was frequently included in puritan attacks on the stage.

133 *flesh*: Initiate in bloodshed (as at I.1.149).

135–6 *When that ... thou*: 135–6 are addressed to the Prince (but *thou* in 137 is England); *care* implies 'caring for', 'looking after', and 'being anxious or uneasy'; *thy riots* are the excesses of wantonness and debauchery of which the Prince stands accused. The *riot* (136) is the public violence and disorder that the King foresees when England is in the Prince's care. But see V.5.65.

141 *dear*: Grievous.

145 *affect*: Aspire to.

147 *obedience*: Obeisance (kneeling).

155 *The noble change that I have purposèd*: See note to IV.4.75.

161 *thou best of gold art worse than gold*: The *best of gold* is the crown; coupled with the *care* it brings, it is *worse than gold*. At 164–5 the crown itself is seen as having eaten up the King, and at 168 it is treated as his murderer.

162 *carat*: Quality.

163 *medicine potable*: Aurum potabile (a liquid supposed to contain gold, credited with great medicinal powers).

167 *try*: Fight out.

169 *quarrel*: Aversion, hostility.

171 *strain*: Tendency.

173 *affection*: Inclination.

178 In F this speech begins with the line *O my Sonne!*, and the Prince's reply (220) begins with *My gracious Liege:*. Neither of these half-lines appears in Q; they echo the opening of the Prince's speech at 139, and they may well be actors' interpolations (see note to 50).

182 *latest*: Last.

184 *crooked*: Devious (one syllable). The guilt and self-justification of the usurper hang heavily over King Henry's speech.

185 *I met this crown*: The word *met* suggests that the King would like to argue that he did not seek the crown – as if he found it unclaimed and put it on (rather as the Prince has just done, technically usurping his father's crown). Richard by no means gave the crown to Henry. In *Richard II* York and Bolingbroke urge Richard to resign the crown (IV.i.179, 189 and 199), but Richard, in a dramatic moment, holds the crown in his hand, places Bolingbroke's hand on the other side, and bids him seize it (181–2). Any member of an audience who had seen *Richard II* would have no doubt that Henry IV did not merely 'meet' the crown. And an audience might remember Falstaff's superbly sardonic comment when the rebel Worcester protests that he has 'not sought the day of this dislike'; Falstaff remarks 'Rebellion lay in his way, and he found it' (*Henry IV, Part I*, V.i.26, 28). However Henry might rationalize his actions, however much he might vow a pilgrimage to the Holy Land, and however bad the state of England under Richard, he usurped the throne and he knew it (see, for example, 189). See also note to III.i.69.

188 *opinion*: Reputation.

189 *soil of the achievement*: Moral taint of any success (punning on *soil* as 'earth').

191 *snatched*: What was *met* is now *snatched*, a description more in line with King Richard's demand that Henry seize the crown (see note to 185).

     boisterous: Two syllables. The word means not only 'energetic' but also 'violent'; Henry means the first but implies the second.

195 *fears*: Objects of fear.

198 *argument*: Subject matter (of a play).

199 *purchased*: Again Henry means one thing ('fairly bought') but implies another (the legal meaning, 'acquired otherwise than by inheritance or descent').

201 *garland*: Crown (with the implication that it can be worn meritoriously).

successively: By right of succession.

203 *griefs*: Grievances.

green: Fresh (and still growing).

204 *my*: Q and F read *thy*, but *my* is surely intended. If Q alone had *thy*, it could be attributed to the compositor, who was inclined to make similar errors in setting *Richard II*. If F's *thy* comes from a source independent of Q, it could be that Shakespeare himself made a mistake, perhaps anticipating the *thy* later in the line (a type of error that is common).

207 *lodge*: Harbour.

211–12 *look | Too near unto*: Pay too much attention to (and consider usurping).

213–14 *busy giddy minds | With foreign quarrels*: The Prince quickly takes this advice, for at V.5.108–11 Prince John is prophesying an expedition to France.

215 *waste*: Weaken. Cf. *wasted* in the next line.

220 See note to 178.

229 *period*: Conclusion.

233 *Jerusalem*: The Jerusalem Chamber in Westminster Abbey took its name from inscriptions round the fireplace mentioning Jerusalem.

234–9 *Even there ... Harry die*: Holinshed recounts the legend that it had been prophesied that Henry would die in Jerusalem, the implication being that his death would occur during his proposed crusade (see note to III.1.104).

V.1

1 *By cock and pie*: A mild oath, meaning 'By God and the book of church services', *pie* being the ordinal of the Roman Catholic Church.

9 *William cook*: William the cook.

11–12 *those precepts ... wheat*: Davy is torn in two ways. It is his duty not only to provide for his master's guests but also to see that the day-to-day work of the farm is carried on and that the process of law continues (even to the point of protecting an *arrant knave*; see 36). Whilst the master can be wholly wrapped up in the excitement of receiving his guests, Davy has to keep his feet on the ground.

11 *precepts*: Writs.

12 *hade land*: Headland (that is, the strip of land left when ploughing so that the plough could be turned without disordering the furrows; it could be worked only after all tasks on the rest of the field had been completed). This is Q's spelling; F uses the more 'correct' version *head-land*.

13 *red wheat*: Late wheat, with a reddish tinge, unlike the white wheat of the main crop.

14 *pigeons*: In Shakespeare's time pigeons (doves) were a source of fresh meat, especially in winter. The large dovecote at his mother's house at Wilmcote, near Stratford-upon-Avon, can still be seen.

15 *note*: Invoice.

17 *cast*: Added up.

19 *link*: Either a rope or chain, or part of one.
bucket: This may mean 'pail', but it could be 'yoke' (see note to III.2.256–7).

21 *Hinckley*: A market town some thirty miles north-east of Stratford-upon-Avon.

22 *answer*: Answer for, make amends for.

23 *short-legged hens*: Preferable to those with long legs, because they had more and better flesh.

24 *tiny*: F reads *tine* here and *tyne* at V.3.56, an example of the tendency for a later edition to make a difficult word easier, for at the time when *Henry IV, Part II* was written, 'tine' was the more common version of the word. 'Tiny' is first recorded in 1598 and 1599, and 'tine' seems to have dropped out fairly quickly thereafter, perhaps because the second syllable added to the sense of diminutiveness.
kickshaws: Fancy extra dishes (from the French '*quelques choses*').

29 *backbitten*: By lice.

31 *Well conceited*: Very witty.

33-4 *William Visor ... o'th'Hill*: It is not possible to be
certain of these identifications, but *Woncot* is a local
pronunciation for Woodmancote in Gloucestershire,
and a family named Visor (or Vizard) lived there in
the early seventeenth century; the nearby Stinchcombe
Hill could be *th'Hill*, and there was a Perkis (or
Purchase) family there. Shakespeare almost certainly
knew this area: in *Richard II*, when Bolingbroke
is marching through Gloucestershire, Hotspur, asked
how far it is to Berkeley Castle, replies that it
stands 'by yon tuft of trees' (II.3.53); and Berkeley
can be seen in a copse less than four miles from
Stinchcombe Hill.

42 *bear out*: Help.

44 *honest friend*: Good friend (not implying that he is
either honest or good in anything but his friendship
with Davy).

46 *shall have no wrong*: Shall be fairly treated. It has
been suggested that Shakespeare is depicting petty
corruption of the magistracy here. This argument
is partly based on an accusation made in the House
of Commons in 1601 that a Justice of the Peace
would for half a dozen chickens 'dispense with a
whole dozen of penal statutes'. Doubtless there was
dishonesty among justices, but Shakespeare's point
here is surely the reverse. Shallow is shown to be
rather silly and very naive, but basically kind and
human; Davy is concerned only to ensure that his
friend has a fair hearing – which Shallow grants.

46-7 *Look about*: Look sharp!

52 *tall*: (1) Lofty (ironically, the Page being small);
(2) valiant.

56 *quantities*: Little pieces.

58 *a wonderful thing*: Falstaff's comments suggest that
he is being purely ironic, yet there is much to be
admired in the relationships Shakespeare dramatizes
in Gloucestershire. Bolingbroke imagined executive
efficiency could replace the mystique of kingship,
and Touchstone (in *As You Like It*) thought his court

wit superior to the natural sympathy and understanding of the shepherd Corin; so Falstaff imagines
his cunning and worldly wisdom are superior to the
good-natured folly of Shallow and the dutifulness
of Davy.

58–9 *semblable coherence*: Close correspondence.

61 *conversing*: Associating.

62 *married in conjunction*: Intimately united.

63 *with the participation of society*: By their participating
with one another, associating together.

64–8 *If I had ... servants*: Falstaff explains how to present
a request indirectly. Had he a favour (*suit*) to beg
of Shallow he would humour his servants, stressing
in what close confidence they were with their master;
if · he wanted something of the servants, he would
flatter (*curry with*) their master that he (Shallow) had
them wholly in his control.

66 *near*: Intimate with.

69 *carriage*: Behaviour.

70–71 *let men take heed of their company*: Proverbial; Falstaff
apparently fails to recognize its relevance to Prince
Henry.

73, 74 *six fashions ... four terms ... two actions*: Four law
terms make up the lawyer's year. Falstaff sees *fashions* changing rapidly – a new one every two months
– but *actions* (lawsuits) proceeding slowly, a single
action taking two *terms*. The legal references (and
the Latin *intervallums*: 'intervals') may have been
designed to appeal to law students in the audience.

76 *sad*: Serious, grave.

76–7 *never had the ache in his shoulders*: Falstaff may
mean simply that Shallow has never had to bear the
problems of the 'real' (city) world on *his shoulders*
and so is not bowed down with pain. But he may
refer to experience of another kind: *ache* was used
of the pain of veneral disease (as in 'incurable bone-
ache', *Troilus and Cressida*, V.1.20–21), and although
Shallow has known whores (III.2.193–4 and 304) he
seems to have escaped venereal disease. The noun

ache (but not the verb) was pronounced 'aitch' in
Shakespeare's time.

78 *like a wet cloak ill laid up*: Creased like a wet cloak
that was not properly hung up to dry.

V.2

7–8 *The service ... injuries*: The Lord Chief Justice fears
that Prince Henry, now King Henry V, will seek
revenge for his action against him (see I.2.54 and
note). His fears resemble those expressed by the dead
King at IV.5.118–38, especially in the first line of
that passage, *Pluck down my officers, break my decrees*.

13 *fantasy*: Wildest imaginings.

14 *heavy issue*: Sorrowful descendants.

15 *temper*: Disposition.

18 *strike sail*: Submit.

22 *forgot to*: Forgotten how to.

23 *our argument*: The subject of our conversation.

30 *to find*: To expect.

31 *coldest expectation*: Bleakest anticipation.

34 *your stream of quality*: The current of your dignity.

38 *raggèd*: Mean, beggarly.

forestalled remission: This is a little difficult to interpret. The Lord Chief Justice has yet to be accused
by the new King of having performed his office
incorrectly, and *forestalled* is probably to be taken
as 'intercepted' – he will not ask pardon before a
charge has even been laid against him – but it could
also mean 'that will certainly be refused'.

42 *Blunt*: See note to the stage direction at III.1.31. Q's
direction is retained (and expanded) here because it
seems unlikely that the King would enter unattended
(as in F).

44–5 *This new and gorgeous garment ... me*: This suggests
an understanding of kingship that Shakespeare also
demonstrates in the lines in *Henry V* beginning,
'And what have kings that privates have not too, |
Save ceremony' (IV.1.231 onwards), and the passage
in *Richard II*, IV.1, where Richard proceeds to
'undo' himself, separating from himself the insignia

of kingship until, when he has completed this task, '"God save King Henry," unkinged Richard says' (IV.1.219). The notion that king and man were not indissolubly united runs as an undercurrent through all four plays of this sequence; in the political affairs of the Stuarts it was to be fought out soon after, and disastrously for Charles I. Kingship is like a garment that can be put on and off; and, as Shakespeare shows in his characterization of Macbeth, kingly garments may not fit a usurper.

48 *Amurath*: A topical allusion to a current example of tyranny: in 1574 Sultan Murad III, known as Amurath, on succeeding his father, killed all his brothers; and his successor did the same when he came to the throne in 1596. Amurath was the subject of a play, *The Courageous Turk*, performed at Oxford in 1619.

52 *deeply*: Profoundly and seriously.

63 *strangely on me*: As if I were a stranger.

65 *measured*: Judged.

70 *Rate*: Admonish.

71 *easy*: Insignificant.

72 *Lethe*: A river in Hades (the underworld); to drink it – not to be *washed in* it – brought forgetfulness.

73 *use the person of*: Represent. The expression is technically exact; judges represent the King in administering justice.

74 *image*: Symbol.

79 *presented*: Represented.

84 *garland*: Crown. See note to IV.5.201.

86 *awful*: See note to IV.1.174.

87 *sword*: In the coronation service the Archbishop officiating offers the sovereign the Sword of Spiritual Justice and says, 'With this sword do justice'; it is then worn briefly by the sovereign and carried naked before him for the rest of the ceremony. It is to this sword that the Lord Chief Justice refers. See also 103 and 114.

90 *your workings in a second body*: Duties as carried out by your representative.

92 *propose*: Imagine. This passage recalls the play-acting of *Henry IV, Part I*, II.4.

97 *soft*: Gently, quietly.

98 *considerance*: Reflection.

99 *in your state*: From your throne, in your capacity as king.

102 *right justice*: There is no punctuation between these words in Q and F. Some modern editors (but not all) add a comma after *right*. The more difficult reading preferred here gives the sense 'justice itself'. *weigh*: Consider, judge.

103 *still bear the balance and the sword*: See first note to stage direction at I.2.52.

109 *proper*: Own.

115 *rememberance*: Reminder.

119–21 *My voice . . . directions*: A good monarch was advised, among many other things, to listen to and act upon the advice of elder statesmen.

123–4 *My father . . . affections*: The obvious implication is that Prince Henry's youthful wildness has been buried with his father, but there is a sense in which Henry IV's wildness – his guilt in usurping the throne – is also buried. Cf. IV.5.184–5. Several interpretations of *affections* are possible, and one need not exclude the others. 'Natural disposition' – that which will be modified by cultivation and civilizing influences – may be implied; or the reference may be to the Prince's (past) inclinations – the *riots*, excess, mentioned by Henry IV at IV.5.135 – or, simply, to lusts.

125 *sadly*: Gravely.

126 *mock*: Disprove.

129 *After my seeming*: According to my outward appearance. (See note to IV.4.75.)

130 *proudly*: Overbearingly, unreasonably.

131 *Now . . . sea*: Nature is returning to normality. Cf. IV.4.122–5 (esp. 125) and notes.

132 *state of floods*: Majesty of the oceans.

134 *we*: Only now does the new King adopt the royal plural. His father was quicker to use it and even

quicker to execute justice as if he were already king
(*Richard II*, IV.1.90, III.1).

135 *limbs*: Members (of the body politic).

141 *accite*: Summon.

142 *remembered*: Mentioned.

    state: Men of rank, government.

143 *consigning to*: Endorsing.

V.3

3 *graffing*: Grafting.

    caraways: Sweetmeats containing caraway seeds.

8 *Spread*: Lay the cloth on the table. Cf. *cover*, II.4.10.

9 *well said*: Well done. Cf. III.2.267.

11 *husband*: Husbandman, steward.

16 *Ah, sirrah*: An exclamation addressed to the world
in general and no one in particular.

17–22 Silence's songs are set as prose in Q and F, except
for the one at 32–5, which F prints as verse. All of
them sound traditional but only the one at 73–5 has
been identified; it is from a drinking song called
'Monsieur Mingo' which Orlando di Lasso set to
music. Its popularity can be gauged from the fact
that snatches from it appear in plays by Nashe,
Jonson, Chapman and Marston.

19 *flesh*: See note to II.4.339.

22 *ever among*: All the while.

27 *Proface*: May it do you good (a polite formula before
eating or drinking, derived from the French '*bon
prou vous fasse*').

28 *want*: Lack.

29 *bear*: Put up with things.

34 *wags*: The singular form for the plural.

38–9 *I have ... now*: As Silence is drinking, *merry*
may mean 'slightly tipsy'; or, as his song at 32–5
suggests, it may mean 'happy'. A third possibility
is that he claims he can, on occasion, be amusing.
In the theatre Silence certainly is a source of
laughter, but not because he is himself witty; the
nearest he gets to wit is at 89–90 and that may
be accidental.

38 *twice and once*: The formula was evidently a stock type of inversion suggesting frequency.

40 *leather-coats*: Russet apples (which have rough, tough skins).

46 *leman*: Sweetheart, lover.

52 *let it come*: A drinking cry, 'pass it round'.

53 *a mile to th'bottom*: Another drinking term; Silence undertakes to drain the cup even if it is a mile deep.

56 *tiny*: See first note to V.1.24.
   thief: Wretch. Lady Percy uses the word affectionately of Hotspur in *Henry IV, Part I*, III.1.229.

58 *cabileros*: Gallants.

59 *once*: One day.

63 *pottle-pot*: Two-quart tankard (twice the amount that Shallow has mentioned).

64 *By God's liggens*: The origin of this oath is not known.

65 *out*: Drop out.

72 *done me right*: Done the right thing by me (by drinking as much as I have). *Do me right* (73) was a common drinking challenge.

73–5 *Do me right ... Samingo*: See note to 17–22. *Dub me knight* refers to the Elizabethan practice of 'knighting' whoever drank the most or drank urine; *Samingo* is probably a corruption of 'Sir Mingo' ('*mingo*' is Latin for 'I urinate').

79 *somewhat*: Something worth doing (as a drinker).

87 *greatest*: (1) Most important, because Prince Henry is King; (2) largest, which meaning Silence takes up in his comment. Whether he is being deliberately witty or comically uncomprehending is not clear, but the latter seems more likely.

89 *but*: Apart from.
   goodman: Title for those, such as yeomen and farmers, below the rank of gentleman.

90 *Barson*: No particular place is necessarily intended; but there is a Barston between Solihull and Coventry, some fifteen miles north-east of Stratford-upon-Avon, and a Barcheston (sometimes pronounced Barston) twelve miles to the south-east.

92 *recreant*: One who has broken faith or yielded in battle.

93–6 *Sir John ... price*: Pistol has a new verse style: for the moment he has abandoned his rant and lets fly a joyous jingle.

97–8 *like a man of this world*: That is, in plain words.

99 *A foutre for*: An indecent expression of contempt.

101–2 *O base Assyrian ... thereof*: Falstaff joins in Pistol's game, imitating his style. No particular *Assyrian knight* is referred to; Assyrians were thought of as brigands by the Elizabethans, and that occupation is close enough to Pistol's. An old ballad telling the story of *Cophetua*, an African king who 'cared not for womenkind' but saw, loved and married a beautiful beggar-girl, was published in 1612. Shakespeare also refers to it in *Love's Labour's Lost* (I.2.104–9, IV.1.67–9), *Romeo and Juliet* (II.1.14) and *Richard II* (V.3.79).

104 *Shall dunghill curs confront the Helicons*: The *Helicons* were the Muses. Pistol, still incensed at Silence's mention of *Puff*, turns on the poor old man again and complains of his singing a line of a ballad in competition with the outpourings of one who is (or has) a true muse, Pistol himself.

105 *baffled*: This was a fairly new word in Shakespeare's time, and its meaning was uncertain and shifting. Its primary sense is related to the public disgracing of a knight who had committed perjury – the *recreant* that Pistol calls Silence (92), though he is a Justice of the Peace, not a knight; Pistol may be accusing Silence of treating the *news* with contempt. But Shakespeare may have had in mind the sense 'confounded' or 'foiled': Silence, by joining in, is hindering the telling of the news (although the chief hindrance is, of course, Pistol himself).

106 *Furies*: In classical mythology, avenging goddesses; see also V.5.37, Alecto.

108 *therefor*: For that.

113–15 *Under ... thine office*: Shallow's *office* as Justice of the Peace has automatically terminated on the death of the King.

113 *Besonian*: Knave (literally, raw recruit); the word, from Italian, gives an excellent high-sounding impression.

118–19 *do this ... Spaniard*: *fig me* is a variant of *foutre* (99), and Pistol accompanies it with the traditional gesture (*this*), putting the thumb between the first and middle fingers. This originated in Spain, hence *The bragging Spaniard*.

120 *just*: Exact, true.

123 *double-charge*: Pistol will be doubly loaded with honours. The expression plays on his name.

133 *sick*: Longing.

134 *take any man's horses*: Falstaff does not mean to steal the horses, but to ride post-haste, hiring horses on the strength of the King's name. The owners will forgo only hiring fees, not the horses themselves. Nevertheless, in taking the King's name so, Falstaff presumes too much; the outcome for him (and for Shallow) is sadder and more serious than was the outcome for Prince Henry in presuming to take the crown before his father's death.

134–6 *the laws of England ... Lord Chief Justice*: This 'terrible sentence', as William Empson described it, might be guaranteed to shock an Elizabethan audience, which would be appalled that the law could be held in contempt by sectional interests. Falstaff's comic role would not protect him here; his attitude would be rejected, and it is no coincidence that he is given these lines at this point. Even if an Elizabethan audience had missed all the earlier signals (as modern audiences are liable to do), King Henry's rejection some eighty lines later would come as no surprise to them after Falstaff's words here. Shakespeare gives a similar sentiment to Northumberland: *Let order die!* (I.1.154); Northumberland and Falstaff are two aspects of Rebellion – Northumberland the political rebel, Falstaff 'that reverend Vice, that grey Iniquity' (see *Part I*, II.4.441 and note to 131–2 there). Falstaff's attitude is apparent to the Lord Chief Justice as early as II.1.128–9 when he says, *You speak as having power to do wrong*.

137 *Let vultures ... also*: Pistol may be alluding to Tityus
    (whose liver was gnawed by vultures) or Prometheus
    (whose liver was gnawed by an eagle). He makes
    the same reference in *The Merry Wives of Windsor*,
    I.3.80: 'Let vultures gripe thy guts!' Similar expres-
    sions occur in other plays of the period, which no
    doubt are again Pistol's source here, rather than a
    reading of the classics themselves.

138 *Where ... I led*: A line, also quoted in *The Taming
    of the Shrew*, IV.1.126, from a poem, now lost, in
    which a lover laments the loss of his freedom.

V.4

We now approach the end of the play, and two
important events are to be dramatized: the coronation of Henry V and the rejection of Falstaff. One
is a matter for rejoicing and the other (however
much it is deserved) a matter for regret. Shakespeare
now introduces a little scene, partly to allow dramatic
time for Falstaff and Shallow's journey (though even
the strewing of rushes at the beginning of V.5 would
suffice for that). Adapters have often omitted this
scene, but its sordidness is essential. To remove it
is to romanticize the end of the play (indeed, the
whole play) and to lose that vital contrast between
the pomp of coronation and the other side of the
coin – Hal's past and Falstaff's present.

0 *Enter Beadles ... Doll Tearsheet*: Q has *Enter Sincklo
    and three or foure officers* (with no mention of the
    Hostess and Doll). John Sincklo's name appears in
    other plays, *Henry VI, Part III*, *The Taming of the
    Shrew*, Marston's *The Malcontent* and the 'plot' (the
    outline indicating entries) of *Seven Deadly Sins, Part
    II*. It seems, from the part he plays here (see 8, 10,
    18, 20, 27–30) and the other roles for which he is
    named, that Sincklo was unusually thin and pale,
    and it is suspected that Shakespeare wrote a number
    of other small parts with him specifically in mind:
    possibly Snare (II.1) and Shadow (III.2) in this play,
    the Apothecary in *Romeo and Juliet*, Pinch in *The*

Comedy of Errors and Holofernes in *Love's Labour's Lost*. Sincklo is not among the *Principall Actors* listed at the beginning of the first Folio, probably because he was only a small-part actor.

Beadles: Minor parish officers, responsible for punishing petty criminals.

3 *drawn my shoulder out of joint*: Constables and other officers had a reputation for grabbing their victims' shoulders vigorously.

5 *whipping-cheer*: Whipping fare, all the whipping she wants (whipping being the punishment meted out to whores – and actors who toured without a licence).

6 *about her*: Either 'because of her' or 'in her company'.

7 *Nut-hook*: Literally, a hooked stick like a shepherd's crook, used for drawing down branches (applied to beadles and constables, perhaps because they, like the *Nut-hook*, catch hold of what they are after).

8 *tripe-visaged*: If this is a specific rather than a general insult, the Beadle's face is presumably pale and pock-marked, like tripe.

8–9 *the child I go with*: Doll maintains that she is pregnant, probably in the hope that this will save her from rough handling. The Beadle is not taken in, and at 14–15 he implies that she has stuffed her dress with a cushion.

12–13 *I pray ... miscarry*: As at 24 the Hostess says the opposite of what she means.

17 *amongst*: Between.

18 *thin man in a censer*: Censers (perfuming pans) often had figures embossed on them in low relief.

19 *swinged*: Thrashed.
bluebottle: Elizabethan beadles wore a blue livery.

20 *correctioner*: An official of the House of Correction or jail – Bridewell.

21 *forswear half-kirtles*: Give up wearing skirts. A kirtle was a bodice and skirt, a half-kirtle the skirt part.

22 *knight-errant*: Here, one who errs at night, i.e. a prostitute.

24 *right ... might*: See note to 12–13.

25 *of sufferance comes ease*: The Hostess may be confusing
'sufferance' and 'suffering', though in Elizabethan
English the words were closer in meaning than
they are now. The phrase is proverbial, the Hostess
comforting herself that her suffering will earn her
freedom from pain at some future date.

29 *atomy*: The Hostess means 'anatomy' (which F prints)
but she uses – rather appropriately – the Elizabethan
word for 'atom'.

30 *rascal*: Young lean deer; Doll has already used the
term at II.4.39.

V.5

There is a strange difference between the arrangement of this scene in F and in Q. Q has a procession to the coronation and then another for the
return (as reproduced here); F misses out the first
procession. If actors' parts underlie the F text (see
An Account of the Text, pp. 125–7), the omission
would be understandable, for the procession involves
no lines for the actors to speak. It might be expected
that, if Q were being at all closely consulted, the
first procession would be picked up from it, but
possibly whoever left it out was in some way misled
by the Third Groom's speech with its reference to
coming *from* the coronation (see note to 3–4). F might
represent a cut – even a cut made by Shakespeare
– but it seems reasonable to expect that, having gone
to the trouble of arranging and providing for one
procession, the company would wish to delight the
audience with more than one sight of the spectacle.

Henry VIII, performed some fifteen years after
Henry IV, Part II, also includes a coronation procession (IV.1.36). From the way in which it is
described it seems clear that Shakespeare's company
had appropriate ceremonial costumes for it; and we
know from details of expenditure that plays in
Shakespeare's time were often sumptuously dressed,
so it is very probable that the procession in *Part II*
was lavishly presented.

There is also a christening procession in *Henry VIII*, and the dialogue (V.4) and the stage direction (V.5) suggest that it came down steps at one side of the stage, past the groundlings standing in front of the stage, forcing them back out of the way, up steps at the other side of the stage, and then, as F's direction puts it, '*The Troope passe once about the Stage*'. In this way part of the audience would become 'extras' in the stage production; and there would be full opportunity for all the audience to see every detail of the procession. In *Henry IV, Part II* the procession may have done no more than *passe ouer the stage*, as Q has it; but it would be surprising if an opportunity for pageantry were not used to the full in the Elizabethan theatre.

1 *rushes*: Strewn on floors or, as here, in the street as a mark of deference.

3–4 *two o'clock ... coronation*: Since (in Q's version of the scene) the King is about to appear on his way to the Abbey, it is strange that the Groom should speak of his return. If, as in F, the first procession is cut, there is no need for such haste – and F does not include the words *Dispatch, dispatch* (it also omits the Third Groom himself, his two lines being given to the First Groom). There may be an authorial error here.

6 *grace*: Honour.
leer upon him: Falstaff would be expected to bow his head as the King passes, but he proposes to cast a sly glance (*leer*) at him to attract his attention.

12 *bestowed*: Laid out.

15, 17, 19 *SHALLOW ... PISTOL ... PISTOL*: These lines are distributed here as in F. Q gives line 15 to Pistol and agrees with F in giving him lines 17 and 19. Many editors follow F at 15 and reassign 17 and 19 to Shallow. But if the tentative suggestion that actors' parts underlie the F text (see An Account of the Text, pp. 125–7) is correct, then F's allocations have a claim to be respected. The difficulty is that 19, if not 17 too, is reminiscent of Shallow's habit of repeating what he says several times in succession. However, Falstaff has just called up Pistol to stand behind him, and it is surely not beyond Pistol to mimic the old Justice. Most of his language imitates that of plays he has heard and there would be a certain humour in his now imitating the language of a character in the play in which he is appearing. It is also more effective on the stage to have dialogue shared between more than two of the characters appearing together, and Pistol's mocking of Shallow's mode of speech would provide a useful scrap of interaction.

22 *shift me*: Change my clothes.

28 *semper idem . . . est*: The two Latin tags mean 'ever the same' and 'apart from this there is nothing'.
    obsque: An error for 'absque', but it is impossible to tell whether the blame lies with Shakespeare, Pistol, or the compositor.

28–9 *'tis all in every part*: It is not clear what this means, and probably it was not absolutely clear in the copy or to the compositors. It is usually explained as an English proverb roughly equivalent to the sense of the Latin: ''Tis all in all and all in every part.' Q does not have *all*, and F has either restored what Q left out or added it to bring it close to a proverb of the day. Shakespeare may have intended ''tis in every part', Pistol adapting the proverb to his own use as he does with the plays he quotes from.

31 *liver*: See first note to I.2.177.

33 *Helen*: The name of Helen of Troy was often used for wives and mistresses. But its application to Doll is absurd, and it must sharply remind an audience that the prostitute hauled away, cursing, in the last scene is Falstaff's Doll.

34 *contagious*: Foul, injurious to life (other than by disease).

36 *mechanical*: Of a mechanic (labourer).

37 *Alecto's snake*: Alecto was one of the Furies (see note to V.2.106), who were described as having snakes writhing in their hair.

38 *in*: In prison.

43 *imp*: An obsolete word for a descendant of a noble house.

46 *vain*: Foolish. There is something particularly chilling in having the Lord Chief Justice, of all people, *speak to* Falstaff.

50 *I know thee not, old man*: The rejection of Falstaff is discussed in the Introduction, p. lvii. Henry as king has adopted a new style of speech, just as he has put on a *new and gorgeous garment* (V.2.44). He speaks with a new authority, taking on the judicial accent of the Lord Chief Justice, whose advice he has said he will now take: *My voice shall sound as you do prompt mine ear* (V.2.119).

56-8 *the grave ... fool-born jest*: An eighteenth-century editor, William Warburton, described this as 'one of Shakespeare's grand touches of nature'. For a brief moment the King slips back into his former self, jesting about Falstaff's bulk (though a trifle sardonically); and then, before Falstaff can respond in like kind, he pulls himself together: *Reply not to me ...*

65 *riots*: A word the King's father has used about him – for example at IV.4.62 and IV.5.135.

69 *competence of life*: Sufficient for living comfortably.

71 *we*: The royal plural; see V.2.134 and the note.

79 *That can hardly be*: There is no good reason why Shallow cannot have his money back, for even Falstaff has not had time to *bestow* it yet (see 11-13).

89 *but a colour*: Only a pretence.

90 *colour*: (1) Appearance; (2) halter (collar).
     die: (1) Die (by hanging); (2) dye (*colour*).

92 *Lieutenant*: Pistol's promotion may be a gift that Falstaff feels he can bestow at no cost to himself.

93 *soon at night*: Towards evening (a common Elizabethanism).

94-5 *carry Sir John ... with him*: This detail is added by Shakespeare, and it has been suggested that it is an act of personal revenge by the Lord Chief Justice. But the Fleet prison had not then acquired its bad reputation, and Queen Elizabeth was accustomed to send there courtiers who had displeased her. It has also been pointed out that the banishment from the court could not immediately be made effective whilst the coronation festivities were in progress, and that being held in the Fleet would be an interim measure until the Lord Chief Justice had time to hear Falstaff and his *company*, which, as he says, will be soon. Nevertheless, all explanations made, the action of the play does not require Falstaff's imprisonment (still less Shallow's), and, if it is a kind of joke, as has also been suggested, it is pretty sour, coming hard on the rejection. The imprisonment of Falstaff and his companions, even if it is brief, and less uncomfortable than we might imagine, is nonetheless a reminder of the cold Lancastrian wind that is blowing through the land.

  99 *Si fortuna ... contenta*: See the note to II.4.176.

 103 *conversations*: Behaviour.

108–10 *ere this year ... France*: See IV.5.213–14 and note.

 109 *civil swords*: Swords recently engaged in civil strife.

EPILOGUE

Many editors have assigned the Epilogue to a dancer because of the references at 17–18 and 32. There is no evidence that there was any such dancer, but there was certainly a member of Shakespeare's company who was famous for his dancing: the clown, William Kemp. We know that Kemp played Dogberry in *Much Ado About Nothing*, probably written a year or so after *Henry IV, Part II* but published in the same year (1600). It cannot be more than a guess, but it seems at least likely that this Epilogue, either wholly or in part, was spoken by Kemp (but see note to 21–2).

    After a line of introduction, the Epilogue is divided into three paragraphs, which may represent three stages of development. The first paragraph could be the original Epilogue. In Q (as in this edition) it concludes with an indication that the speaker kneels *to pray for the Queen*; in F this is transferred to the very end of the Epilogue. There are epilogues in other plays – for example, in *A Nice Wanton* (an interlude published in 1560 but written in the reign of Edward VI) – that invite the audience to pray for the sovereign, and one would expect that to mark the conclusion of this Epilogue. The second paragraph might be an extension of the first, but it could be a complete Epilogue in its own right. The last paragraph is introduced in a way that may suggest that it is an addition, but it must have been written before *Henry V* (see note to 27). All three paragraphs might have been used on their own on different occasions. Thus the reference at 8–9 to *a displeasing play* could only be made when it recalled some particular event known to the audience (unless the company had a habit of performing displeasing plays).

 1 *curtsy*: Bow (by either sex).

 6 *doubt*: Fear.

 7 *venture*: Attempt (at his speech).

8–9 *a displeasing play*: This has not been identified. See also headnote above.

 11 *ill venture*: Unsuccessful expedition.
    break: (1) Break my promise; (2) go bankrupt.

 14 *Bate me*: Let me off.

21–2 *All the gentlewomen here have forgiven me*: J. Dover Wilson suggested that this might appropriately be spoken by the Page.

 27 *with Sir John in it*: Falstaff does not appear in *Henry V* (though his death is mentioned). Consequently this part of the Epilogue could hardly have been written after Shakespeare had started *Henry V*, probably within a year of completing *Henry IV, Part II*. At this point he evidently expected Falstaff's fortunes to revive; why they did not can only be conjectured.

 29 *sweat*: Plague or venereal disease.

30 *Oldcastle*: It is very surprising that Shakespeare's use of the name Oldcastle in the original version of *Henry IV, Part I* should have seemed again to need explanation. Someone, however, must have thought a disclaimer essential.

The National: three theatres and so much more...

www.nationaltheatre.org.uk

In its three theatres on London's South Bank, the National presents an eclectic mix of new plays and classics, with seven or eight shows in repertory at any one time.

And there's more. Step inside and enjoy free exhibitions, backstage tours, talks and readings, a great theatre bookshop and plenty of places to eat and drink.

Sign-up as an e-member at www.nationaltheatre.org.uk/join and we'll keep you up-to-date with everything that's going on.

NATIONAL THEATRE
SOUTH BANK
LONDON SE1 9PX

PENGUIN SHAKESPEARE

HENRY IV, PART I
WILLIAM SHAKESPEARE

WWW.PENGUINSHAKESPEARE.COM

Prince Hal, the son of King Henry IV, spends his time in idle pleasure with dissolute friends, among them the roguish Sir John Falstaff. But when the kingdom is threatened by rebellious forces, the prince must abandon his reckless ways. Taking arms against a heroic enemy, he begins a great and compelling transformation – from irresponsible reprobate to noble ruler of men.

This book includes a general introduction to Shakespeare's life and the Elizabethan theatre, a separate introduction to *Henry IV, Part I*, a chronology of his works, suggestions for further reading, an essay discussing performance options on both stage and screen, and a commentary.

Edited by: Peter Davison

With an introduction by Charles Edelman

General Editor: Stanley Wells

PENGUIN SHAKESPEARE

HENRY VI, PART II
WILLIAM SHAKESPEARE

WWW.PENGUINSHAKESPEARE.COM

Henry VI is tricked into marrying Margaret – lover of the Earl of
Suffolk, who hopes to rule the kingdom through her influence. There is
one great obstacle in Suffolk's path, however – the noble Lord
Protector, whom he slyly orders to be murdered. Discovering this
betrayal, Henry banishes Suffolk, but with his Lord Protector gone the
unworldly young King must face his greatest challenge: impending
civil war and the rising threat of the House of York.

This book includes a general introduction to Shakespeare's life and the
Elizabethan theatre, a separate introduction to *Henry VI, Part II*, a
chronology of his works, suggestions for further reading, an essay
discussing performance options on both stage and screen by Rebecca
Brown, and a commentary.

Edited by Norman Sanders

With an introduction by Michael Taylor

General Editor: Stanley Wells

PENGUIN SHAKESPEARE

KING JOHN
WILLIAM SHAKESPEARE

WWW.PENGUINSHAKESPEARE.COM

Under the rule of King John, England is forced into war when the French challenge the legitimacy of John's claim to the throne and determine to install his nephew Arthur in his place. But political principles, hypocritically flaunted, are soon forgotten, as the French and English kings form an alliance based on cynical self-interest. And as the desire to cling to power dominates England's paranoid and weak-willed king, his country is threatened with disaster.

This book includes a general introduction to Shakespeare's life and the Elizabethan theatre, a separate introduction to *King John*, a chronology of his works, suggestions for further reading, an essay discussing performance options on both stage and screen, and a commentary.

Edited by R. L. Smallwood

With an introduction by Eugene Giddens

General Editor: Stanley Wells

PENGUIN SHAKESPEARE

RICHARD III
WILLIAM SHAKESPEARE

WWW.PENGUINSHAKESPEARE.COM

The bitter, deformed brother of the King is secretly plotting to seize the throne of England. Charming and duplicitous, powerfully eloquent and viciously cruel, he is prepared to go to any lengths to achieve his goal – and, in his skilful manipulation of events and people, Richard is a chilling incarnation of the lure of evil and the temptation of power.

This book includes a general introduction to Shakespeare's life and the Elizabethan theatre, a separate introduction to *Richard III*, a chronology of his works, suggestions for further reading, an essay discussing performance options on both stage and screen by Gillian Day, and a commentary.

Edited by E. A. J. Honigmann

With an introduction by Michael Taylor

General Editor: Stanley Wells

PENGUIN SHAKESPEARE

JULIUS CAESAR
WILLIAM SHAKESPEARE

WWW.PENGUINSHAKESPEARE.COM

When it seems that Julius Caesar may assume supreme power, a plot to destroy him is hatched by those determined to preserve the threatened republic. But the different motives of the conspirators soon become apparent when high principles clash with malice and political realism. As the nation plunges into bloody civil war, this taut drama explores the violent consequences of betrayal and murder.

This book includes a general introduction to Shakespeare's life and the Elizabethan theatre, a separate introduction to *Julius Caesar*, a chronology of his works, suggestions for further reading, an essay discussing performance options on both stage and screen, and a commentary.

Edited by Norman Sanders

With an introduction by Martin Wiggins

General editor: Stanley Wells

Read more in Penguin

PENGUIN SHAKESPEARE

All's Well That Ends Well
Antony and Cleopatra
As You Like It
The Comedy of Errors
Coriolanus
Cymbeline
Hamlet
Henry IV, Part I
Henry IV, Part II
Henry V
Henry VI, Part I
Henry VI, Part II
Henry VI, Part III
Henry VIII
Julius Caesar
King John
King Lear
Love's Labour's Lost
Macbeth
Measure for Measure
The Merchant of Venice

The Merry Wives of
    Windsor
A Midsummer Night's
    Dream
Much Ado About Nothing
Othello
Pericles
Richard II
Richard III
Romeo and Juliet
The Sonnets and A Lover's
    Complaint
The Taming of the Shrew
The Tempest
Timon of Athens
Titus Andronicus
Twelfth Night
The Two Gentlemen of
    Verona
The Two Noble Kinsmen
The Winter's Tale